A SYSTEMS APPROACH
TO SMALL GROUP
INTERACTION

A SYSTEMS APPROACH TO SMALL GROUP INTERACTION

FIFTH EDITION

STEWART L. TUBBS

Dean, College of Business

Eastern Michigan University

McGRAW-HILL, INC.

New York   St. Louis   San Francisco   Auckland   Bogotá
Caracas   Lisbon   London   Madrid   Mexico City   Milan
Montreal   New Delhi   San Juan   Singapore
Sydney   Tokyo   Toronto

This book is printed on recycled, acid-free paper containing 10% postconsumer waste.

1 2 3 4 5 6 7 8 9 0 DOH DOH 9 0 9 8 7 6 5 4

ISBN 0-07-065512-X

This book was set in Plantin by The Clarinda Company.
The editors were Hilary Jackson, Fran Marino, and David Dunham;
the production supervisor was Denise L. Puryear.
The cover was designed by John Hite.
R. R. Donnelley & Sons Company was printer and binder.

Library of Congress Cataloging-in-Publication Data

Tubbs, Stewart L., (date).
    A systems approach to small group interaction / Stewart L. Tubbs.
—5th ed.
      p.   cm.
    Includes bibliographical references and index.
    ISBN 0-07-065512-X
    1. Work groups.   2. Small groups.   3. Organizational behavior.
I. Title.
HD66.T82   1995
302.3'4—dc20   94-20888

ABOUT THE AUTHOR

Stewart L. Tubbs is dean of the College of Business and professor of management at Eastern Michigan University. He received his doctorate in communication and organizational behavior from the University of Kansas. His master's degree in communication and his bachelor's degree in science are from Bowling Green State University. He has completed postdoctoral work in management at Michigan State University, the University of Michigan, and Harvard Business School.

Dr. Tubbs has also taught at General Motors Institute and at Boise State University, where he was chairman of the Management Department and later associate dean of the College of Business.

He has been named an Outstanding Teacher three times, an Outstanding Scholar twice, has consulted extensively for Fortune 500 companies, and is past chairman of the Organizational Communication division of the Academy of Management. He recently received the outstanding leadership award in London from the Academy of Business Administration and was also inducted into the Distinguished Alumni Hall of Fame by Lakewood High School in Lakewood, Ohio. Dr. Tubbs is the co-author, with Sylvia Moss, of *Interpersonal Communication* and *Human Communication*. He is also listed in *American Men and Women of Science, Contemporary Authors, Directory of American Scholars,* the *International Who's Who in Education,* and *Outstanding Young Men of America.*

To the memory of
my father and mother

CONTENTS

3   Group Circumstances and Structure   89

4   Leadership and Social Influence Processes   125

5   **Communication Processes**   **182**

6   Conflict Resolution and Decision-Making Processes   233

7   Consequences   280

PREFACE

You can hardly read a newspaper or a magazine today without encountering an article about the increasing use of teams in our society. Whether it is in public schools, hospitals, universities, businesses, or government, it seems that everybody is finding the value of small group activities.

This book explores the myriad ways that groups and teams can be used to help achieve successful results. It is intended as a primary text for courses in group communication. Since it was first published, it has been used by over 50,000 students. This fifth edition represents the most dramatic revision and updating of any edition thus far.

While the systems model of small group interaction has been retained as the book's organizing framework, numerous other parts of the book have been changed. Four of the seven chapters have new chapter-opening case studies. All seven chapters have either a new case study or new student exercises at the end of the chapter. In addition, ten out of the fourteen sample readings are new in this edition. New material has been added from over 100 sources, the vast majority of which have been published since the fourth edition of this book was published in 1992.

DISTINCTIONS OF A SYSTEMS APPROACH TO SMALL GROUP INTERACTION

This book's format—text, with student experiential exercises and selected readings—is unique among the small group texts available. Each chapter begins with a brief chapter preview, followed by a glossary of terms used in that chapter. Next is an opening case study designed to stimulate student class discussions. The case study is followed by the chapter text material. Following each chapter are several experiential exercises designed to offer opportunities to practice the small group interactions discussed in the chapter. Finally, each chapter ends with two reading selections chosen for their direct relevance to the subjects discussed in that chapter. The readings are intended to offer further depth or to illustrate applications of the concepts discussed in that chapter.

PLAN OF THE BOOK AND NEW FEATURES OF THE FIFTH EDITION

Chapter 1, entitled "What Is Small Group Interaction?" offers key definitions and offers a "Systems Approach" conceptual model that serves as the organizing framework for the remainder of the book. New in this edition are:

- The opening case study about college student drinking behavior.

- A new, more concise definition of teams.

- New material on the use of work teams on the job.

- An entirely new section on empowerment.

- Condensed discussion of the small group model to replace dated material.

- The exercise on cloning humans.

- A new case on "Baby Jessica."

- Inclusion of the movie *Wind* as a case example to demonstrate the Tubbs Model of Group Interaction.

- The first reading selection which discusses some of the common reasons why people join groups.

- The second reading selection which discusses general systems concepts.

Chapter 2, "Relevant Background Factors," discusses six characteristics of individual group members that will influence the group's functioning: personality, sex, age, health, attitudes, and values. New in this edition are:

- The opening case study about a group murder in Africa.

- Research findings on attraction to the group itself.

- Findings on involvement in group decision-making resulting in higher satisfaction.

- Research findings on the impact of group member differences in age, team tenure, and prestige of university as predictors of group-member turnover.

- Research findings on how health is influenced by people's jobs.

- Research findings on romantic relationships at work.

- Research that differences in attitudes between the sexes increase as age increases.

- Research findings on male-female communication styles.

- Information on cultural diversity in groups.

- A new "Interaction Exercise."

- The second reading selection has been thoroughly revised for this edition.

Chapter 3, "Group Circumstances and Structure," discusses the group's physical environment, group size and structure, and different types of groups. New in this edition are:

- The opening case study about teams in a pharmaceutical company.

- Information on group size and team effectiveness.

- An entire new section on self-directed work teams (SDWT).

- An entire new section on computer-assisted groups.

- A new case on "Gays in the Military."

- The first reading selection which offers some practical tips for participating in groups.

- The second reading selection which offers some additional tips for getting the most out of group members.

Chapter 4, "Leadership and Social Influence Processes," discusses status, power, leadership, group norms, and conformity pressures. New in this edition are:

- New information on leadership.

- Condensed coverage of the U.S. Table of Precedence, following the suggestions of reviewers.

- Material on SuperLeaders and SuperTeams.

- Information on situational leadership

- The revised Hersey and Blanchard Situational Leadership model.

- A new case on "Doctor Assisted Suicides."

- A revised first reading selection on situational leadership.

- A new second reading selection which applies groupthink to the Challenger shuttle disaster.

Chapter 5, "Communication Processes," deals with the unique aspects of communication in the small group setting. It covers language behavior, self-disclosure, and interaction roles. New in this edition are:

- Information on various nonverbal behaviors in different cultures.

- An example of nose rings influencing job applicants.

- Material from Stephen Covey's books.

- Examples of the systems approach as illustrated by fights among group members in aerobics classes.

- A new case on the "National Endowment for the Arts."

- A new reading selection has been added which discusses communication behaviors of effective groups.

Chapter 6, "Conflict Resolution and Decision-Making Processes," examines the various methods for organizing group problem solving as well as the topic of conflict resolution. New in this edition are:

- Material on "Tacit Bargaining."
- Tips for effective negotiating.
- More information on negotiating effectiveness.
- A new continuum of decision-making behavior.
- A new case on "Gun Control."
- The first reading selection with some tips on how to more effectively run a meeting.
- A new second reading selection which describes some of the best ways to negotiate through a conflict anywhere around the world.

Chapter 7, "Consequences," is devoted to the outcomes of group activity. It covers solutions to problems, changes in interpersonal relations, improved information flow, increased risk-taking, interpersonal growth, and organizational change. New in this edition are:

- The opening case study about teamwork among lifeguards at a swimming pool.
- One of the two reading selections has been changed.
- The section on acceptance of solutions has been significantly rewritten.
- The section on changes in interpersonal relations has been significantly rewritten.
- The section on organizational change has been entirely rewritten.
- New material on the ways to measure group effectiveness.
- New cases on "Health Care Reform" and "The Use of Aborted Fetus Eggs."
- The second reading selection.

Much of the new material shows applications of group dynamics to real-life settings, thus continuing the book's strong integration of research and theory with life and career applications.

INSTRUCTOR'S MANUAL

The instructor's manual that accompanies the text has sample syllabi, additional class exercises, suggested films, and a variety of test questions that cover each chapter. The goal, as in the previous editions, is to make the book as usable as possible for the instructor.

ACKNOWLEDGMENTS

I would like to thank the reviewers whose valuable suggestions helped guide this latest revision. They are Barbara Adler, Concordia College; Timothy Ashmore, Eastern New Mexico University; Barbara Blackstone, Slippery Rock University of Pennsylvania; Brian Polansky, University of Arkansas, Little Rock; Harry Russell, Mid-America Nazarene College; and Raymond Zeuschner, California Polytechnic State University. Finally, I would especially like to thank Fran Marino, and Hilary Jackson of McGraw-Hill, for their wonderful professional advice and encouragement, and Mary Schmaltz for her excellent help in various stages of the manuscript preparation, and Barbara Brown for her research assistance.

Stewart L. Tubbs

A SYSTEMS APPROACH
TO SMALL GROUP
INTERACTION

What Is Small Group Interaction?

PREVIEW

Chapter 1 is dedicated to laying the groundwork for the rest of the book. It begins with a definition of small group interaction. It includes a section that explains why studying small groups is useful to you. It also has a section on empowerment. Chapter 1 also introduces systems theory along with a general systems model. The Tubbs Model of Small Group Interaction identifies three categories of variables: relevant background factors, internal influences, and consequences. Ten general systems concepts that apply to the model are explained briefly.

GLOSSARY

Empowerment: Empowerment is a leadership style that enables group members to more effectively utilize their talents, abilities, and knowledge.

Input: Input is the raw material of small group interaction. It includes the six relevant background factors: personality, sex, age, health, attitudes, and values. It also includes information the group receives from outside the group.

Throughput: Throughput refers to all the actual verbal and nonverbal behaviors that occur in the course of a group discussion.

Output: Output is often referred to as encompassing solutions, interpersonal relations, improved information flow, risk taking, interpersonal growth, and organizational change. It is sometimes called the end result of group interaction.

Cycles: A cycle is characterized by the results of group interaction being fed back to the group and becoming input for future interactions. For example, a team's success adds strength to the group's cohesion in future activities.

Negative Entropy: Entropy is characterized by all systems moving toward disorganization or death. Negative entropies are the forces that maintain the organization of a system.

Feedback: Feedback is the receiving of information by groups in order to modify themselves.

Dynamic Equilibrium: Dynamic equilibrium is reached at a point at which the forces to change and the forces to resist change are equal.

Differentiation: Differentiation is the specialization that occurs among people in small group communication.

Integration: Integration in small group communication is synonymous with organization. It is the coordination of the various parts of the group.

Equifinality: Equifinality is the potential for adaptation that groups possess. This allows for various possible approaches to achieve a goal.

CASE STUDY: Students Defy Efforts to Keep Campus Sober

The students have retaken Ann Arbor. The University of Michigan's favored by 24 points in its home opener. The weather's incredible, and there're no classes until next Thursday.

That meant Jamie Borteck, a junior from Scarsdale, N.Y., and 10,000 or so of his closest friends on campus were planning to—in his words—get "foozed, sloshed, salty."

To illustrate the point, he demonstrated a "keg stand"—a hand stand on the sweating rim of a rapidly emptying beer keg, drinking directly from the hose while two companions hold his legs aloft."

I started partying at 11 A.M.," said Borteck, who was doing his pre-game imbibing at a Saturday lawn party on Oakland just south of Hill Street. "I'll finish about 4 A.M. after maybe 24 beers, some screwdrivers, some Jack Daniels."

Meanwhile, on the porch of the Chi Phi fraternity on Washtenaw Avenue, Dave Mollicone, a senior from Bingham Farms, was 30 shots into his pre-game "century club"—a shot of beer every minute for 100 minutes.

Doing a century, keg stands and the language of booze are part of a tradition of student inebriation, a tradition U-M experts say is both as old as college itself and proving to be stubbornly resistant to change despite a variety of efforts both at Michigan and elsewhere."

It is a cultural expectation passed from generation to generation that there will be a lot of heavy partying in college. Currently that expectation is fulfilled," said Lloyd D. Johnston, a U-M research scientist who oversees annual national surveys of drug and alcohol use among young people."

If getting drunk wasn't important, they wouldn't have so many names for it."

In one effort to cope, the U-M mailed out a 25-page list of sober things to do in and around campus to all new students before they arrived, said Maureen Hartford, vice president for student affairs.

Particularly worrisome, she said, was the long time span between move-in, which began last Thursday, and the start of classes later this week.

On Saturday, an informal survey of pre-game parties, where students and friends got extra time to drink because of the television-dictated late game start, suggested her worries weren't unfounded.

In a second effort to cope, the Ann Arbor Police Department's party patrol was mobilized at 9 P.M. Saturday to try to put the damper on the excessive decibels of drunkenness.

The plan, said Chief Douglas Smith, was to put virtually every uniformed officer in the field, ticket the repeat violators of the city's noise ordinance and shut down those parties that wouldn't quiet down when warned.

Smith praised the work of the Interfraternity Council in struggling to put the cork in the bottle and said he believes some of the wildness has gone out of the fall parties in the last couple of years.

In gearing for the long haul, psychiatrist Frederick B. Glaser, head of the U-M substance abuse center, is overseeing the implementation of a series of task force recommendations that range from the requirement that every unit on campus develop a drug policy to the hiring of two more substance abuse counselors.

There is even a computer program for self-diagnosing whether one is getting into trouble with alcohol or drugs that students are accessing at the rate of "several hundred a month," he said.

Glaser, in talking about the enduring nature of the problem, noted that Benjamin Franklin in 1758 compiled and published a list of 238 terms for being drunk.

Here's a sampling of some of the revelers the U-M is up against, their party plans for the weekend and the names they would submit to an updated Ben Franklin list:

- Eric Raker, a senior from Des Moines, Iowa, who was planning to party off of his fraternity's keg but was nonetheless returning three cases of bottles to get some funding to replenish his personal stash: "Loaded, lit, blitzed."

- Andrew Shepard, a senior from West Bloomfield, who figures he will probably consume 10 beers, but says he is a big bourbon fan: "Buttered, broiled, sauced, shellacked."

- J. J. Fireman, a graduate from White Plains, N.Y., who was back in town for several weeks to catch some games and assault a keg or two: "Trashed, hammered."

- Joe Kutka, a graduate back from Salt Lake City, "where they definitely drink less," who figures he will drink 15 to 20 beers: "Toasted, inebriated."

- Brad German, a fifth-year senior from St. Joseph, who is thinking in terms of 12 to 15 beers: "Slammed, fubar, which is an expression that came out of the Vietnam War."

- Craig Pastolove, a sophomore from Dix Hills on Long Island, who beat Borteck in an impromptu beer-chugging contest on the way to an evening he "very realistically" estimates will include half a fifth of vodka plus a six-pack of beer: "Out of my head."

- Tom Cunningham, a graduate who flies back from Atlanta for all the games and figures he's good for 15 beers out of the two cases he just bought: "Juiced, plastered, crushed."

- Dave Mollicone, who refers to it as "getting drunk or wasted," is looking forward to his "bell party" in January. That's when all the fraternity brothers who've turned 21 during the year wear bells around their necks—bells that are inscribed with the time of consumption of the 21 beers they are obliged to drink during the party. He says they keep the bells as treasured mementos.

"We're up against a great deal in trying to control this type of binge drinking," said Glaser. "There is tremendous pressure to relate socially to women through drinking, but the evidence that it actually works as a social lubricant is equivocal."

"There is a widespread belief that friends and colleagues drink more than they actually do. If they can do that without suffering the consequences, that gives you an excuse to drink more than you should."

Most students who drink heavily in school do not develop later problems, but some do, he said.

And the numbers are staggering. According to Johnston's surveys, 43.9 percent of college students in 1980 engaged in binge drinking—five or more drinks in a row—during the two weeks prior to the survey. Twelve years later, that number has dropped to only 41.4 percent.

Glaser said a still-to-be published U-M survey puts the university at "about the national average."

1. What does this case study tell you about the influence that groups have on individual behavior?

2. Identify and discuss as many examples as you can of group influences on college students' behaviors.

3. From your own experience, how do you think groups can be used to have positive influences on college students? What about people in other age groups?

4. What would you most like to learn from this course?

From Stephen Cain, "Students Defy Efforts to Keep Campus Sober," *The Ann Arbor News,* September 5, 1993, pp. A1, A10.

The opening case study illustrates the powerful influence that social groups have on our behavior and on our lives. How much drinking do you think people would do in college if they were all by themselves? Probably not much. Alcohol has been called a "social lubricant." Drinking is very much a social behavior, and drinking makes many social situations more fun.

In this book we will be looking at many group situations. Beginning with our family group and continuing on throughout our lives, groups have a very significant impact on all of us. This book is dedicated to helping you learn more about groups and the very significant influences that they have on us all.

A DEFINITION

If you were going to define the term "small group interaction," how would you do it? First, you would probably want to consider size. Would two people constitute a group? How about fifty people? Most (although not all) experts agree that a group consists of at least three people. Because this book is about small groups, we can arbitrarily consider "small" to range from three to about twenty people.

But size is only one consideration. Shaw (1976) has proposed six different considerations in identifying a group. They are (1) perceptions (do members make an impression on others?); (2) motivation (is the group rewarding?); (3) goals (working together for a purpose); (4) organization (each person has some organized role to play, such as moderator, note taker, etc.); (5) interdependence (each person is somewhat dependent on the others); and (6) interaction (the group is small enough to allow face-to-face communication among members). A group may be defined in any of the above ways.

What do we mean by "interaction"? Interaction simply means communication. This includes talking and listening, head nods, gestures, glances, pats on the back, smiles, frowns, and any other behavior to which people assign meaning. Because communication occurs in an ever-changing context, we refer to this as the *process* of communication. The analogy that is often used is that of a movie or a videotape as opposed to a snapshot of group behavior. In fact, these days, most people agree that the speed of the videotape seems to be increasing. Conner (1993) surveyed thousands of people, 90 percent of whom felt that the speed of change in their daily life is increasing rapidly. This led him to conclude that three years from now, we will look back at today as "the good old days" (p. 46).

To summarize, *small group interaction* is the process by which three or more members of a group exchange verbal and nonverbal messages in an attempt to influence one another.

What is the difference between a group and a team? The term "group" is more general. A team is a type of group. Francis and Young (1992) define a team as "a high performing task group whose members are actively interdependent and share common performance objectives" (p. 9). The word "team" also has come to connote closer cooperation and cohesiveness than the term "group." So when we use the word "team," it implies closeness as well as cooperation.

A recent handbook of tips for your career contains the following advice: "Team-work will become more and more important. Learn what it is and how to be a good team member" (Moran, 1993, p. 247).

Why Study Small Groups?

Modern organizations are undergoing a radical transformation designed to better utilize human potential, primarily through the increased use of small groups. In fact, *Fortune* magazine calls effective work groups "the productivity breakthrough of the 1990's" (Dumaine, 1990, p. 52). For example, Saturn Corporation was created with a revolutionary new organizational structure that uses groups as the basic leadership unit. In fact, the name "Saturn" was chosen to reflect the concentric rings of decision-making teams that run the organization. Experts argue that this is the prototype of the organizational structure of the future.

However, in a national survey of worker attitudes, Lundin and Lundin (1993) found that "actions lag well behind all the words about teambuilding; nearly 61% of all respondents claim there's something akin to a 'dog eat dog' atmosphere where they work" (p. 33). Cummins suggests that this may be in part because "getting employees involved . . . is more easily said than done. Organizations are discovering that employee involvement is far more complex and difficult than previously imagined. . . . Employee involvement generally requires fundamental changes in leadership practices, skills, and abilities, information sharing, and rewards. These changes go to the core of the organization's values, beliefs, and norms about work behavior" (quoted in Cotton, 1993, p. vii).

In your lifetime, and in your career, you will undoubtedly be very much affected by these organizational changes. The exciting thing about all this is that the world of work will be more enriching and interesting than it was for your parents' generation. However, the challenge is for you to improve your proficiency in small group situations. This book is dedicated to that end.

In over twenty years of college teaching, the one question that students have asked me the most is "How can I become a success?" Students are often surprised by the answers. The effective use of small groups has been found to be essential to

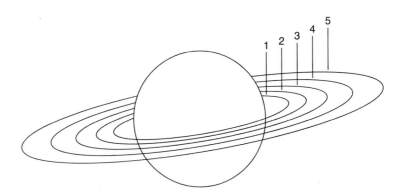

career success. After extensive examination of successful people, Whetton and Cameron (1991) have identified what they consider the nine most important skills required for career success. They are:

1. Development of self-awareness

2. Managing personal stress

3. Solving problems creatively

4. Establishing supportive communication

5. Gaining power and influence

6. Improving employee performance through motivation

7. Delegating and decision making

8. Managing conflict

9. Conducting effective group meetings

Of these nine, only the second (managing personal stress) is not a part of the material covered in this book. In other words, this book is devoted to improving your understanding of the major action skills required for your career success. However, the important thing to remember is that we are talking about behavioral skills, not just knowing about those skills. Like all skills, development begins with new information and proceeds with practice, practice, and more practice, with continual modification and improvement based on feedback from previous performance.

Small groups can help you in college as well as in your career. For example, Fiske (1990) reported a Harvard University study conducted at twenty-one universities that showed that students who study in small groups learn more effectively than those who don't. Also, small group study experiences correlate with overall satisfaction in college (p. A1). For years Harvard Business School has required that its students form study groups and remain in those groups throughout the course. However, one recent article mentioned that Harvard Business School is being criticized for still not having enough "group exercises and projects assigned to students to develop teamwork and leadership skills" (Byrne, 1993, p. 65). Furthermore, Sorenson, Savage, and Orem (1990) surveyed 440 schools in the United States, Canada, and South America and found that an increasing number were adding small group communication courses to their required curriculum because of the increasing relevance to student needs. For example, Connecticut General Life Insurance Company (1975) found that the average executive spends over 700 hours a year in meetings, or almost two out of every five working days totally spent in small group meetings.

Learning to work effectively in small groups can save you time and money. The chart on page 8 shows the value of people's time as their salary increases. If we can learn to improve our meeting effectiveness and thus cut the number and length of meetings, it can yield a measurable savings. Westinghouse reportedly installed electronic numerical keypads in meeting rooms and had each group member enter

THE VALUE OF PEOPLE'S TIME

Salary Year	Salary Week	Benefits = 40% Total Salary	Total Week	Value per Hour	Value per Minute
$ 1,000	$ 19.23	$ 7.69	$ 26.92	$ .67	$ .01
2,000	38.46	15.38	53.84	1.35	.02
3,000	57.69	23.08	80.77	2.02	.03
4,000	76.92	30.77	107.69	2.69	.04
5,000	96.15	38.46	134.61	3.37	.06
6,000	115.38	46.15	161.53	4.04	.07
7,000	134.62	53.85	188.47	4.71	.08
8,000	153.85	61.54	215.39	5.38	.09
9,000	173.08	69.23	242.31	6.06	.10
10,000	192.31	76.92	269.23	6.73	.11
20,000	384.62	153.85	538.47	13.46	.22
30,000	576.92	230.77	807.69	20.19	.34
40,000	769.23	307.69	1076.92	26.92	.45
50,000	961.54	348.62	1346.16	33.65	.56
60,000	1153.85	461.54	1615.39	40.38	.67
70,000	1346.15	538.46	1884.61	47.12	.79
80,000	1538.46	615.38	2153.84	53.85	.90
90,000	1730.77	692.31	2423.08	60.58	1.01
100,000	1923.08	769.23	2692.31	67.31	1.12

his or her salary into the computer as he or she came into the room. Then the computer was started as the meeting began and gave a continuous readout of the cost of the meeting as time went on. Over a few months' time, corporatewide, Westinghouse cut its meeting times in half by simply making participants aware of the cost of each meeting and the cost of each person's comments. Evidently, this important feedback made people more consciously weigh the real value of their comments and encouraged them to waste less time.

Leaders are increasingly learning to improve their use of small groups to effectively accomplish organizational goals. Few leaders in today's complex society can succeed on their own without the help of competent and committed team members.

Bradford and Cohen (1984, pp. 10–11) have argued persuasively in their best-selling book, *Managing for Excellence,* that the Manager as Hero style, which worked well in the past, has given way to the Manager as Developer, which is the style for today and for the future. They identify four myths of the heroic management style:

1. The good manager knows at all times what is going on in the department.

2. The good manager should have more technical expertise than any subordinate.

3. The good manager should be able to solve any problem that comes up (or at least solve it before the subordinate can).

4. The good manager should be the primary (if not the only) person responsible for how the department is working.

They go on to say:

> The solution that worked yesterday is only slightly appropriate today and will be irrelevant tomorrow. Task complexity virtually assures that no one person can have all the necessary knowledge which forces a heightened degree of interdependence among subordinates (and a much greater demand for coordination) if work is to be successfully accomplished, especially at an excellent level. . . . Heroism may be motivating for the superior but it has the opposite effect on subordinates. . . . Today there are far more subordinates who want to be challenged by work; they place "challenging jobs" and "a chance to grow and develop" ahead of such rewards as pay, status, and job security. (pp. 12, 15)

One recent survey revealed that Federal Express has over 4000 employee teams; Motorola has over 2200 problem-solving teams; Cadillac has over 60 percent of its workforce working in teams; and Xerox has over 75 percent of its workforce working in teams (Blackburn and Rosen, 1993). In another study, employees who were seen as acting like "the Lone Ranger" on the job often failed, while those who excelled at building teams early in their time on the job succeeded (Louis, 1990). Clearly, more and more organizations are moving toward a stronger emphasis on teamwork. In fact, many believe that you will need to have some team-based experience on your résumé to get a job within the next few years.

John Gardner (1990), in his best-selling book, *On Leadership,* emphasized the same point of view when he wrote, "When I use the word leader, I am in fact referring to the leadership team. No individual has all the skills—and certainly not the time—to carry out all the complex tasks of contemporary leadership" (p. 10). Similarly, Manz and Sims (1990), in their book entitled *Super-Leadership,* write, "SuperLeaders marshal the strength of many, for their strength does not lie solely in their own abilities, but in the vast, multiple talents of those that surround them" (p. xvi). On a broader scale, anthropologist Walter Goldschmidt argues that every person in every human society needs group affiliation. He has observed this need in such diverse groups as street gangs, yuppies in corporate America, and the Tlingit Indians in Alaska (Hendrix, 1990, p. B5).

As you read further in this book, you will find that a strong understanding of group dynamics and the skills to use that understanding will be among the most important factors in your success as a leader and as a person. Although this book is primarily about problem-solving groups, its focus is broader than that. The lessons contained herein also apply to your friendship groups, your family, and your classroom groups.

INDIVIDUALISM VERSUS COLLECTIVISM IN SELECTED COUNTRIES

Individualism Score*	Country	Individualism Score*	Country
91	United States	53	Spain
90	Australia	48	India
89	Great Britain	46	Japan
77	Canada	46	Argentina
75	Denmark	38	Brazil
74	Italy	32	Mexico
74	Belgium	25	Hong Kong
71	Sweden	20	Singapore
70	Switzerland	17	Taiwan
70	France	16	Venezuela
55	Israel		

*Highest Individualism score = 100.

Source: Frank L. Acuff, How to Negotiate Anything with Anyone Anywhere around the World *(New York: American Management Association, 1993), p. 70.*

Just in case you think that these skills are easy, Acuff (1993) found in his research that Americans are the most individualistic and least team-oriented culture in the world. Therefore, it is harder for Americans to work together as a team than it is for any of the other nationalities he studied. His findings are presented in the chart above.

EMPOWERMENT

The national front-page story on December 17, 1992, was the decision by General Motors to shut down its huge Willow Run (Michigan) assembly plant and move the business (assembling Chevrolets) to its sister plant in Arlington, Texas. According to a confidential GM memo, the reason was that "the Willow Run local [union] hasn't accepted the team concept" (George and Morrow, 1992, p. A1).

In other words, modern organizations are basing multi-billion-dollar decisions, in part, on the use of teams. Among the many other companies using teams are Westinghouse, Federal Express, Carrier, Volvo, Ford, General Electric, General Mills, AT&T, and Dana Corporation. More and more organizations are moving toward greater teamwork and empowerment in an all-out attempt to remain competitive in today's global economy. Your own future jobs and career will no doubt be dramatically impacted by this national trend (Solomon, 1993).

Empowerment is a leadership style that enables the leader to more effectively utilize the talents, abilities, and knowledge of others and, at the same time, increase his or her available time to work on more strategic activities, rather than on "putting out fires." Stephen Covey (1991) writes:

> Empowerment basically means, "Give a man a fish and you feed him for a day. Teach him how to fish and you feed him for a lifetime." When you fully empower people, your paradigm of yourself changes. You become a servant. You no longer control others; they control themselves. You become a source of help to them. (p. 256)

In his book *The Empowered Manager,* Block (1987) writes, "The concept of empowerment has exploded into the national consciousness . . . and rightly so" (p. xii). He goes on to say that we should all "stop searching and waiting for examples of where empowerment is working. All of us have to conduct the experiment in our own . . . lives" (p. xiv).

At Tropicana Products, Inc., in Bradenton, Florida, sales employees have been empowered to conduct promotions analyses that had previously been conducted at much higher levels in the company. Using on-line computer information, employees can analyze external data gathered from checkout scanners at retail grocery stores. This is an attempt to move decision-making downward in the organization and to better utilize employees (Portnoy, 1992).

Empowerment is also being used in the public schools. Windsor (1993) reports that groups of parents, teachers, and administrators are working together more and more in an attempt to improve the quality of public schools. In addition, Adams (1992) reports that school administrators are attempting to empower schoolteachers more in an effort to better utilize their talents and ideas.

Saturn Corporation has been at the forefront of implementing empowerment in the auto industry. In 1993 the union members voted more than two to one to keep their current empowerment system, rather than go back to the traditional methods of working (West, 1993). Notice in the diagram on page 12 how Saturn implements the empowerment concept in small work groups (Rodes, 1992).

Empowerment has certain inherent advantages. For example, it leads to greater productivity, quicker response to problems, improved quality of communication between groups, increased individual motivation, and improved overall organizational effectiveness.

On the other hand, there are some potential challenges and disadvantages as well. Empowerment can cause frustration, since traditional sources of authority have been changed. Ambiguity as to who is responsible for what can also occur. New behaviors must be learned, new relations between groups must be established, and new levels of trust must be developed. Covey (1991) writes: "Technique is relatively unimportant compared to trust, which is the result of our [behaviors] over time. When trust is high, we communicate easily, effortlessly, instantaneously. We can make mistakes and others will still capture our meaning. But when trust is low, communication is exhausting, time-consuming, ineffective, and inordinately difficult" (p. 18).

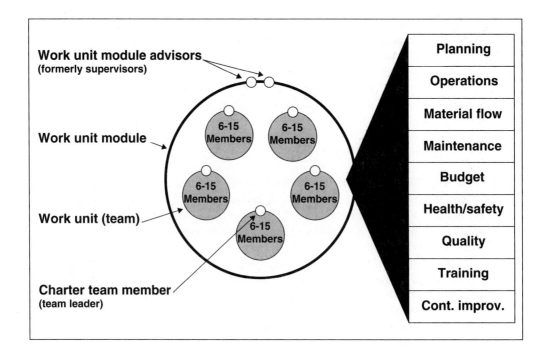

If you are interested in empowering groups in which you are a member, you will find many portions of this book directly relevant to this topic. (See also Fisher, 1993, and Beyerlein and Johnson, 1994.)

A CONCEPTUAL ORIENTATION FOR SMALL GROUPS

Small group interaction is very complicated and involves a large number of factors that act and interact simultaneously. In addition, these factors are in a continual state of flux. Think of the difficulty of trying to describe and analyze all the behaviors that occur at just one party! We have all been to parties that generate far more reactions than we would have thought. Any attempt to provide a conceptual orientation for small group interaction or any social process must be highly simplified.

GENERAL SYSTEMS PERSPECTIVE

The remainder of this book is organized around the idea that small group interaction can most adequately be thought of as occurring in a system of interdependent forces, each of which can be analyzed and set in the perspective of other forces. This idea represents a so-called general systems theory of thinking about small groups.

The general systems theory originated with Ludwig Von Bertelanffy, a theoretical biologist, as a way to think about and study the constant, dynamic adjustments of living phenomena. An *open system* such as a group is defined as an organized set of interrelated and interacting parts that attempts to maintain its own balance amid the influences from its surrounding environment.

Let us look at an example. In July 1990, there was an unusually high number of babies born in and around San Francisco. It took officials only a short while to count back nine months to October 17, 1989, when the same area suffered a large earthquake. The 1990 babies then were referred to as "quake babies." One hospital official was quoted as saying, "We had a blackout situation, but not a lot of devastation from the quake in our area. And people had a lot of time on their hands" (Associated Press, 1990a). This is an example of systems theory. Elements in a system are interrelated, and a change in one part of the system (blackouts in the early evening) can cause changes in another part of the system (the birth rate nine months later).

Norman Cousins, a writer, stumbled upon the interrelationship of psychological systems and physiological health through his own serious illness. His discoveries have led to a renewed interest in a systems approach to health called holistic medicine. He writes:

> Emotional states have long been known to affect the secretion of certain hormones—for example, those of the thyroid and adrenal glands. It has been recently discovered that the brain and the pituitary gland contain a heretofore unknown class of hormones which are chemically related and which go by the collective name endorphins. The physiological activity of some endorphins presents great similarity to that of morphine, heroin, and other opiate substances which relieve pain, not only by acting on the mechanisms of pain itself, but also by inhibiting the emotional response to pain and therefore suffering. (Cousins, 1980, p. 20)

Finally, as suggested by the open systems model, the consequences, or outputs, of the group are fed back into the system through the feedback loop. Katz and Kahn (1978) describe an open system this way: "Activities can be examined in relation to the *energic input* into the system, the *transformation of energies within the system,* and the *resulting product or energic output*" (italics added; p. 17). They also say that "our theoretical model for the understanding of [social] organizations is that of an input-output system in which the energic return from the output reactivates the system (p. 16).

Let's look at it in less theoretical terms. A highly successful baseball team develops a renewed sense of energy from having a winning season. This energy is reinvested in the team by new attitudes of becoming even more successful, admiring each other more, and so forth. This new energy and motivation level may allow team members to enjoy a higher level of status, a new and more democratic style of leadership, and a more luxurious physical environment within which to work or live. (This entire process of multiple causation is indicated by the two-headed arrows in the model; see Figure 1.1.) Keep in mind that the model appears to be static, like a photograph. But in reality, small group behaviors should be modeled by a movie, with each of the parts *moving* in relation to the others.

Different levels of systems analysis and the type of system studied include:

- Astronomy—universal systems
- Ecology—planetary systems
- Political science—political systems
- Sociology—social systems
- Psychology—human systems
- Physiology—organ systems
- Molecular biology—microscopic systems

General systems theory has been applied to many different fields of study, including biology, engineering, mathematics, and psychiatry. Systems analysis has become a particularly popular way of analyzing human behavior in organizations and has been written about in several sources (Katz and Kahn, 1978; Hughes et al., 1993; Woodman et al., 1993).

Ancona (1990) has written emphatically that teams or groups should be analyzed from an "open systems" framework identical to that described throughout this book.

FIGURE 1.1   THE TUBBS MODEL OF SMALL GROUP INTERACTION

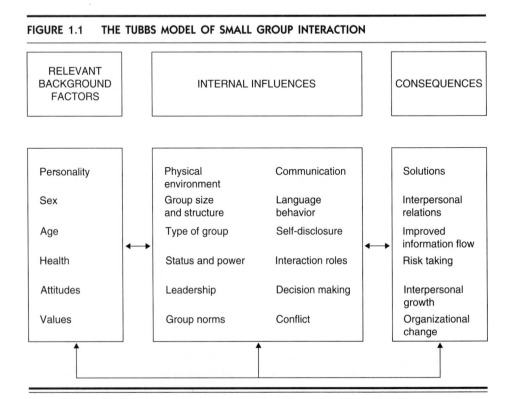

GENERAL SYSTEMS CONCEPTS

With some of this background in mind, let us look briefly at ten general systems concepts that apply to small group communication and are suggested by our general systems model (Katz and Kahn, 1978, pp. 23–30).

INPUT   Input refers to the raw material of small group interaction. It includes all six of the relevant background factors depicted in the model. It also includes information the group receives from outside the group. For example, problem-solving group members in the midst of a discussion may notice that they are running short on time. This new information will probably influence the group to change procedures (e.g., stop talking about side issues) and focus more directly or efficiently on solving the problem at hand.

A system that has inputs from outside is called an *open system*. An open system is said to interact with its environment, in contrast to remaining isolated. Gross (1964, p. 113) identifies four phenomena characteristic of open systems:

1. Entries and exits, which transform outsiders into members and members into outsiders

2. Multiple membership, which results in members' loyalties to outside groups

3. Resource exchange, which involves the absorption of inputs in the production process and in the delivery of output produced

4. Mutual or reciprocal influence on the part of both members and outsiders

Anyone who has ever felt torn between two different groups will be able to understand the relevance of Gross's four points.

THROUGHPUT   Throughput refers to the internal influences depicted in our model. It means all of the actual verbal and nonverbal behaviors that occur in the course of a group discussion. It includes the process of creating and modifying ideas in the course of a discussion. Throughput is the heart and in some cases the entirety of what most small group communication books discuss. Chapters 3 through 6 will discuss these variables in detail.

OUTPUT   Output is referred to in the consequences section of our model. Outputs are sometimes called the end results of group interaction. However, as we shall soon see, end results imply a beginning and an end, which is somewhat misleading, because groups often have an ongoing life history, during which these outputs, or consequences, are continually being modified on the basis of continuing interaction. Chapter 7 is devoted to discussing the consequences, or outputs, of small group interaction.

CYCLES   Often the outputs of group interaction are fed back to the group and become inputs for future interactions. For example, a severe personality conflict in one meeting (of a group) may reduce the level of cohesiveness or interpersonal closeness of group members. As a result some members may refuse to attend future meetings, some may attend but will not participate as openly, or some may try harder the next time to be more diplomatic in their remarks in order to avoid a recurrence of the conflict. The arrows at the bottom of our model (Figure 1.1) indicate what is commonly called a *feedback loop*. This loop represents the cyclical and ongoing nature of group processes and also implies that the process does not begin and end anew with each group meeting, but rather builds on all the past experiences of each group member.

NEGATIVE ENTROPY   The entropic process is a universal law of nature in which all systems eventually move toward disorganization or death. Recently, we have seen the entropic process overtake Frontier Airlines, several hundred banks, Osborn Computers, Addressograph-Multigraph, and many others. To combat the process of disorganization and/or death, a system must employ negative entropy. If you have ever been in a meeting that seemed to be completely out of control and was a total waste of time, you know how easily entropy can overtake a group.

Max DePree (1989), chairman of the board of Herman Miller Furniture Company, writes:

> Some months ago, I was on what is known in the financial industry as a "dog and pony show." Our team was in Boston making a presentation to some sophisticated financial analysts. After the presentation and during the question-and-answer period, one of the analysts said to me, "What is one of the most difficult things that you personally need to work on?" He seemed very surprised when I said, "The interception of entropy."
>
> I am using the word "entropy" in a loose way, because technically it has to do with the second law of thermodynamics. From a corporate management point of view, I choose to define it as meaning that everything has a tendency to deteriorate. One of the important things leaders need to learn is to recognize the signals of impending deterioration. (p. 98)

FEEDBACK   All systems must receive feedback to modify themselves. Think of a bowling game in which you saw the ball go down the lane and through a black cover and you never saw which pins you hit and never heard the sound of the ball striking the pins. You would never play a second game. Or imagine going to school year after year and never getting an assignment back and never getting any grades or comments from an instructor. We all want feedback on our performance. In a rather funny example of feedback modifying a group's behavior, the City Council of Boise, Idaho, decided to change its meetings from Monday night to Tuesday night because of Monday night football. The council had been meeting on Monday nights since 1929. However, because the public turnout was so poor, the council decided to modify its meeting time in response to the feedback that the televised football games were just too much competition (Popkey, 1986).

DYNAMIC EQUILIBRIUM   Management and labor have reached an unspoken agreement in virtually every organization of what constitutes "a fair day's work for a fair day's pay." This is an example of an equilibrium. Similarly, students and teachers often negotiate throughout the course of a term. However, should students fail to read their assignments, teachers will often react by throwing "pop" quizzes, thus upsetting the equilibrium. Once the students change their performance, equilibrium returns. Similarly, when an organization finds itself losing market share or profit margins, it often has to upset the fair day's work for a fair day's pay equilibrium. In 1985 General Motors decided to eliminate the Cost of Living Allowance (COLA) for its salaried workers. This seemed to change the "fair day's pay" side of the equation. Salaried employees decided not to work so hard, thus restoring their feeling of equilibrium. In groups, we each decide if membership is worth what we are putting into it. If not, we slack off and may even eventually quit the group to find one that more nearly meets our sense of equilibrium.

DIFFERENTIATION   Ever since the industrial revolution began, organizations have become increasingly more specialized. It is no longer adequate to have generalists; organizations must now have specialists in production, inspection, materials handling, transportation, legal affairs, accounting, payroll, sales, engineering, plant layout, maintenance, management information systems, distribution, service, real estate, finance, public relations, and labor relations, for example. In groups we also see different people gravitating toward certain roles. In addition, it is a rare group in which all members' attitudes are the same toward any topic.

Conner (1993) found that as organizations got larger, they became more and more decentralized and, ironically, participation in decision making increased due to the increased need for individual departments to work independently from one another.

INTEGRATION   As groups and organizations become more complex and differentiated, the need for integration and coordination of the various parts increases. Without integration, the group or organization becomes chaotic. Imagine being in a hospital in which the lab results or x-rays couldn't be communicated to the physician for interpretation or the pharmacy couldn't get your prescription in order to obtain your medication. Or worse yet, imagine a scenario in which the emergency room wasn't accessible because the driveways were blocked for repair. In groups, if too many subgroups talk at once, coordination soon breaks down, as it does if each person is trying to follow a different agenda (or no agenda). Integration, then, is synonymous with organizing.

Drucker (1990, p. 101) wrote in the *Harvard Business Review* that all manufacturing plants in the future will need to be set up using a "systems approach." He offered the following contemporary example:

> When Honda decided six or seven years ago to make a new, upscale car for the U.S. market, the most heated strategic debate was not about design, performance, or price. It was about whether to distribute the Acura through Honda's well-established dealer

network or to create a new market segment by building separate Acura dealerships at high cost and risk. This was a marketing issue, of course. But the decision was made by a team of design, engineering, manufacturing, and marketing people.

EQUIFINALITY   You have undoubtedly heard the expression, "There is more than one way to skin a cat." This expression captures part of what is meant by the term "equifinality." This concept means that, although two groups may have different members, leadership styles, decision-making methods, and so on, they may still arrive at the same solution to a given problem. There is an incredibly large number of combinations of all the variables in our small group model. These combinations may in some cases interact in such a way as to produce the same group consequences, but from dramatically different processes. Conversely, two groups may attempt to use the same procedures but end up with different outcomes. Thus, equifinality refers to the unpredictability and potential for adaptation groups possess.

For readers who are familiar with small group literature, a synthesis of different small group models is offered in Figure 1.2. You will note the considerable similar-

FIGURE 1.2   SYNTHESIS OF GROUP MODELS

Homans (1950)	External system			Internal system	
Stogdill (1959)	Member inputs		Mediating variables	Resultant variables	
Thibaut and Kelley (1959)	Exogenous variables		Endogenous variables	Resultant variables	
McGrath and Altman (1966)	Properties of group members	Conditions imposed on group	Interaction process	Performance	
Kibler and Barker (1969)	Antecedents		Messages	Consequences	
Fisher (1971)	Inputs		Mediating variables	Outputs	
Gouran (1973)	Context of communication		Communication behaviors	Group outcomes	
Tubbs (1978, 1995)	Relevant background factors		Internal influences	Consequences	
Brilhart and Galanes (1992)	Input		Throughput	Output	
Hughes et al. (1993)	Input		Process	Output	
Wilson and Hanna (1993)	Inputs		Processes	Outputs	
Ellis and Fisher (1994)	Entry elements		Process elements	Outcomes	

ity of conceptual approaches that span more than thirty years of writing. Note, however, that the Tubbs model was one of the first to explicitly emphasize the dynamic and simultaneous interaction of all the component parts. (See also Ellis and Fisher, 1994.)

THE SYSTEMS PERSPECTIVE: THE TUBBS MODEL

As an undergraduate and then as a graduate student, I took a total of nine courses in group dynamics. In each course I always felt a certain sense of discomfort with my inability to get an overall "feel" for the big picture of small group interaction. Each textbook took a different approach, and each approach seemed to somewhat contradict the other. Few if any of the books had a conceptual model which explained the relationships of all the important variables related to small groups.

As a result, when I began to teach my first small groups course, I had difficulty in picking out a textbook. As I studied various group communication texts, I found that all of them covered many of the same topics such as leadership, communication, problem solving, etc. I found, however, that the topics were like so many playing cards which could be shuffled and reshuffled to form a book's table of contents. There was no conceptual model which integrated the topics in a meaningful way. It was only when I studied advanced theoretical books on groups that I found conceptual theories and models that did a better job of tying all the important topics together. These books, however, were not intended for beginning undergraduate students. When I tried using them as texts, students were very unhappy with the choices.

At about the same time, I began to study more and more of the literature on organizational behavior. I read the late Rensis Likert's (1967) now-classic text which organized the variables in that discipline into three categories: (1) causal variables, (2) intervening variables, and (3) end-result variables. This was the closest I had come to finding the conceptualization which made sense. Likert's model seemed to be lacking, too, as it implied a beginning and an end (e.g., causal, intervening, and end-result variables).

Finally, I found the missing link in the general systems literature, which at that time had never been applied in a small group text. The systems approach advanced the idea that all the various component parts of the model are interrelated and that a change in one often creates changes in other parts of the system. In addition, in an open system, so-called end results are fed back into the beginning of the group and become causal variables for future behaviors.

Over time, I began to develop my own materials and eventually developed an open systems model of small group interaction (Figure 1.1) which seemed to provide what I had been looking for. My model conceptualized the small group field and could be adapted for a text written for the introductory student. This systems model grew out of the conceptual groundwork which had been laid by several other authors. Figure 1.2 summarizes those authors' models.

The Tubbs Model organizes the important small group variables into three major categories: (1) relevant background factors, (2) internal influences, and (3) consequences. This model offers several advantages over previous introductory small group books. First, it helps students grasp the conceptual overview which I had not found in books when I was a student. Second, this model shows the dynamic interactive nature of all the variables in the model, and avoids the cause-and-effect thinking of earlier models. Third, it explicitly shows how consequences, or outputs, of one small group experience can become background factors or inputs to the next group experience.

This model is reinforced throughout the text with real-life case studies, student exercises, and carefully selected readings. I hope that this book's combination of theory and application will be useful to you.

The 1992 movie *Wind,* starring Matthew Modine and Jennifer Grey, provides a wonderful example of the systems model of group behavior. In the movie, a group of young people from varying backgrounds work on a task to design, build, and race a sailboat in the America's Cup race in Australia. It beautifully illustrates the various *relevant background factors* of the group members, the dynamic interplay of the many *internal influences* of the group's workings, and the ultimate *consequences* (e.g., winning the race) of the group's activities. If you get a chance, rent this film and use it to see how well it illustrates the model around which this book is written.

Relevant Background Factors

Relevant background factors are attributes within the individual participants that existed prior to the group's formation and that will endure in some modified form after the group no longer exists. These background factors influence the group's functioning; in turn, the group process affects the group's outcomes, or results.

Let us look at a few of these factors. Each of us has a distinct personality. The mix of personalities will undoubtedly have some influence on the "chemistry" or working relationships within the group. For example, when filming *The Godfather III,* Al Pacino and Diane Keaton broke off their long-running relationship, which caused severe setbacks in filming the movie. This illustrates both personality conflict and the influence of sex or gender on the group's functioning. Obviously, any group membership that includes both sexes involves a very volatile element. In fact, many companies have policies that do not allow husbands and wives to work in the same department. Obviously, any time the two sexes interact, there is the potential for romantic relationships to influence the group's functioning.

Age is certainly a factor important to group activities. Age itself is probably not as important as the different attitudes that tend to accompany different age groups. Therefore, groups containing members of a similar age group tend also to be somewhat more similar or homogamous with regard to attitudes. For example, how different would a group discussion concerning Madonna be if your parents were in the group?

Health also plays a role in influencing groups. If individuals are suffering from health problems, their energy level and the stamina with which they address problems are often reduced. In one work group, a member who had chronic pneumonia was consistently the most outstanding contributor at each meeting of the group that she was able to attend. However, her frequent health-related absences handicapped the group.

Values also exert a powerful influence in groups. Think about a discussion on the subject of abortion, gun control, or racism. Think how quickly the values of the group members will come into play and how they will most likely affect both the group's processes and its outcomes. Keep in mind that all six of these relevant background factors are constantly interacting with one another. For example, values and attitudes are closely related, as are age and health, and sex and personality. And all of these factors (except sex) are constantly changing over the course of our human experiences. The relevant background factors are the subject of Chapter 2.

Internal Influences

The second set of variables in the model is referred to as *internal influences*. These factors influence the actual functioning of the group. Imagine how physical environment plays a role when the group meets in a quiet conference room with comfortable furniture compared to meeting in a noisy corner of a room with poor ventilation, heavy cigarette smoke, poor lighting, and a hot temperature. Similarly, imagine the way a group interacts when there are only four or five members compared to fifteen to twenty. Typically, the smaller the group, the higher the individual satisfaction of group members with the discussion.

The *type of group* refers to a group's general nature. A group may be, for example, an educational group, a social group, or a work group. Obviously, each of these would perform differently. Chapter 3 discusses in greater depth the factors of physical environment, group size and structure, and group type.

Chapter 4 is devoted to three very important topics: (1) status and power, (2) leadership, and (3) group norms. Status and power strongly influence group outcomes. If a group such as the President's cabinet is meeting to discuss a problem, obviously, the President has the highest status and resulting power. Similarly, if the Dallas Cowboys are meeting, Troy Aikman and Emmett Smith would have an especially high level of status within the group, and their opinions would most likely be more powerful than those of any other members of the group.

Leadership is probably one of the two most important *internal influences*. Thus, we have devoted quite a bit of attention to it. As mentioned earlier in this chapter, many people learn how to increase their own leadership by studying small group interaction. The trend of the present and most definitely of the future is for greater participative leadership, which heavily utilizes group interaction. For example, Dumaine (1993) writes: "Managers who master skills such as team building . . . will likely be in the best position to get tomorrow's top corporate jobs. That's because the role of the top executive is becoming more like that of a team player and broker of others' efforts, not that of an autocrat" (p. 81).

The third topic in Chapter 4 is group norms. These are unwritten rules that strongly influence our behaviors. Usually norms are so much a part of our thinking that we become aware of them only when someone violates them. For example, if someone dresses (or undresses) in a fashion that is completely out of place, this violates our sense of what is comfortable (or *norm*al). Conformity pressure to adhere to group norms is a powerful influence on every small group.

Chapter 5 discusses (1) communication, (2) language behavior, (3) self-disclosure, and (4) interaction roles. Communication is the other most important *internal influence*. Thus, we have dedicated a significant amount of coverage to it. Virtually every human behavior has the potential to communicate, and so communication permeates all aspects of group behavior.

Language behavior focuses on the verbal part of communication and the intimate relationship between words and thoughts. This body of knowledge is often referred to as *semantics*. Several language-related communication difficulties are discussed, and practical methods for improvement are included.

Self-disclosure refers to the amount we reveal about ourselves to others. Too little self-disclosure results in an isolation from others. However, too much self-disclosure with virtual strangers is inappropriate. The contexts of appropriate self-disclosure as a method for personal growth and development are discussed.

Chapter 6 covers two important topics—decision making and conflict. Many traditional small group books have been exclusively devoted to the topic of decision making. The skills covered in this section will serve you throughout your entire lifetime as you solve literally thousands of problems.

Conflict is something all of us experience. This section discusses the dynamics of conflict and attempts to better equip you for managing conflicts in your life, especially in group situations.

Consequences

Finally, Chapter 7 looks at the reasons why we engage in group activities in the first place—that is, the results that can be obtained from groups. They are the raison d'être of a group, the reason the group is formed. These are (1) solutions to problems, (2) improvements in interpersonal relations, (3) improvements in the flow of information between and among people, and (4) organizational change. Each of these end results, or consequences, of group interaction is a worthwhile goal.

As you read this book, keep in mind the consequences that are possible. As you focus on what is often referred to as "the bottom line," you will better understand how the systems approach ties all these variables together.

SUMMARY

We opened this chapter with a look at a real-life example of a small groups team. The college student drinking case illustrated both the challenge and potential of effective small group management. The case study is reinforced with key definitions of the language and terms unique to the study of small groups. The section "Why Study Small Groups?" highlights the many advantages of this area of study.

Having laid this initial groundwork, we examined the topic of empowerment and then a conceptual orientation of the small group. The "General Systems Perspective" section examined the many theories presented that help categorize the elements of group communications. Drawing from these general philosophies, this textbook is based upon a *new* theory of small group interaction: The Tubbs

Model—A Systems Perspective. The Tubbs Model is a conceptual model that illustrates and defines the relationships of all the important variables of the small group.

In the next six chapters and the accompanying readings, each part of the model will be discussed in greater detail: Chapter 2 covers *relevant background factors*, Chapters 3 to 6 are devoted to *internal influences*, and Chapter 7 deals with the *consequences* of small group interaction.

EXERCISES

1. First Impressions

Each person in the class should introduce himself or herself. Class members should feel free to ask each person questions to get a more complete impression. After the introductions, each person should write down some first impressions of the other class members (if you each display a large name card, this is much easier). Those who want to may share their first impressions with the class. Then reactions to those impressions also may be shared and discussed.

2. Interpersonal Perceptions

Separate into groups of five, and fill out the Preliminary Scale of Interpersonal Perceptions on each of the other four group members. Pass the completed scales to each person in the group. Examine the feedback you get, and discuss it with the others in the group. You may want to share with one another the behaviors that led to these perceptions.

PRELIMINARY SCALE OF INTERPERSONAL PERCEPTIONS

Group Member's Name_____

On the scale below each question, circle the number that best describes the way you see this person's participation in group discussion. Try to distinguish between those areas where the person rates high and those where he/she rates less well.

1. How well does this person understand himself/herself in relation to this group? (Circle one numeral)

5	4	3	2	1
He/she has a very good understanding				He/she has very little understanding

2. How effective do you think this person is in contributing ideas, insights, and suggestions that help the group solve problems and achieve its goals? (Circle one numeral)

5	4	3	2	1
He/she is exceptionally effective				He/she is very ineffective

3. How effective do you think this person is in performing functions that build the group and keep it working well? (Circle one numeral)

5	4	3	2	1
He/she is exceptionally effective				He/she is very ineffective

4. In your opinion, how able is this person to express himself/herself freely and comfortably in the group? (Circle one numeral)

5	4	3	2	1
He/she is exceptionally free and comfortable				He/she is very restricted and tense

5. To what extent do you feel that this person really understands your ideas and feelings? (Circle one numeral)

5	4	3	2	1
He/she has a very good understanding				He/she has very little understanding

3. Group Consensus Activity

Form into groups of five, and then read and discuss the following article on cloning. As an agenda, try to answer the questions that follow the article.

CLONING CLAMOR *
By CONNIE CASS, The Associated Press
   WASHINGTON—Suddenly, it seemed possible to ponder the imponderable: Could humans be copied and mass-produced? Could parents one day choose designer embryos?
   Fertility researcher Jerry Hall says his research—cloning human embryos—is all part of helping couples who can't have babies. But to some, it eerily echoes science fiction and crosses an ethical boundary. The Vatican branded his experiment "perverse."

*From *The Ann Arbor News*, October 26, 1993, A4.

Hall says such far-fetched ideas as mass-producing humans may never be possible and certainly can't be done now.

At a news conference Monday, the George Washington University researcher seemed puzzled that his experiments on short-lived embryos in a petri dish raised such specters.

"We did not implant these into any women; we did not intend to implant them," Hall said. "No child has been born from this procedure."

Nevertheless, some ethicists say Hall crossed a line when he conducted the first known cloning of human life. They fear that other scientists will now charge across that same divide.

"Once you start tampering with the reproductive process, it's hard to decide about where to stop," said Ray Moseley, director of the Medical Humanities Program at the University of Florida College of Medicine.

Cynthia Cohen, head of the National Advisory Board on Ethics and Reproduction, said the research raises "chilling" possibilities for the future. She and others called for a moratorium on further human embryo research until clear limits can be set.

"The fact that there is a total moral vacuum in this whole area is now finally being realized," Cohen said.

What are the implications of this case for the cloning of humans? Would clones be human? Would they have souls? What rights should they have? Is it desirable to clone humans? What should be U.S. policy toward the cloning of humans?

4. Ice-Breaking Exercise

Fill out the two forms that follow; then get into groups of five or so, and share answers. Later, you can discuss what you as a group experience from these exercises.

1. The person in the group I would like to get to know better is

   _____

2. The person in the group who seems to be most like myself is

   _____

3. The person in the group whom I would like to know and whom I care and am concerned about, is

   _____

4. The person who has been the most helpful is

   _____

5. A person I would like to hitchhike around the country with is

   _____

6. A person I would trust to fold my parachute before jumping from an airplane is

_____

7. A person I would like to have a deep discussion with is

_____

8. A person I would like most to keep in touch with is

_____

9. A person I would trust with my secrets is

_____

10. A person whom I feel I know least well is

_____

What other things would you like to say to someone in this group? Take a risk (be constructive).

_____

_____

What person in this group:

_____ 1. Has the darkest eyes?

_____ 2. Has the longest name?

_____ 3. Could hide in the smallest place?

_____ 4. Has the biggest hands?

_____ 5. Has the oldest brother or sister?

_____ 6. Can give the biggest smile?

_____ 7. Can make the scariest face?

_____ 8. Has the most brothers and sisters?

_____ 9. Has the fewest brothers and sisters?

_____10. Has the lightest hair?

_____11. Has the most freckles?

_____12. Can make the highest mark on the wall without jumping?

_____13. Is wearing the most colors?

_____14. Has the longest hair?

_____15. Has the shortest name?

_____16. Has lived in the most places?

_____17. Has had the most pets?

_____18. Can hum the lowest note?

_____19. Has the smallest waist?

_____20. Can stand on one foot for the longest time without holding on to something?

5. Group Decision Making

Separate into groups of five or so. Read the case described below, and decide as a group what you would do in the situation. Then discuss your group processes.

The "Baby Jessica" Story   "Baby Jessica" was adopted shortly after her birth in 1990 by Jan and Roberta DeBoer of Ann Arbor, Michigan. Her birth mother, Cara Schmidt of Blairstown, Iowa, signed the paperwork giving Jessica up for adoption. She was not married at the time. Later, Dan Schmidt found out that he was the father and filed suit for custody of Jessica. Subsequently the Schmidts got married. A two and a half year legal battle followed. In late 1993 the Schmidts were awarded custody of Jessica. She was shown on national television crying and screaming while being taken from the DeBoers' home. Public opinion polls showed that respondents were strongly in favor of the DeBoers keeping Jessica.

READINGS: OVERVIEW

The systems model presented in Figure 1.1 shows the interrelated nature of twenty-four variables relevant to the study of small group interaction (six variables in each of the four columns in the model). Wilson and Hanna's selection offers excellent insights into some of the main reasons why people join groups. It is also interesting to note that these reasons fit quite comfortably within the systems approach to studying small group interaction, which is the conceptual model around which this book is structured.

The second article, by Lipnack and Stamps, shows the complexity of systems theory and its relationship to small groups.

Motivations for Member Participation in Groups

Gerald L. Wilson and Michael S. Hanna

Examine your motives for being a member of a particular group. Do you have a group in mind? If not, stop for a moment and pick one. Now think both of yourself and the other members of the group. A good question to ask yourself is, "What things do members of the group receive that keep them in the group?" See how many different motivations you can list on a piece of paper.

Now check your list against the one presented below to see how you did. Perhaps our words are a little more "academic sounding," but see if your ideas match these. People are motivated to belong to groups because of (1) attraction to others in the group, (2) attraction to the group's activities, (3) attraction to the group's goals, (4) attraction to being affiliated with the group, and (5) attraction to needs outside the group. We will take up each of these ideas, with illustrations of each and suggestions for group development. The motives for belonging that a person brings to a group affect the development potential and direction of the group. These motives can be used to develop other members' motivation to participate. And, in doing so, the development of the group as a decision-making team is affected. The subsequent sections will examine these motives and demonstrate their potential for use in developing groups.

Attraction to Others in the Group

Ask any group of people to describe why they are attracted to one another and you are likely to get a variety of answers. You can gain an appreciation of the complexity of this issue by considering someone you know in a group, to whom you are attracted. Now take a moment to think of several of the reasons you like to be with that person.

Do you find the person physically attractive?

Do you have similar interests?

Do you have attitudes and values that seem to match reasonably closely?

From Gerald L. Wilson and Michael S. Hanna, Groups in Context, 3rd ed. (New York: McGraw-Hill, 1993).

Do your important values match closely?

Do you see yourselves as having similar personality characteristics?

Are you of similar economic status, race, and so forth?

Do you see the person as having abilities similar to yours?

Count the number of times you said yes to these questions. You are likely to have several yeses, because attraction is a complex issue. People are attracted to groups for a variety of reasons. Pete Wells belongs to the Rotary because the members he knows represent an image he admires. Al Smith belongs to a study group at his church because several of its members are interested in tennis. Sally Williams belongs to a group investigating computer needs in her department because she enjoys the people who volunteered to work in the group. Motivations for being part of a group are varied, and not always related to the task of the group.

Attraction is related to pleasing physical characteristics, similarities in attitude, belief, personality, race, economic status, and perceived ability of the other person. Perhaps the strongest of these—and the most often studied—is perceived similarity of attitude. Theodore Newcomb conducted the classic study that demonstrated the strength of similarity. He invited seventeen male students to live in the same house rent-free for two years. After they occupied the house, he gave them a series of tests to measure attitudes and values. He also checked the room assignments and likings of group members. He discovered that liking was based on proximity—how close to one another in the house they were physically situated. Later, when he retested the interpersonal attractions, he found a shift. Now those who perceived themselves to be similar in attitudes had developed attractions. Newcomb concluded that people initially got to know those closest to them. Then, as they were able to know others in the house, they were attracted to those who were similar. Similarity is a good starting place when you look at why members are attracted to groups.

Attraction is also related to personality similarity. Byrne, Griffitt, and Stefaniak, for example, had 151 subjects respond to items on a scale that measures personality characteristics. Then they examined a stranger's responses that agreed with their choices—25 percent, 50 percent, or 80 percent of the time. Next the subjects rated the stranger's attractiveness. The more the stranger agreed, the more the person was liked.

The details of these two studies are presented for two reasons. First, it is useful for you to have an appreciation of how researchers approach and examine issues such as these. Second, the kind of evidence that supports these generalizations is important. There is also support to show that attraction is related to economic similarity, race, and similarity of ability. The findings related to similarity of ability are interesting. Initially people were attracted to those who had previously been successful at a given task. However, when they had the opportunity to shift from their initial choices, in time unsuccessful people chose unsuccessful partners.

Attraction to Group Activities

Sometimes people belong to a group because they enjoy some aspect of the task that members do. This is not always the same thing as valuing the goal of the group. For example, imagine an athletic woman joining the sorority softball team to participate in its athletic program but not really embracing its primary goal of socializing. Some people belong to a civic group to socialize with its members rather than to work toward achievement of its goals. You can imagine how important it could be to realize that particular members are not especially interested in the group's goal. If you try to motivate such people by emphasizing commitment to the goal, your success is likely to be minimal. On the other hand, you may be able to link achievement of their needs to the group goal and be successful. For example, a sorority might show how other athletes are attracted to groups with strong social programs. This may give the woman who joined to participate in athletics a reason to support the social program, too.

Attraction to Group Goal

Perhaps the most important reason for a member to belong to a group from the standpoint of group development is attraction to the goal. Attraction to the goal contributes more to a group than mere achievement of particular ends. Members who are committed to the goal may work hard on being able to get along. They may even be able to put aside differences and hostilities because they value goal achievement. Sherif and Sherif vividly demonstrated this aspect of goal achievement in their famous boys' camp experiment. They created hostility between two groups of boys through various manipulations. For example, they invited both groups to a party in which half of the refreshments were badly damaged. They invited one group earlier than the other so that they had opportunity to serve themselves the undamaged portion of the food. This they did; the other group became predictably angry. Next they tried to manage the conflict by creating a goal to which they thought both groups would be attracted. They arranged a baseball game in which their camp would play a neighboring camp. The embracing of this attractive goal served to ease much of the hostility and created a new group loyalty.

Attraction to Being Affiliated with the Group

Groups allow people to interact and thereby fulfill a need to affiliate with others. You undoubtedly know of people who do not really care about the task of the group, are not really interested in the group's goals, and may even

Develop purpose as a resource for your team, just as people develop procedures and policies using law as a resource. Encourage your members to participate in planning and decision making to internalize the purpose for themselves. Externalize the purpose through explicit plans, information access, and the creation of symbols—logos, nicknames, acronyms. Instead of controlling one another through one-way orders or endlessly detailed policies, boundary crossing teamnet members exercise control through their shared process.

Principle 2: The Best Member Is a Holon

Each of us is a *whole* person who plays a *part* in businesses, families, and communities.

What sorts of things are simultaneously wholes and parts? Everything. Arthur Koestler, the author and systems thinker, coined the word "holon" to stand for this whole/part characteristic of everything. This "systems within systems" feature of nature is fundamental to understanding complexity.

View teamnet members as holons. The autonomy of teamnet members means that they are independent parts; they have their own integrity and own life processes of survival and growth. This is true whether the members are alliances of firms or individual peers on a team.

Parts and wholes have names. Companies, departments, divisions, functions, projects, programs, and teams all have names. From a systems perspective, these names label *categories*. They differentiate the parts of complex systems. Bureaucratic boxes and network nodes both function as categories; they both collect people, things, and activities into coherent clusters. In real life, we are all parts of many categories, many social clusters, many boxes. Sometimes, the same name represents both a bureaucratic box and a network node: an engineering group is both a node in the product development boundary crossing teamnet, and a bureaucratic departmental box at the same time.

There are important differences here. While you play multiple roles in multiple networks, in hierarchies you appear in one and only one box. As a network member, you are relatively independent and demonstrate strong tendencies to autonomy. In a bureaucracy, you are relatively dependent and look for precision fit. When it comes to the independence-dependence continuum, network nodes and bureaucratic boxes lean to opposite poles.

Principle 3: The Interconnected Web of Relationships

Relationships are elusive things. For some people, they are real; for others, they are not. Some people literally cannot see relationships, even indirectly. These people do well in organizations with a rule to govern every aspect of behavior. They don't fare well in teamnets. Relationships are at a network's core.

There are so many relationships involved in life, and so many different kinds of them everywhere you look. To simplify this vast interconnected mess, traditional organizations have many one-way signs. Hierarchies and bureaucracies take an extremely limited approach to how parts interconnect. Generally speaking, orders and information flow in a minimal number of formal channels. Information flows up and commands flow down. This traffic pattern gives rise to the walls, stovepipes, silos, and other hard-to-penetrate boundaries in organizations.

By contrast, in networks, connections are many rather than few. Information and influence flow both up and down the levels through links, as well as horizontally within levels. What is the situation with your boundary crossing teamnet? Do information and influence flow along a two-way highway, or are people stopped for going against the traffic?

Systems thinking has historically emphasized relationships. Peter Senge's book, *The Fifth Discipline,* is an excellent example of a systems approach to complexity for business based on understanding processes and relationships. Gregg Lichtenstein, one of the leading facilitators of flexible business networks, wrote about "the significance of relationships in entrepreneurship" for his doctoral dissertation in social systems science. June Holley and Roger Wilkens have developed a systems dynamics model of flexible networks to guide the development of networks of small manufacturers in southern Ohio.

Principle 4: Representative Leadership

Nothing in groups is as complicated as leadership. One way to simplify complex wholes is to grasp a part that represents the rest. For example, Wall Street is shorthand for America's financial system; the White House stands for the executive branch of government; the Oval Office represents the White House. In the search for simple ways to "grasp a group," leaders come in handy. Leaders are people who stand for a group.

All organizations have leaders, even self-directed groups, where leadership comes from within rather than from without. Networks are rife with leaders. By definition, leaders are partial representatives whose views others need to supplement.

To Americans, hierarchies in the social sense are single-pointed pyramids. Unfortunate as the burden is impractical, in a hierarchy everything supposedly comes together at the top in one perfect person. In a hierarchy, the rule is the fewer the leaders the better—with as little change as possible for as long as possible.

The same is not true in networks. As we stress repeatedly, the more leaders the better. In the best of networks, everyone is a leader. Everyone provides guidance in specific realms of expertise, their talents and knowledge all contributing to the success of the group. People alternate between leadership and followership roles in fast-moving networks with many parallel interconnected activities.

Principle 5: Hierarchical Levels

While in some ways boundary crossing teamnets are very different from hierarchies, in others they are the same. Do not despair. This is not some sort of depressing truth that makes us want to say, "See? I knew there was nothing different here, after all." Consider it instead a great source of comfort. Since you already know a great deal about hierarchies, draw on your experience as a source of strength.

Were you schooled in the analytic, "break-it-down," mechanistic, one-size-fits-all strategy approach to anything complicated? We were, and so was nearly everyone else in the West. This half-brained approach to thinking has its strengths but also its limitations in solving life's problems. From a systems perspective, it ignores the parallel value of synthesis, the "build-it-up" holistic strategy, critical for all living systems, including human ones.

What systems am I part of? What environments is the team part of? What contexts is the company part of? What systems . . .

One of the great ironies of systems science lies in the term "hierarchy." Hierarchy is the most common principle threading through the multitude of systems theories. Every comprehensive systems theory uses it, regardless of its native discipline. According to Herbert Simon, the father of information science, hierarchy is nature's "architecture of complexity." Confusion over the word, which literally means "priestly rulership," has kept this idea from being widely understood where it is needed most, in human affairs.

Hierarchy is what we mean by *levels*.

The social use of the term "hierarchy" includes the scientific one, levels of organization. Unfortunately, when people apply the word to organizations, they also add another characteristic: vertical control. In social hierarchies, the higher you are, the better off you are, and the more power you have; the lower you are, the worse off you are, and the less power you have.

As true as this may be in your local hierarchy, let us say most emphatically that *top-down* is only one of many possible relationships between levels. Exclusive one-way control is *not* natural in nature's hierarchies. Rather than dominating one another, levels are interdependent. More inclusive levels have critical dependencies on lower levels. Molecules would have a tough time without atoms. Organisms wouldn't be much without cells, which rely on molecules. The life of cells follows its own rules quite apart from an organism's life, which has its own special rules. These are all examples of hierarchy in the natural scientific sense.

Complex boundary crossing teamnets *are* "systems of systems within systems." Every teamnet is a hierarchy of wholes and parts. Teamnet members are systems of systems. The systems principles of segmentation and inclusion apply every time a group splits up into task teams or an alliance jells.

Love and Marriage, Horse and Carriage: The Complementarity of Co-opetition

"Co-opetition" brings the complements of cooperation and competition into one word. This dynamic between the self and others is one of many ways *complementarity,* the second fundamental principle of systems (after hierarchy), shows up in networks. When you see your teamnet as both structure and process, you see complementary views of the same thing.

Both hierarchy and complementarity appear everywhere in nature and society. They are grand boundary crossing concepts that cross many terrains of knowledge. Physicists use complements like positive and negative charges, matter and antimatter, and right and left spins. They see fundamental reality as both particles and waves at the same time. In biology, we see life and non-life, birth and death, male and female, as basic complements. In society, people struggle between *self* and *group,* a natural dynamic that is central to families, communities, and nations alike.

Tension erupts when complements begin to grate against one another. In reality, the tension of duality is always there. When the system begins to shake, stress becomes noticeable as relationships form, break, and re-form. You can use the principle of complements as a simple tool in many teamnet situations. For example, you can take a complementary approach to conflict, using such simple homilies as "There are two sides to every story."

Phases of Growth

The teamnet concept of process derives from a key pattern recognized by general systems theory. "General systems"—initiated half a century ago by the biologist Ludwig von Bertalanffy and the economist Kenneth Boulding among others—is a scientific discipline that focuses on common patterns, mathematical and otherwise, found in physical, biological, and social systems.

The S curve, also known as the "logistic growth curve," which we use to represent the change process, appears in the original paper von Bertalanffy wrote establishing the field of general systems. It was his first example of an "isomorphy," a general principle that holds across scientific disciplines. *An isomorphy is a boundary crossing principle.*

To track the cumulative progress of some change over time, add a second dimension to the simple time line. Now, the straight-arrow process path

Timeline

Time

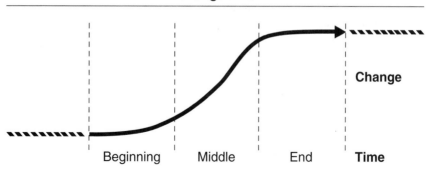

Change Line

Beginning   Middle   End   **Time**

Change

looks like an S curve. It generates a *plane of change,* a very typical result when you plot change data against time.

The S curve does equally well at charting the growth of bacteria in a petri dish and the rate at which new technology spreads, for example, the penetration of a cable television franchise into a new area. "Limits to growth" is the common factor in these processes, a major law of all life on this planet.

> *The S curve charts the common dynamic when change starts small, develops slowly, then "suddenly" takes off, rapidly filling out the available opportunity, slowing as it reaches limits, and stabilizing into a new slow- to no-growth pattern.*

Well understood in a wide variety of disciplines, the S curve represents great acquired knowledge, available to those who want to deepen their understanding of process.

The S curve becomes the "stress curve" when you pay attention to the turbulence associated with the two bends in the curve. . . . The stress curve is a very handy pocket tool for anyone involved with teamnets. Use it as an extremely valuable process aid to plan meetings and conferences of all sizes. Look to the points of turbulence in the process. Use them as alpine skiers do the bumps on the downhill trail: racers anticipate and prejump the bump, leveraging momentum from the bump's back side rather than being thrown for a loop by flying off the front.

Smarter Groups

Human evolution has progressed by substituting brain for brawn.

We see the possibility of much smarter groups as new forms of teamnets integrate with the electronic world of technology networks. Remember:

Only a few generations of humans have had instantaneous electronic communications, and only now are we launching groups linked with the historically unique cognitive (digital) technology of computers.

In the broad cultural context, electronic and digital technology stimulates and shapes the sociological response of global networks. Networks are the unique response to the driving forces of information, just as hierarchy developed in the Agricultural Era and bureaucracy matured in the Industrial Era.

But we don't have to wait for tomorrow for smarter groups. Most people have at some time or another been a member of a group that really "clicks"—a family, work, political, religious, or volunteer effort. Most people intuitively know the tremendous personal satisfaction that is possible with high group performance. Only a small but critical general improvement in people's ability to think and act collectively may have a great impact on solving all the world's problems.

Relevant Background Factors

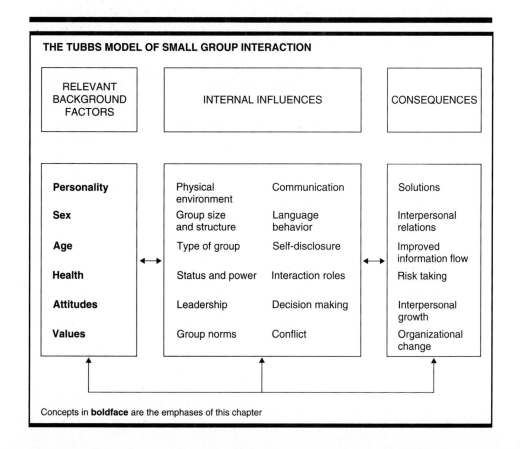

THE TUBBS MODEL OF SMALL GROUP INTERACTION

RELEVANT BACKGROUND FACTORS	INTERNAL INFLUENCES		CONSEQUENCES
Personality	Physical environment	Communication	Solutions
Sex	Group size and structure	Language behavior	Interpersonal relations
Age	Type of group	Self-disclosure	Improved information flow
Health	Status and power	Interaction roles	Risk taking
Attitudes	Leadership	Decision making	Interpersonal growth
Values	Group norms	Conflict	Organizational change

Concepts in **boldface** are the emphases of this chapter

PREVIEW

The purpose of Chapter 2 is to study closely the relevant background factors that partially compose the Tubbs Model of Small Group Interaction. The six relevant background factors are personality, sex, age, health, attitudes, and values. These six factors relate directly to "why we do what we do" when placed in situations involving a small group. The chapter also discusses Maslow's hierarchy of needs. These needs tend to help explain further the six relevant background factors.

GLOSSARY

Inclusion: Inclusion is our need for belonging, feeling a part of and being together with others.

Control: Control is our need to influence, lead, and develop power over others or to be influenced, led, or have others exert power over us.

Affection: Affection refers to the friendship and closeness between people.

Attitudes: An attitude is a mental state that exerts influence over an individual's behaviors. Attitudes have three components: (1) a cognitive component, which refers to a concept, (2) an affective component, which is emotion, and (3) a behavioral component, which is the readiness to act.

Consistency Theories: Consistency theories all are based on the assumption that human beings have a strong psychological need for consistency. This is often referred to as a need to maintain cognitive balance.

Values: Values are fewer in number than attitudes and serve as important predictors of behavior. They appear to be more stable and long-lasting than attitudes.

CASE STUDY: Adventures in Kenya

Renee Huckle

May 18, 1993
journal entry

Just when I think I'm used to life in Kenya and I've seen it all—that nothing could really surprise me anymore—wham, I'm rudely awakened to the fact that yes, I'm still in Africa.

Today I got up and made my way into Nairobi from Westlands to meet Kika at the Masai Market. She leaves Friday, so we were going to do the market thing and grab some lunch. We met at the Harvest Restaurant and decided to check out the market first as we both weren't that hungry yet. At the market I ran into a couple of students from another college program and Betty, who I'm sure was more than happy to leave the embassy basement and spend her lunch time out of the office.

The Masai Market has got to be one of the most interesting places to visit in Nairobi. Every Tuesday the place is alive with people weaving in and out of the rows of women sitting on the ground selling their handicrafts. The Masai women are so interesting, so "African," whatever that really is, and their beadwork is absolutely amazing. I started talking with two women from whom I wanted to buy a rungu stick, one of the clublike things the Masai use/used as protection from animals. One of the women said I can use it to beat my husband with, so I thought, hey, could come in handy one day!

Just as I was about to pay for it, mass confusion broke out. People were suddenly scrambling to pack up their things and run. It was so weird—I couldn't figure out what was happening. I quickly gave one of the women my money and took the stick I wanted. Like the others hurrying past me, she too had a look of panic on her face that I didn't understand. I just stood there trying to make sense of the scene before me. Many people were running to the far end of the market where I stood. They were running away from something unknown to me, and in less than two minutes one could hardly tell where the market had been. I asked the woman who sold me the stick what was happening and she said, *"Mwezi,"* Swahili for thief. The way everyone was clearing out I thought maybe there was a bunch of bandits rampaging the place; but that wasn't the case.

Then I saw the mob forming on the opposite side of the market from where I stood. I had heard about mob justice, where some unfortunate soul stupid enough to steal something pays the ultimate price for the crime—death, or something close to it. I couldn't see exactly what was happening, but the group was obviously surrounding someone. I found Kika and we just stood there taking in the whole scene. She said that they were using some concrete bricks that were lying around to beat somebody. We were standing about 40 feet from the mob with others who hadn't fled. A man and woman were standing near us and filled us in on what was happening.

Apparently, a couple of young people came to the market and stole something and were caught. Someone probably called *"mwezi,"* and as happens with mob justice, people grabbed and surrounded them and then started beating the thieves. The people selling things then scrambled to get out of the way so if the thieves broke free and started running, the mob that followed wouldn't trample all of the things lying on the ground for sale. A couple of times as we stood there, people would suddenly panic and start running, which would perpetuate the mob hysteria that seemed to mesmerize everyone witnessing the gruesome event. Despite the fact that I no longer had an appetite and felt almost sick to my stomach, I felt compelled to stay and experience the mob justice phenomenon that I'd heard occurred all too often in this country.

After perhaps ten minutes, a man appeared from the crowd who from a distance looked as if he had blood on his head and was roughed up. But the most startling sight was the limp woman whom he carried on his back. She too had blood on her and was either unconscious or dead. People followed slowly behind as he walked under a clump of trees. At this point I asked someone if the woman was dead and if they would "necklace" the two people. I'm not so sure if this is unique to Kenya, but often if someone is caught stealing, the mob will place a tire around the person and light it, essentially burning the person to death. In this case, the police showed up, and apparently then there's no "torching." However, the woman was probably already dead from multiple blows to her head with the cement blocks, so further punishment would obviously be unnecessary.

I had heard so much about mob justice from people who had witnessed similar incidents, but not until I saw it for myself did I fully understand the horror of it. In a country like Kenya, where the police can't always be trusted to fight crime, and where people have so few valuables, citizens are incredibly intolerant of thieves and it is socially acceptable for people to take the law into their own hands in such cases.

Kika and I walked away from the scene in a daze. I still can't fully comprehend the fact that we probably witnessed a murder. Justice was rendered, right? What ever happened to "innocent until proven guilty"? In Kenya you are guilty until proven innocent, but all too often it's too late.

1. What issues and/or problems can you identify in this case?

2. How does this case illustrate the systems model for analyzing group interaction?

T his case clearly illustrates the very complex systems nature of group dynamics. The attitudes and culture of the Masai were at the heart of the situation. The short-term result was a loss of life. The longer-term result was that civil order was maintained. Although the case doesn't follow up the incident, probably the group's attitudes will be strengthened and its cohesiveness increased; a new thief will likely face an even more close-knit society.

In this chapter we will examine six factors that we refer to as relevant background factors. They are personality, sex, age, health, attitudes, and values. One of the basic premises of systems theory is that all these factors are interrelated, so that a change in one part of the system creates changes in other parts of the system.

EXPLAINING WHY WE DO WHAT WE DO

Perhaps you may have wondered why the Masai acted the way they did. Or more generally, why do any people behave the way they do? This question has intrigued people for centuries. Behaving in specific ways is usually seen as an attempt by the individual to meet certain needs. For example, have you ever been in a group situation and wondered why you were there? Suppose you look out a classroom window and see a beautiful sky; it is a great day for being outside. You begin to experience competing needs—the need to go outside and have fun and the need to accomplish whatever the group's purpose is (such as studying for an upcoming exam). Whichever need is more intense will most probably determine the behavior you pursue.

Probably one of the best-known models for explaining people's needs is Maslow's (1970) hierarchy of needs (see Figure 2.1).

FIGURE 2.1   MASLOW'S NEED HIERARCHY

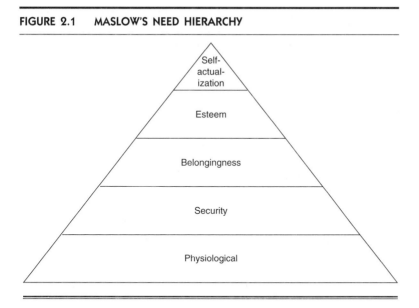

Physiological needs must be met in order to survive. Some groups were formed in the days of the cave dwellers to fight off saber-toothed tigers, as well as unfriendly cave people, and to help gather food.

Security needs often motivate the formation of groups by individuals who lack sufficient power on their own. This is demonstrated by the union movement, which resulted from the fact that there were far more workers than jobs. With ten people waiting to fill each job, workers were somewhat hesitant to make demands of bosses. Unions helped workers gain power and, eventually, job security.

Belongingness needs are easy for most people to identify with. Think about what you felt like during your first week as a college freshman. One student member of a freshman discussion group wrote about this belongingness need not being fulfilled:

> During our discussion, I felt like I wasn't even supposed to be in my group. The others seemed like they were all very familiar with each other and discussed almost entirely among themselves. They took over the discussion basically by looking only at each other and asking a lot of questions of each other (and cracking a lot of really funny jokes). I tried to contribute but felt ignored. It was very uncomfortable and I became quiet after a few more attempts to contribute. I'm glad I didn't receive a grade on that discussion because I was annoyed at how little I participated.

Eventually, the feelings of aloneness begin to subside as people develop their own circles of friends (social groups).

Esteem needs may also be met by groups. Often people are attracted to certain fraternities or sororities because of the prestige of membership, which adds to their feeling of self-esteem. All people need to feel that they are important, and being a part of a good group or organization is one very good way to accomplish that goal.

Self-actualization needs are the highest-level needs Maslow identified. A person may be attracted to a group because of the need for self-development. Encounter groups are one particular type of group devoted to the growth and development of members. Educational groups or work groups also may help individuals achieve a higher lever of human potential.

Maslow argued that the needs lowest on the hierarchy must be satisfied before the higher-level needs are activated. For example, we worry less about self-actualization in a job when we are unemployed and the bills haven't been paid.

Probably one of the reasons Maslow's theory has been so popular is because it seems intuitively valid. It is important to have an understanding of what motivates people (including ourselves). When we are in a group and one person talks a lot, it may be that he or she is trying to meet a belongingness need. If people brag, they are probably trying to satisfy an esteem need. If they consistently offer creative ideas that seem quite unusual, they may be trying to meet a self-actualization need.

PERSONALITY

Because each of us is a member of numerous groups throughout our lives, have you ever wondered what motivates us to join groups in the first place? Although there are many personality theories, one seems particularly relevant to small group behavior. Schutz (1958, 1967, 1971) hypothesized that most people share three needs that groups help fulfill: needs for inclusion, control, and affection. You will find Schutz's theory explained in detail at the end of this chapter. It is called the *FIRO-B theory.* FIRO-B stands for Fundamental Interpersonal Relations Orientation—Behavior. It means that individuals relate or orient themselves to others in ways that can be identified, measured, and predicted. If you are trying to lead a work group, it is very useful to be able to understand what motivates you and your group members.

Schutz's work began at the Naval Research Laboratory in Washington, D.C. The FIRO-B test has been used to select submarine crews as well as astronaut teams whose members would have personality styles that would help them work more efficiently together under high-stress conditions. The major premise of Schutz's theory is that people need people and that we join groups to help fill this need. Each person, from childhood on, develops a fundamental interpersonal relations orientation with differing levels of needed inclusion, control, and affection.

All of us have felt the need for inclusion. If you have ever been in a physical education class in which teams were chosen, you know this feeling. Do you remember waiting to be chosen and fearing not being chosen? Some people have also experienced the need for control. If you are trying to lead a group, and several conversations are going on simultaneously, the situation brings out the need to control the discussion. Finally, if a group pays a lot of attention to certain members, this can make us feel the need to have some attention and affection directed our way, too. These are important needs in all people, but obviously they vary in intensity from person to person.

Inclusion

Inclusion refers to our need for belonging, feeling a part of and being together with others. Have you ever been in a group in which you felt ignored? Perhaps you have felt this way in this very class, especially on the first or second day. This is because you were not being responded to as much as your need for inclusion required. Other people may not necessarily disagree with what you are saying; they just may not be responding. Such behavior violates our need to be included in the group. On a more basic level, it also makes us doubt our self-worth. If this exclusion happens over and over, most of us will begin to doubt our intrinsic worth as people.

On the job, if people go to lunch and don't invite us, our need for inclusion may not be met. On the other hand, if we prefer to do things on our own and people are constantly around us, this violates our *low* need for inclusion. Most of us want to be included in some groups and prefer to avoid others. If we are ignored by the attractive groups and sought after by the unattractive groups, this also violates our need for inclusion.

Even the rich and famous need to feel included. In her book on the tragic life of NBC News anchorwoman Jessica Savitch, Blair (1988) writes:

> Recently, however, Savitch had asked Linda Ellerbee to dinner at Hurley's. "Jessica wanted to be one of the guys, to be associated with those of us who did what we were paid to do," Ellerbee said. "She wanted to talk journalism war stories, but hers all had to do with hairdressers and missed planes and missed opportunities." As Ellerbee sat there listening to Savitch, who was talking so loudly that other diners' heads were turning, she felt any remaining envy dissolve into pity for the blond anchorwoman. "NBC was a good place for women to work," Ellerbee said. "We stuck together. But Jessica never got into any of that. She was terrified of being found out, so she never got close to anybody at work. She never trusted any of us." (p. 334)

The late Sammy Davis, Jr., experienced the opposite of inclusion (exclusion) when he first went into his group in the U.S. Army in 1942. Here is his gripping description of the incident:

> It was impossible to believe they were talking about me.
> "Yeah, but I still ain't sleepin' next to no nigger." . . . The corporal beckoned from the doorway. "Okay, c'mon in," he snapped, "on the double." We picked up our gear and followed him through the door. I felt like a disease he was bringing in. . . . I looked around the barracks. The bed nearest ours was empty. All the cots were about two feet apart from each other except ours, which were separated from the rest by about six feet—like we were on an island. . . . A sergeant came in and from the center of the barracks announced, "I'm Sergeant Williams. I'm in charge of this company. . . . There is only one way we do things here and that's the Army way! There will be exactly three feet of space, to the inch, between every bed in this barracks. You have sixty seconds to replace the beds as you found them. *Move!*" (Davis and Boyar, 1989, pp. 6–7)

The inclusion issue raises its head over and over throughout our lives. Each time we take a new job, join a new work group, or meet a new group socially, we feel excluded. Problems occur when we are not sensitive to someone who is new in the group. That person is experiencing the feeling, but we may not be tuned into his or her needs. Often, when a person comes in late for a meeting, the others do not make any attempt to orient that person or bring him or her up to date. All of us have a need for inclusion that must be met before we are able to function fully in a group. Keep in mind that this need recurs, much as our need to eat.

Control

Control refers to our need to influence, lead, and develop power over others or to be influenced, led, or have others exert power over us. If you have ever been in a group with no appointed leader, you know how uncomfortable it is to break the ice and get the discussion started. Those who attempt to get the group organized are trying to exert control over the others. At first, this may be welcomed, but often people begin to resent the control takers and will eventually ask them to stop being so pushy, with comments such as, "Who died and left you boss?" The issue of who is in control remains alive throughout the life of any group. Especially as membership changes, the pecking order is reshuffled and has to be reestablished. Here is an account of a class exercise in which resentment of a control taker is very obvious:

> The group consisted of seven people. The purpose of the class exercise was to form a manufacturing company and produce products. One individual chose himself as General Manager and also appointed an Assistant General Manager. The remaining members formed the assembly line workers. . . . The General Manager was a very forceful, energetic individual. He chose his own Assistant and appointed himself almost before we had formed the group. He is a very impatient individual. His entire manner left everyone in doubt as to the final outcome of the exercise. . . . The practice run was a complete disaster. We didn't know what the product was, let alone how to build it. Step by step instructions were available for everyone to read, but we weren't given time to read them. The General Manager didn't pay attention to his duties. He was more interested in production line speed than he was in purchasing materials or financial matters. He couldn't get quality products because of the haphazard organization of the work force. We had to start over again and again. The third time through, we got fairly decent quality. By that time it was too late. Dissension in the ranks of the group was rampant. . . . We were not motivated to do a good job, the only challenge was to beat the opposition (i.e., management).

Control, power, and leadership are closely related subjects. Why do you suppose so much has been written about them? Who is in control seems to be one of life's basic issues. Some studies have shown that whenever two people meet for the first time, a dominant-submissive relationship is established within the first sixty seconds. The perceptions of who is dominant between two people have been found to correlate over 90 percent with carefully constructed personality tests measuring the same phenomenon. Some books on power and control go to extreme lengths to help people gain control over others. Korda (1975) suggests that in order to gain and hold control over others, you should position your desk with your back to a window so that the other person has to look into the sunlight, thus putting him or her at a disadvantage.

The control issue is relevant to every organization on a daily basis, from the formal organization and the so-called span of control to who talks the most in meetings. Supervisors typically talk more than subordinates. They also usually control the topic of conversation. Control is often demonstrated in rather subtle ways, too. I once saw a professor throw a report on a secretary's desk. He said, "Sandy, I need to have this typed for the 3 o'clock class today." You could tell by her expression that she did not like the way he talked to her. Later that day, he came to pick up the finished report. She said, "Gee, Dave, I'm really sorry. I just didn't have time to get it done. Dr. Jenkins [the department head] had me on another project all day." She was giving Dave a lesson in organizational control. Any experienced supervisor knows how much control his or her subordinates have if they choose to use it.

Affection

Affection refers to the friendship and closeness among people. Often our best friends are coworkers. Why is it that when we have time off from the job, we will organize bowling leagues, golf outings, and baseball leagues with coworkers? Some of these activities, such as the company picnic or Christmas party, may be more or less required. But for the most part, we socialize off the job as well as on because we want to; picture the many winning-team locker-room scenes with the champagne pouring over people's heads and players hugging each other as extreme examples of this affection.

Schutz (1967) compares inclusion, control, and affection in the following way:

> A difference in inclusion behavior, control behavior, and affection behavior is illustrated by the different feelings a man has in being turned down by a fraternity, failed in a course by a professor, and rejected by his girl. . . . Inclusion is concerned with the problem of in or out, control is concerned with top or bottom, and affection with close or far.

In each of these areas we have both the need to receive these behaviors from others and the need to express such needs toward others. Wanted inclusion would be hoping to be asked to go to lunch or for coffee or to have a beer with the group; expressed inclusion would be inviting someone else to go. A compatible need level would exist when a person's wanted and expressed needs are at about the same level of intensity. Compatibility among individuals seems to occur when their needs are similar on the inclusion and affection dimensions and complementary or different on the control dimension. A group may suffer from too many power struggles if members are all high in need to control. Compatibility on these three dimensions tends to reduce conflict and increase group cohesiveness and satisfaction.

A carefully controlled laboratory study found that Schutz's predictions were substantiated. Liddell and Slocum (1976) constructed groups that were neutral, compatible, or incompatible on the basis of FIRO-B scores. When the groups were allowed to work on a problem-solving task, the compatible groups completed their tasks significantly faster than the neutral groups, which were significantly more efficient than the incompatible groups.

FIRO-B also has been found to be useful in organizational development. Varney and Hunady (1978) conducted a study in a fifty-year-old heavy-metal production plant with 900 employees and 95 managers. They used the FIRO-B test as a tool to give feedback to the work groups regarding their own individual needs and to give them insight into each other. The plant manager originally described the organization's needs in the following summary:

> There is a considerable amount of disagreement and disharmony among members of the management staff, resulting in a failure on the part of individuals as well as the team as a whole to accomplish set tasks. The performance indictors for the plant are in almost all cases below the normal, and we ranked among a total of six plants in our division as the lowest performer. The basic problem seems to be that people cannot work together when it comes to sorting out problems, and they spend a lot of time blaming each other for the failures that occur. (p. 445)

As a result of the study, the researchers reported numerous changes in the behavior of the employees involved in the study. They concluded, "FIRO-B is a powerful stimulus to change. In the research reported here, we have demonstrated the value of the use of a "high energizer" such as the FIRO-B in team-building interventions" (p. 445).

Although personality is one of the most important background factors in small group communication, other factors are also involved. *Organismic factors* or variables are those that are part of the organism. These include a number of characteristics, but three seem to be especially pertinent to small group interaction: sex, age, and health.

SEX

Perhaps the most obvious thing about groups that include both sexes is that they are most interesting! Schutz (1971) writes, "Usually, if there's a girl in the group who attracts me I find more interest in the group as a whole, and must watch myself because I tend to find everything she says and does somehow much more fascinating than I do anyone else's contribution" (p. 226). Women emphatically point out that the increased arousal brought about by a member of the opposite sex is every bit as much a part of the feminine response pattern as it is the masculine.

Sex does seem to play an increasing role in work groups. Blotnick (1986) surveyed 1800 professional women between the ages of 18 and 45. They had a median age of 32 and an average income of $26,000. He found that an astonishing 56 percent reported having had an affair with a coworker, customer, or client. This compared to only 7 to 9 percent in the 1970s and even lower percentages in the 1950s and 1960s. These statistics lead to the conclusion that sex is a volatile and extremely relevant background factor to consider in work group settings.

More recently, Maineiro (1990) wrote of recent surveys involving sex and the work group:

> Over eighty-six percent of the employees whom they interviewed had been aware of, or had been involved in, an office romance. A survey of 444 readers showed . . . over fifty percent of those surveyed had been sexually propositioned by someone at work; a quarter had sex in their place of work and another eighteen percent had sex with a co-worker during work hours! (p. 5)

In a survey of 3144 people reported by Grantham (1992), 30 percent of the men and 29 percent of the women answered "yes" to the question "Have you ever made love at (your) place of work?" He also cites that "four out of five employees said they either knew a co-worker who was involved in a romantic relationship at work or were involved in one themselves" (p. F1).

These statistics are even more shocking given that Thomas (1986, p. 26) reports that 53 percent of all the full-time workers in America are women and that of all the women in the country between ages 25 and 35, fully 66 percent are working full time.

Differences in behavior between the sexes have for years been known to be a function of cultural influences and childhood learning experiences. Margaret Mead (1968) found as early as 1935 that certain behaviors the Western world had assumed were innately masculine or feminine were, instead, culturally determined. In her studies of New Guinea tribes, she found certain societies in which women dominated. She writes: "Among the Tchambuli the woman is the dominant, impersonal, managing partner, the man the less responsible and the emotionally dependent person" (p. 259). Mead describes the husband, on the other hand, as being catty toward other men but charming toward women. He danced in the tribal ceremonies, spent hours on his personal makeup, and gossiped about the other *men* in the village. Obviously, such behaviors cannot be an inherent function of one's sex.

One recent study of car-buying decisions found that women of younger ages (25 to 44) tend to be significantly less different from men than are older women (45 to 65). The authors specifically identify the interaction of age, sex, and attitudes to explain the findings. In other words, younger women have attitudes much more similar to those of men than do older women (Widgery and McGaugh, 1993).

It would seem that the same futility presently exists in attempting to predict *group* communication behaviors on the basis of sex alone. However, it is important to emphasize that certain stereotypes concerning male and female roles are probably outdated and that new research is needed to establish whether any sex differences do exist regarding small group behaviors. For example, review the stereotypes listed below:

How to Tell a Businessman from a Businesswoman

A businessman is aggressive; a businesswoman is pushy.

A businessman is good on details; she's picky.

He loses his temper because he's so involved in his job; she's bitchy.

When he's depressed (or hung over), everyone tiptoes past his office.

She's moody, so it must be her time of the month.

He follows through; she doesn't know when to quit.

He's confident; she's conceited.

He stands firm; she's impossible to deal with.

He's firm; she's hard.

His judgments are her prejudices.

He is a man of the world; she's been around.

He drinks because of excessive job pressure; she's a lush.

He isn't afraid to say what he thinks; she's mouthy.

He exercises authority; she's power mad.

He's close-mouthed; she's secretive.

He's a stern taskmaster; she's hard to work for.

It seems reasonable to predict that groups comprised of both sexes will be different from those whose members are all of the same sex. We might expect that sexually heterogeneous groups would have more socially oriented behaviors and fewer task-oriented behaviors because their members would be more interested in promoting social relationships than those in homogeneous groups. A clever study by Rosenfeld and Fowler (1976) found that sex and personality combined to influence an individual's leadership style. The most interesting finding of this study seems to be that men and women who act similarly are perceived differently. According to Rosenfeld and Fowler, "Whereas democratic males were characterized as forceful, analytical, and as valuing the love of people . . . democratic females were characterized as open-minded and nurturing. The democratic male may appear to group members as analytical and thereby aloof, while the democratic female may appear to be warm and affectionate" (p. 324). This study illustrates what is meant by the systems aspects of small group interaction. Personality, sex, style of leadership behavior, and the resulting perception of the person behaving are all interrelated.

Morrison, White, and Van Velsor (1990, p. 290) conducted extensive interviews with seventy-six successful women in Fortune 100 companies. On the basis of this research, they identified six factors associated with women's career success. They are:

1. *Help:* Mentors from above offered advice and inspiration.

2. *Achievement:* A track record of proven successes.

3. *Desire:* This is demonstrated through hard work, long hours, and personal sacrifice.

4. *Management:* The ability to get people to perform while maintaining their respect and trust.

5. *Risk taking:* Career moves requiring relocation and travel were examples.

6. *Tough, decisive, and demanding:* Being aggressive, making hard decisions, and being willing to fight for what they believed was right.

It would seem from this list that there is nothing that would differentiate these characteristics from those of successful male executives. However, Loden (1990) found that women approach teamwork and participatory management differently from men. She found that "they are less likely to 'pull rank' and more likely to stress cooperation than competition" (p. 298).

Two recent best-selling books focus in depth on the difficulties of male-female communication. One, by Gray (1992), is entitled *Men Are from Mars, Women Are from Venus.* That should give you some idea of the vastness of the communication gap. The other book, by Tannen (1991), is strongly research-based. Tannen writes: "Study after study finds that it is men who talk more—at meetings, in mixed-group discussions, and in classrooms . . . [in university faculty meetings]. The men's turns [to talk] ranged from 10.66 to 17.07 seconds, while the women's turns ranged from 3–10 seconds" (p. 75). She goes on to say that, nonverbally, "the men sat with their legs stretched out, while the women gathered themselves in" (p. 130).

Suffice it to say that communication between the sexes will continue to be both complex and interesting.

AGE

Obviously, communication patterns differ from childhood through adolescence to adulthood and old age. Older group members in college-age groups (for example, married students, veterans, and so forth) tend to be more influential, on the basis of their relatively greater number of years of experience. Although this may not always hold true, it is usually the case. There is some evidence (Bass, Doll, and Clair, 1953) that older college women are held in higher esteem than younger college women. It generally takes time to develop leadership qualifications. In fact, one study (Quinn, 1973) indicated that one reason younger people in general have lower job satisfaction is that they tend to have lower-level jobs, which are inherently less satisfying. On the other hand, as they gain in age and experience, they move into more challenging job capacities and gain in satisfaction.

Zenger and Lawrence (1989) found that age similarity of group members had a positive effect on the communication of information within project groups. This stems from earlier notions that people tend to communicate with those who are similar to themselves. Similar age ranges lead to similar life experiences and interests. Communication channels produced by non-work-related conversations will influence the ease of work-related communications.

Finally, Shaw (1981), summarizing the literature on age and group behavior, states:

> There is good evidence that chronological age of the group member is related to several aspects of group interaction. With increasing age, the individual has an increasing . . . selectivity of contacts and greater complexity of . . . interaction. . . . Age is related to behavior in groups, it provides the time required for the individual to learn appropriate social responses, . . . [and] in most cases it is not the mere fact that the individual has aged that is important, but rather that he has had greater experience in social situations. (pp. 181–182)

It is also interesting to speculate that groups with age heterogeneity would perform differently than those with age homogeneity. A number of studies indicate that some member heterogeneity relates positively to such group outcomes as cohesion (Hare, 1962). It is apparent that age, and the experiences that go along with age, will affect group interaction and subsequent group outcomes. For the time being, however, the exact nature of these relationships is not clear.

HEALTH

Although health may not be a highly significant factor in the study of small groups, it does play a part. Deficiencies in both physical and mental health would seem to impede group performance. A member who fails to attend meetings or who is unable to carry his or her portion of the group workload will sooner or later reduce total group output. Also, physical health frequently affects stamina. Strength and stamina may not be important in relatively short discussions (lasting up to an hour); however, discussions and conferences frequently last for days. Labor-management negotiations may go twenty hours a day for a week or longer. In one case, a local labor agreement was settled after a prolonged strike; the week after the agreement was reached, the local union president died of a heart attack. So physical health and stamina can play an important part in small group interaction.

A recent study by Fox et al. (1993) showed that people's blood pressure was higher both at work and at home when they had too much to do at work and had very little empowerment. On the other hand, even those who had too much to do had lower blood pressure when they were given more empowerment. The use of groups and teams is one of the methods most often employed to increase empowerment. Think about situations in which you feel overwhelmed but can decide how to change things. Such situations are much less stressful than those in which you can't do anything to change things (i.e., you are between a rock and a hard place).

Those who are spaced out on drugs or who are hung over from the night before will also harm group performance. In one case a college professor was consistently abusive and aggressive in department meetings. He later admitted that he had been so high on drugs he didn't even remember being at the meetings. Yet his behavior caused severe setbacks in his department, because he argued vociferously against all attempts to cover the items in the group's agenda; he also seriously hurt the feelings of other group members through his verbal assaults. Physical and mental health factors are out of the control of other group members, yet they have an effect on the group's end results.

Bo Schembechler, the legendary former football coach of the University of Michigan and former president of the Detroit Tigers, gives the following account of how health affects his life:

> Sure enough, five weeks later, I was in the hospital for another catheterization when I started to have that second heart attack, and a day that was supposed to be back-to-work turned into the day they cut my chest open and did my second open-heart surgery. That one, I thought, would be the clincher. *God, just let me live.* My heart was becoming like an old car; parts were hard to find. I really figured my life would change after that, and I'd be lucky to be walking, let alone coaching, again. . . .
>
> So what have I learned from my troubled heart? Well I figure it's God's way of keeping me in check. Just like my bowl record. Without that, I'd have nothing but success in football; my ego would go through the roof. Same thing with my heart. Without that, I might lose all sight of what life is really about. I might just coach myself into oblivion, let little things depress me, never have a good laugh or shoot the breeze with players. But because of all the times I've been in that damn hospital wondering if I'd ever get out, I've really come to enjoy life, as crazy as it is.
>
> My heart has given me a certain perspective. I never get depressed. Little things don't upset me anymore. I'm a different guy than most people figure from watching the games or reading newspapers. All my screaming and carrying on is strictly in football—and most of that is for effect. Privately, I'm a fairly sensitive person, and I enjoy life, and I have a decent sense of humor. I like to laugh, I like people, and I'm pretty easy to please when it comes to doing things or going places. Why worry?
>
> As long as I hear that ticky, ticky, ticky, I'm a happy guy. (Schembechler and Albom, 1989, pp. 225–226)

One small company president (Stack, 1992) wrote about the health factor in the following way:

> Several years ago, I took up bass fishing for my health. It was near the end of 1983, the first year after the buyout, and the pressures were getting to me. My hair was falling out in clumps. I couldn't eat or sleep. I missed steps when I walked. I called a doctor, who told me it was either Lou Gehrig's disease or multiple sclerosis. The next doctor was more encouraging. He said it was stress. (p. 235)

As each of us develops through childhood and adolescence, a myriad of experiences shape our view of the world. Because we each have different experiences, we would expect our outlooks to differ also. These experiences are called *developmental factors,* and we will look at three that are related to small group interaction: attitudes, values, and anxieties.

ATTITUDES

Almost sixty years ago, Allport (1935) defined an *attitude* as "a mental and a neural state of readiness, organized through experience, exerting a directive or dynamic influence upon the individual's response to all objects and situations with which it is related." According to Triandis (1971), attitudes have three components: (1) a cognitive component, which refers to an idea or a concept, such as "Chevrolets," (2) an affective component, or the emotion toward the idea (Chevrolets are good), and (3) a behavioral component, which is the readiness to act (that is, to drive or buy a Chevrolet).

Group members may hold several types of attitudes that are relevant to their participation in small groups. For example, they have attitudes toward the task itself, toward the situation within which the group is operating, toward people inside and outside of the group, and toward other issues that may be related to the one under discussion. All these attitudes will ultimately affect their behavior in the group, which in turn will affect the group's results. How many times have you been a member of a project team or group in which either you or others in the group have found that you just couldn't seem to get too enthusiastic about accomplishing the task? Or perhaps you would ordinarily be interested in the task, but it comes at a time when you are preoccupied with other things, such as romantic difficulties or financial worries. These illustrations help to indicate the important role that attitudes may play in determining one's actions in the group.

Recently, Fulk (1993) found that group members who had strong attraction to their group tended to hold similar attitudes on other important topics. She measured attraction to the group on such items as the extent to which members "(1) cooperate with each other, (2) regard each other as friends, (3) know that they can depend on each other, (4) stand up for one another, and (5) work together as a team" (pp. 933–934).

Another variable in the background factors of small group communication is race. Perhaps it is difficult for you to recognize the relevance of discussing race differences in small group communications. Remember that each group member brings his or her own individual history to the group. Race and religious persuasion have proved to be associated with attitudes.

When we speak about organizations as groups, access discrimination has been successfully reduced within the last few years. But in many organizations, treatment discrimination is holding fast. Greenhaus and others (1990) found that although minority groups, particularly blacks, have come to occupy considerably more managerial positions in organizations in the last few years, they still receive fewer opportunities to excel in the organization. Compared to white managers, black managers felt less accepted in their organizations, perceived themselves as having less discretion on their jobs, received lower ratings from their supervisors in job performance and promotability, were more likely to have reached career plateaus, and experienced lower levels of career satisfaction.

A group environment that is conducive to equal opportunities should produce minimal race differences and will result in a more successful group effort.

Some of the most intuitive yet provocative theories concerning attitudes are the so-called cognitive consistency theories. These closely related theories are all based on the assumption that human beings have a strong psychological need for consistency. Heider (1958), the first of the consistency theorists, refers to this as a need to maintain *balance*. He reasons that if we hold an attitude X and another person holds the same value, then we are likely to feel positively toward that person. For example, if Lance likes motorcycles and Brad also likes motorcycles, Lance is like-

FIGURE 2.2

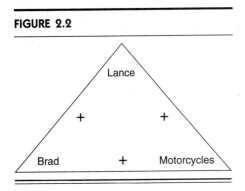

ly to have positive feelings toward Brad. This is illustrated in Figure 2.2. If, on the other hand, Brad does not like motorcycles, Lance would feel some imbalance and would be motivated to resolve it in one of several ways. First, he could try to change Brad's evaluation of motorcycles. Second, he could change his feeling toward Brad. Finally, he could change his own evaluation of motorcycles. The specific alternative Lance chooses would depend on the relative strength of his attitudes toward Brad and toward motorcycles.

Heider predicts that balanced triads are rewarding, or pleasant to experience, whereas imbalanced triads result in pressure to restore balance. An easy rule of thumb for differentiating between balanced and imbalanced triads is that if the algebraic product of the three elements in the triad is positive, the triad is balanced. If the algebraic product is negative, the triad is imbalanced. Which of the triads in Figure 2.3 is imbalanced, thus creating pressure to restore balance? How could balance be restored?

A related consistency theory is called *cognitive dissonance theory* (Festinger, 1957). In this theory, *consonance* is the same as Heider's concept of balance, and *dissonance* is equivalent to imbalance in that it serves to motivate a change back to consonance. One of the interesting finds of research in this area is that a severe ini-

FIGURE 2.3

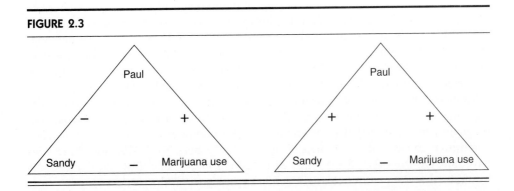

tiation for attaining group membership creates a high level of dissonance, which is usually resolved by the person's valuing membership in the group more than if the initiation were less severe (Aronson and Mills, 1959).

Fraternities and sororities have used pledging as a device to increase the severity of initiation into membership. The result is usually that one who endures these experiences reduces the dissonance caused by them and begins to believe they are necessary and even desirable for the new pledge class to endure. The traditional pride in being a U.S. marine has also resulted largely from the severity of initiation experienced in Marine Corps boot camp. The 1992 movie *A Few Good Men* provides a good example of this.

Group interaction may also create dissonance. If you are confronted in a discussion with an opinion contrary to your own, some degree of dissonance will result. The dissonance will increase if you value the other person and if the issue over which you disagree is one of high relevance. According to Festinger and Aronson (1968) you may reduce the dissonance in these five ways (starting with the most likely and going to the least likely approach): (1) Devalue the importance of the issue; (2) derogate the disagreeing person; (3) attempt to change his or her attitude; (4) seek additional social support for your view; and (5) change your attitude. Aronson (1973) posits that although people like to think of themselves as rational animals, they are more likely than not "rationalizing animals." It is important to point out that we all use these methods of dissonance reduction, and we need to have them. Although rationalizing may sound like something we should avoid, it can be a helpful tool if we are consciously aware of using it.

VALUES

Although an overwhelming amount of research has been conducted on attitudes and attitude change, Rokeach (1968, 1971, 1973) has argued that people's *values* are also important as a predictor of behavior. His rationale is that we have thousands of different attitudes, but we have only several dozen values. Values, then, are seen as more fundamental than attitudes and are more stable and long-lasting. For an exercise concerning your own values and how they relate to the values of others, see Exercise 1 at the end of this chapter.

People are both products and producers of their environment. As outlined in a social cognition theory by Wood and Bandura (1989), *reciprocal determinism* represents the "bidirectional influence" of our behavior. We respond, with our own personal values and experiences, to others, with their own personal values and experiences. Others respond to our responding to them, and our behavior determines and is determined by our environment. The process is both reciprocal and perpetual.

Value differences may significantly influence the course of any given group discussion. Suppose you are in a group attempting to determine a policy regarding pregnancy leaves of absence for employees of a company. Suppose also that your committee consists of six women, three who have been to college and three who have not. On the basis of the study data in Figure 2.4, how likely do you think it would be that the committee might achieve consensus on this issue?

FIGURE 2.4
Bar graph from the *Flint Journal,*
November 13, 1974

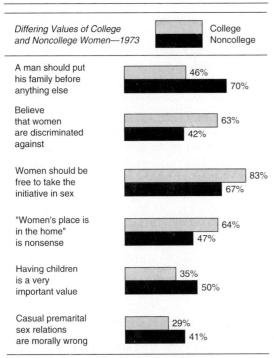

*Differing Values of College
and Noncollege Women—1973*

☐ College
■ Noncollege

A man should put
his family before
anything else — 46% / 70%

Believe
that women
are discriminated
against — 63% / 42%

Women should be
free to take the
initiative in sex — 83% / 67%

"Women's place is
in the home"
is nonsense — 64% / 47%

Having children
is a very
important value — 35% / 50%

Casual premarital
sex relations
are morally wrong — 29% / 41%

Women's movement has had its warmest reception
on America's campuses. The recent Yankelovich "Study
of American Youth" reports that the values of Women's
Lib have created a wide schism between women in college
and women who do not have a college education.

This research indicates that educational differences would generate severe value differences between the two subgroups on the committee. If one group, the non-college women, basically valued motherhood and devalued careers for women, it would probably be difficult for them to agree with the others on a leave-of-absence policy decision. Similar difficulties arise in discussions dealing with sexual behaviors, obscenity, abortion, religion, and politics, for example. Any discussion on a topic on which people have strong value differences is likely to be complicated by such differences.

With the graduating class of 1986, there were two nationally publicized examples of values influencing graduation committees' decisions. At Rice University in Houston, Texas, two graduates who were vegetarians asked administrators to allow them to have diplomas printed on paper rather than on sheepskin. One of the graduates said, "I don't participate in eating meat. If I draw the line there, why not draw it one step further?" (Associated Press, 1986b). At Tufts University in Boston, the medical school students no longer wanted to take the 2000-year-old Hippocratic oath because they no longer believed in the values it upheld. Instead, they vowed to "stress prevention over cure, tend to their patients' psychological needs, seek help from others, and, above all, 'not play God'" (Associated Press, 1986a).

At every university, committees decide such policies. It is conceivable that the values of the administrators on those committees played a part in determining the decisions described above. In fact, Naisbitt (1982) argues that these are simply examples of one "megatrend," which he calls "From either/or to Multiple Option." As another example, he cites the number of television channels that used to be available (three networks) compared to the ever-increasing number offered by cable television.

Earlier we discussed the influence of age on values and behaviors. Payne, Summers, and Stewart (1973) studied subjects from three generations (college students, their parents, and their grandparents). The subjects were asked to respond on a seven-point scale—from (1) "not at all bad" to (7) "extremely bad"—to each of eighty-five items. Sample items were:

- Becoming involved in unusual sex practices with persons of the opposite sex

- Being unpatriotic

- Cheating on your income tax

- Cheating on an exam and getting caught

- Going to a party in casual clothes and finding that everyone is dressed up

- Having to go on welfare to feed or clothe your children adequately

The researchers found that college students were significantly less severe in their judgments than were their parents, who were in turn less severe than the grandparents.

Although differences exist among generations, it is also likely that major differences exist among individuals in the same age group. A question arises as to the degree of value differences that can be tolerated in a group before these differences become a major obstacle to group functioning. Fortunately, some related research sheds light on this question. Rogers and Shoemaker (1971) discussed this issue with regard to homophily and heterophily of relationships. *Homophily* is defined as "the degree to which pairs of individuals who interact are similar in certain attributes (beliefs, values, education, social status)" (McCroskey, 1971, p. 174). Rogers and Bhowmik (1971) state: "Heterophilic interaction is likely to cause message distortion, delayed transmission, restriction of communication channels, and may cause cognitive dissonance, as the receiver is exposed to messages that may be inconsistent with his existing beliefs and attitudes, an uncomfortable psychological state" (p. 213). In other words, two students would probably communicate more easily than a student and a professor. Although considerable research has been conducted on the effect of homophily-heterophily on the diffusion of innovations, more research is needed to determine the effects these factors have on group functioning and group outcomes.

One promising outcome of recent studies is that groups comprised of culturally diverse individuals learn to work more effectively over time. Groups of four were formed of one white American, one African American, one Hispanic American, and a foreign national from another country. The homogeneous groups consisted of four white Americans. Initially, the homogeneous groups were more effective (as measured by quantity and quality of solutions to problems). However, over the course of seventeen weeks the diverse groups became as proficient as the homogeneous groups (Watson et al., 1993).

With the increase in international trade, it is more than likely that most of you will at some time be involved in a group project with someone raised in a culture different from your own. Also, it is important for you to remember that there are many different cultures right here in the United States. You don't have to go across the ocean to find someone with cultural values different from your own. As Weisinger (1989) points out, it is important not to force a person to act in a way that contradicts his or her cultural norms. If such a situation arises, make sure that everyone in the group knows one another's cultural rules. Being aware of such differences will help group members learn the best way to respond to one another.

THE SYSTEMS PERSPECTIVE

As we pointed out in Chapter 1, small group interactions are the result of influences that can be labeled inputs, throughputs, and outputs. These factors are in a constant state of simultaneous and reciprocal influence. This chapter has focused on some of the inputs—namely, the relevant background factors of the group members. Through the discussion of personality, we tried to illustrate the role personality plays in shaping individual behavior. For example, those high on inclusion will probably be more inclined to join groups in the first place (if we assume that membership is voluntary). Those high on affection are very likely to smile more, express more feelings both verbally and nonverbally than low affiliators, give more direct eye contact to more members of the group, and agree more than low affiliators. We would expect that high-affection members would have higher satisfaction resulting from harmonious group experiences, and greater dissatisfaction with groups that experience a high degree of conflict and disagreement. The person low on need for inclusion would tend to avoid meetings and group memberships whenever possible and would avoid talking in the groups he or she was forced to be in. Group interaction would generally be viewed by the introvert as threatening and therefore less satisfying than engaging in the same activity alone. However, if the group were conducted by a supportive and nonthreatening leader, the introvert's satisfaction level would increase dramatically.

High-control members tend to enjoy working on task-oriented projects, because they are more task-oriented than most others and find that the group tends to slow down their progress. The exception, of course, would be a group composed of a lot of high controllers. In this case, high cohesion or high conflict might result, depending on the way the members decided to reward their efforts. Thus group norms, leadership style, and communication patterns all tend to influence the satisfaction level of group members.

The three organismic factors discussed in this chapter were sex, age, and health. A group with both sexes tends to have more socially oriented communication patterns and fewer task-oriented comments resulting.

Age seems to be somewhat similar to attitudes and values in that the more similar group members are (in age, attitudes, and values), the easier it is for them to communicate in a way that leads to higher satisfaction. One recent study (Wiersema and Bird, 1993) found that groups that had members with highly diverse ages, team tenure, and university prestige tended to have much more group membership turnover than groups that had member similarity. It stands to reason that it is more comfortable to be in groups with people like ourselves (in terms of age, attitudes, and values) than it is to be in groups in which we feel we "don't fit in" as well. However, some of the most interesting experiences occur when we meet someone of a drastically different age group who shares our attitudes and values. Conversely, even people of one's own age may differ so much in attitude or personality that hard feelings result.

Even organizations can promote certain values. Saturn Corporation includes the following in the company values that it advertises (Stoney, 1993):

> *Teamwork*
> We are dedicated to singleness of purpose through the effective involvement of members [employees], suppliers, dealers, neighbors, and other stakeholders. A fundamental tenet of our philosophy is the belief that effective teams engage the talents of individual members while encouraging team growth.

Small wonder that Saturn has become one of the major organizational success stories of the twentieth century.

In the readings at the end of this chapter, William Schutz shows the importance of the need for inclusion, control, and affection in relation to several aspects of group behavior. The second selection, by Widgery and Tubbs, attempts to apply attitude change theory to real life.

EXERCISES

1. Employee Selection Problem

You are a member of a personnel selection committee. You need to hire two people as first-line supervisors in an industrial foundry. The supervisors would be in charge of thirty-person (mostly male) work groups who do machining processes (grinding, drilling, polishing) on metal castings made from molten metal in a different part of the foundry. Examine all five information sheets, which describe the candidates who have passed the physical examination and are available for immediate employment.

1

NAME: Sally A. Peterson　　　　　　　AGE: 23

MARITAL STATUS: Married　　　　　　Number of Children: 0

NUMBER OF DEPENDENTS OTHER THAN SELF (explain relation): 1—husband

EDUCATION

	Years	Degree or Diploma	Major (where applicable)
Elementary	8	Yes	
High School	4	Yes	College prep.
College	4	Yes (B.A.)	Sociology

CURRENT EDUCATIONAL OR VOCATIONAL SITUATION: Has been management trainee for four months with XYZ Aircraft Company. Began with XYZ immediately after serving two years with Peace Corps.

VOCATIONAL SKILLS OR EXPERIENCE: None other than a few elementary skills learned while in Peace Corps.

POLICE RECORD: None

ADDITIONAL COMMENTS: Currently active in volunteer community social work. Has taken over Junior Achievement group in underprivileged neighborhood.

2

NAME: Thomas Browne　　　　　　　Age: 26

MARITAL STATUS: Married　　　　　　NUMBER OF CHILDREN: 0

NUMBER OF DEPENDENTS OTHER THAN SELF (explain relation): 1—wife

EDUCATION

	Years	Degree or Diploma	Major (where applicable)
Elementary	8	Yes	
High School	4	Yes	College prep.
College	4	Yes (B.A.)	Economics
	½	(toward M.A.)	Economics

CURRENT EDUCATIONAL OR VOCATIONAL SITUATION: Is completing first year in graduate school working toward M.A. in economics, which should be completed in one more semester. Is classified in top third of his graduate school class. Is currently a research assistant to leading economist in graduate school of business.

VOCATIONAL SKILLS OR EXPERIENCE: None

POLICE RECORD: Arrested with a number of other students involved in campus disturbance—released without charges being made.

ADDITIONAL COMMENTS: None

3

NAME: William Cross   AGE: 20

MARITAL STATUS: Married   NUMBER OF CHILDREN: 0
                                                        (expecting first child in 6 months)

NUMBER OF DEPENDENTS OTHER THAN SELF (explain relation): 1—wife

EDUCATION:

	Years	Degree or Diploma	Major (where applicable)
Elementary	8	Yes	
High School	4	Yes	Vocational
College			

CURRENT EDUCATIONAL OR VOCATIONAL SITUATION: Plumber's apprentice completing second year of apprenticeship. Employed by large building contractor.

VOCATIONAL SKILLS OR EXPERIENCE: Plumbing, some automotive repair skills, welding. General construction work.

POLICE RECORD: Two arrests, no convictions.
First arrest while in high school—no details because of juvenile status. Second arrest for disorderly conduct—charges dismissed.

ADDITIONAL COMMENTS: None

4

NAME: Jane Williams   AGE: 24

MARITAL STATUS: Single   NUMBER OF CHILDREN: 0

NUMBER OF DEPENDENTS OTHER THAN SELF (explain relation): 0

EDUCATION:

	Years	Degree or Diploma	Major (where applicable)
Elementary	8	Yes	
High School	4	Yes	College prep.
College	4	Yes (B.A.)	Sociology
	1½	Yes (M.B.A.)	Production Management

CURRENT EDUCATIONAL OR VOCATIONAL SITUATION: Completing second year of graduate school. Has B.A. in sociology, working toward Ph.D., which should be completed in 3 to 4 semesters. Ranks in middle third of graduate class. Working one-half time as a teaching assistant. Doing volunteer work, and beginning research on urban sociology project.

VOCATIONAL SKILLS OR EXPERIENCE: None

POLICE RECORD: None

ADDITIONAL COMMENTS: None

5

Robert Smith   AGE: 21

MARITAL STATUS: Single   NUMBER OF CHILDREN: 0

NUMBER OF DEPENDENTS OTHER THAN SELF (explain relation): 0

EDUCATION:

	Years	Degree or Diploma	Major (where applicable)
Elementary	8	Yes	
High School	4	Yes	College prep.
College	3½	B.S. expected at end of semester	Business Administration

CURRENT EDUCATIONAL OR VOCATIONAL SITUATION: College senior expecting degree at end of current (spring) semester. "A–" student.

VOCATIONAL SKILLS OR EXPERIENCE: Typing. Has also worked part time in selling, construction work, and on farms.

POLICE RECORD: None

ADDITIONAL COMMENTS: Father unemployed for medical reasons. Mother works to support family. It is known that he has worked his way through college and has incurred a small debt in the form of a student loan.

Group Task   After reviewing all five information sheets, meet as a group for thirty minutes to decide which two candidates should get the jobs. Each of you in the group will be assigned to argue in favor of one of the five candidates. After each of you presents the best "case" for your candidate, you must work together collectively to determine in the best interest of everyone concerned who should be hired. Your company is an equal opportunity/affirmative action employer.

2. Self-Esteem Exercise

Rate yourself on the following list of terms. First put an "I" in the appropriate blank indicating how you would like to be *ideally*. After completing all the items, begin the list again. This time put an "R" in the appropriate blank indicating how you think you *really* are. After you have rated your ideal self and your real self, compare the two. You may want to talk to others to see how their ratings compare.

1. Attractive   ___:___:___:___:___:___   Unattractive

2. Intelligent   ___:___:___:___:___:___   Unintelligent

3. Weak	___:___:___:___:___:___	Strong
4. Passive	___:___:___:___:___:___	Active
5. Fair	___:___:___:___:___:___	Unfair
6. Kind	___:___:___:___:___:___	Unkind
7. Quiet	___:___:___:___:___:___	Loud
8. Introverted	___:___:___:___:___:___	Extroverted
9. Nervous	___:___:___:___:___:___	Relaxed
10. Liberal	___:___:___:___:___:___	Conservative
11. Happy	___:___:___:___:___:___	Sad
12. Boastful	___:___:___:___:___:___	Humble
13. Controlled	___:___:___:___:___:___	Uncontrolled
14. Vulnerable	___:___:___:___:___:___	Invulnerable
15. Excited	___:___:___:___:___:___	Calm
16. Sexy	___:___:___:___:___:___	Unsexy
17. Trusting	___:___:___:___:___:___	Untrusting
18. Powerful	___:___:___:___:___:___	Weak
19. Conforming	___:___:___:___:___:___	Independent
20. Sensitive	___:___:___:___:___:___	Insensitive

3. Personal Styles Exercise

Read the descriptions of the Tough Battler, Friendly Helper, and Objective Thinker that follow. Then anonymously rate volunteer class members on these three dimensions by placing an "X" inside a triangle as illustrated.

After this has been done, distribute the ratings to the people who have been rated. Class members may ask questions to get more feedback on what behaviors create these impressions on fellow students.

4. Interaction Exercise★

- Go place your hand on the shoulder of the person in this room whom you have known the longest.

---

*Adapted from Diana K. Ivy and Phil Backlund, *Exploring Genderspeak: Personal Effectiveness in Gender Communication* (New York: McGraw-Hill, 1994), pp. 179–180.

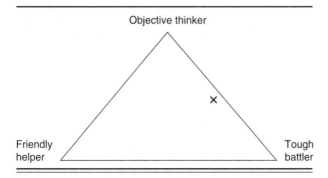

- Go place your hand on the shoulder of the person in this room with whom you spend the most time.

- Go place your hand on the shoulder of the person you think is most similar to you in attitudes, beliefs, and values.

- Go place your hand on the shoulder of the person you most believe you could gain or learn something from and tell her or him what that is.

- Go place your hand on the shoulder of the person you admire and tell him or her why.

Then break into groups of five and discuss the feelings and insights evoked by this exercise. Have each group report about its discussion to the entire class.

5. The New-Hire Case

Andrea Turner was a new faculty member at a small private college (150 faculty members). This was her first teaching job after receiving her Ph.D. from one of the most prestigious graduate schools in the country. She worked in the psychology department, which employed twenty-five faculty and three secretaries. Andrea commuted from a city 50 miles away. Therefore, she came to work only on the three days she taught classes and on other days did her other work at home.

When she was at work, she always kept her office door closed. Most others in the department left theirs open. Occasionally faculty members would go to the student center for coffee breaks in groups of three or four. Andrea was invited but almost never went. After a while, the others stopped asking her to join them. She was busy writing her first book for a prestigious publishing house.

Andrea was an effective teacher and participated on several faculty committees. She was a prolific writer and scholar. Over the course of three years, Andrea performed well above average for a new faculty member.

When it came time for her review for promotion, a great division was apparent among the other faculty members in their attitudes toward Andrea. A

PERSONAL STYLES IN GROUPS AND ORGANIZATIONS

Listed below are three characteristic types that may be found in any group or organization.

	Tough Battler	Friendly Helper	Objective Thinker
Emotions	Accepts aggression, rejects affection	Accepts affection, rejects aggression	Rejects both affection and interpersonal aggression
Goal	Dominance	Acceptance	Correctness
Influences others by	Direction, intimidation, control of rewards	Offering understanding, praise, favors, friendship	Factual data, logical arguments
Value in organization	Initiates, demands, disciplines	Supports, harmonizes, relieves tension	Defines, clarifies, gets information, criticizes, tests
Overuses	Fighting	Kindness	Analysis
Becomes	Pugnacious	Sloppy, sentimental	Pedantic
Fears	Being "soft" or dependent	Desertion, conflict	Emotions, irrational acts
Needs	Warmth, consideration, objectivity, humility	Strength, integrity, firmness, self-assertion	Awareness of feeling, ability to love and to fight

Above are shown characteristic emotions, goals, standards of evaluation, and techniques of influence of each type, and his/her service to the organization.

Each can be overdone and distorted. The *Tough Battler* would be a better manager, a better parent, a better neighbor, and a more satisfied person if he/she could learn some sensitivity, accept his/her inevitable dependence on others, and come to enjoy consideration for them. The Tough Battler would be more successful if he/she recognized that some facts will not yield to pugnacity.

The *Friendly Helper* would be a better manager, parent, citizen, and person if he/she could stand up for his/her own interests and for what is right, even against the pleas of others. This type needs firmness and strength and courage not to evade or smooth over conflicts. He/she must face facts.

The *Objective Thinker* would be a better human being and a better business leader if he/she could become more aware of his/her own feelings and the feelings of others. The Objective Thinker needs to learn that there are times when it is all right to fight and times when it is desirable to love.

Source: This material is adapted from the Reading Book *of the NTI Institute for Applied Behavioral Science associated with the National Education Association. The papers were originally prepared for theory sessions at the institute's laboratories.*

few felt that her work was very strong and that she deserved to be promoted. About two-thirds of the professors on the committee felt that she was too much of a loner and did not contribute to the overall needs of the department, only to her own personal success. After much heated discussion, the decision was made not to promote her.

Within three months, Andrea resigned and took a new teaching job at an excellent university. She left without the usual farewell party for departing colleagues. She apparently cleared out her office one night after everyone had left work. Nobody remembered saying good-bye to her.

Postscript: Several other women faculty members had been promoted in this department, and there was a favorable attitude toward affirmative action among the group. So it can be assumed that sex discrimination was not a factor in this case.

Discussion Questions

1. How would you analyze this case in light of Schutz's theory?

2. How would you analyze it from Andrea's viewpoint?

3. From the department's viewpoint?

4. Would you have done anything about this situation if you had been Andrea's department head?

5. Would you have done anything if you had been one of her colleagues in the department?

6. How typical do you think this case is?

7. What implications does this case (and Schutz's theory) have for you?

READINGS: OVERVIEW

William Schutz has been studying the influence of personality needs on interpersonal and small group interaction for over forty years. During this time he has identified the three basic needs described in this chapter: *inclusion, control,* and *affection.* In this article he elaborates on the manner in which these needs consistently influence our interaction patterns with others.

The second article examines some practical applications of attitude change theory in real life.

The Interpersonal

William Schutz

Our self-concept is largely derived from our relations with other people. In our dealings we exchange various commodities with these people and must make adjustments. In order to understand this interpersonal level I will use a framework first introduced in my book *FIRO.*

Each person has three basic interpersonal needs that are manifested in behavior and feelings toward other people. But this activity is rooted in a person's feeling about himself, his self-concept. The three basic need areas are posited to be *inclusion, control,* and *affection.*

Inclusion refers to feelings about being important or significant, of having some worth so that people will care. The aspect of the self-concept related to *control* is the feeling of competence, including intelligence, appearance, practicality, and general ability to cope with the world. The area of *affection* revolves around feelings of being lovable, of feeling that if one's personal core is revealed in its entirety it will be seen as a lovely thing.

Inclusion behavior refers to associations between people, being excluded or included, belonging, togetherness. The need to be included manifests itself as wanting to be attended to, and to attract attention and interaction. The college militant is often objecting mostly to the lack of attention paid him, the automated student. Even if he is given negative attention he is partially satisfied.

Being a distinct person—that is, having a particular identity—is an essential aspect of inclusion. An integral part of being recognized and paid attention to is that the individual be distinguishable from other people. The height of being identifiable is to be understood, since it implies that someone is interested enough to discover a person's unique characteristics.

An issue that arises frequently at the outset of group relations is that of commitment, the decision to become involved in a given relationship. Usually, in the initial testing of a relationship, individuals try to present themselves to one another partly to find out what facet of themselves others will be interested in. Frequently a member is silent at first because he is not sure that people are interested in him.

Inclusion is unlike affection in that it does not involve strong emotional attachments to individual persons. It is unlike control in that the preoccupation

---

is with prominence, not dominance. Since inclusion involves the process of formation, it usually occurs first in the life of a group. People must decide whether they do or don't want to form a group.

A person who has too little inclusion, the undersocial, tends to be introverted and withdrawn. He consciously wants to maintain this distance between himself and others, and insists that he doesn't want to get enmeshed with people and lose his privacy. Unconsciously, however, he definitely wants others to pay attention to him. His biggest fears are that people will ignore him and would just as soon leave him behind. His unconscious attitude may be summarized by, "No one is interested in me, so I'm not going to risk being ignored. I'll stay away from people and get along by myself." He has a strong drive toward self-sufficiency as a technique for existence without others. Behind his withdrawal is the private feeling that others don't understand him. His deepest anxiety, that referring to the self-concept, is that he is worthless. He thinks that if no one ever considered him important enough to receive attention, he must be of no value whatsoever.

The oversocial person tends toward extroversion. He seeks people incessantly and wants them to seek him out. He is also afraid that they will ignore him. His unconscious feelings are the same as those of the withdrawn person, but his overt behavior is the opposite. His unconscious attitude is summarized by, "Although no one is interested in me, I'll make people pay attention to me in any way I can." His inclination is always to seek companionship, for he is the type who can't stand to be alone. All of his activities will be designed to be done in a group.

The interpersonal behavior of the oversocial type of person is designed to focus attention on himself, to make people notice him, to be prominent. The direct method is to be an intensive, exhibitive participator. By simply forcing himself on the group, he forces the group to focus attention on him. A more subtle technique is to try to acquire power (control) or to be well-liked (affection), but it is still for the primary purpose of gaining attention.

To the individual for whom inclusion was resolved in childhood, interaction with people presents no problem. He is comfortable with or without people. He can be a high or low participant in a group without anxiety. He is capable of strong commitment to and involvement with certain groups, but can also withhold commitment if he feels it is appropriate. Unconsciously, he feels that he is a worthwhile, significant person.

On the physical level, inclusion has to do with penetration of the boundaries between the self and the rest of the world, and therefore deals primarily with the periphery of the body, the skin and sense organs, the eyes, ears, nose, and mouth. Attitudes toward these organs may be related to attitudes toward being included with people. If contact with people is a fearsome thing, then the eyes keep people from intruding by not seeing others clearly, and then in order to see them clearly, it is permitted to put up a barrier—a barrier called glasses. When eyes are in the active process of seeing, and don't really want to see, they become dull and seem to retire toward the back of the head. Ears which don't want inclusion hear people who are close as if they were far away. Closeness is not accepted and people are kept at a distance. The mouth and lips become tight and impenetrable. The skin shies away from being touched; it is easily tickled, gets rashes and hives easily so that people will not come near. The muscles of the skin may also become tightened so that feeling is minimized, resulting in a leathery touch feeling.

All of these devices need not be used by one individual. There are probably special circumstances that bring about the preeminence of one over the other. The rock opera *Tommy* describes a boy who sees his mother in bed with another man and becomes blind, who hears them talking and becomes deaf, and who is told never to tell anyone what he saw and heard and becomes mute. In a dramatic form this is probably a good example for the reason for specifying which sense organ is the preferred one for avoiding inclusion.

On a recent trip that involved discussing work with a large number of people, my voice started getting hoarse, which I took to mean that I didn't want to talk any more. But then I noticed my hearing becoming erratic. Of course it was psychological; I simply didn't want to listen to all these people anymore. I began to understand how desirable and possible it would be to become deaf, at least in that situation.

If being included is important, the body may reflect it by having these peripheral organs perform in the opposite way. The eyes become vigilant, looking for people in order to see them clearly. They try to see people who are far away as actually being closer. Possible outcomes of this are especially good vision and perhaps vertical lines between the eyebrows reflecting the effort put into seeing clearly. You can try this right now by looking at some object, preferably a person, in two ways. First look at him dully, as if your eyes were open but actually way back in your head and seeing as little as possible while appearing to give attention. Then look at the same object and feel your eyes leap out and grab him, taking in every aspect of him. The difference in the two feelings is usually very marked and gives some sense of how voluntary such a common phenomenon as looking can be.

The person with a high need for inclusion will have acute senses of smell and hearing, bringing far things near. The skin is receptive to touch and probably is open and soft. This is the pure inclusion pattern. Very quickly complications arise. The person open to inclusion can be sensitive to rejection and develop a barrier. Or he may allow touch and then be afraid.

An interesting body difference occurred in a class in Rolfing. One man, who was learning to be a Rolfer, reacted to the assaults of the teacher Ida Rolf—who uses assault as a teaching method—by immediately responding with a defense, a self-justification, a counterattack, a lengthy explanation. I on the other hand responded to her attacks with utter coolness and calm, allowing her to continue unabated, sometimes agreeing with her point, possibly joking away some of her steam, while underneath, quietly knowing that I was right.

When it came to Rolfing each of us, a startling difference appeared in the way we responded at the periphery of our bodies, the skin. When my friend was physically penetrated he would scream and holler, ask for time out, complain, cry, and reassess the competence of the Rolf practitioner. I would feel most of those things, too, but be very stoic and allow the practitioner to penetrate quite far. But then he would be disconcerted by two things. When he took his hand out my skin would spring back to where it was like rubber, apparently unaffected by his push. Also, if he pushed deeply enough into the flesh, he met a barrier that felt like steel. In other words, he and I represented in our bodies almost the identical reactions we made psychologically, his immediate response, my apparent acceptance but deeper resistance.

Another possibility in exploring the physical correlates of inclusion comes from a comment about sexual intercourse, and brings up physical function to add to the structural physical considerations I have been talking about. In the sexual act, various phases can be distinguished that parallel inclusion, control, and affection. Inclusion problems refer to the initial phases of the act, the feelings about penetration. A male with problems of inclusion will probably have erection problems. His conflict over whether or not to penetrate would be reflected in the nervous enervation of the penis and its willingness or not to be ready to enter. A similar situation arises for a woman where inclusion problems are reflected in the readiness of her vagina to receive the penis, whether she's loose enough and moist enough. Also, the pelvic muscles for both that should be relaxed for maximum pleasure may be tightened if conflict still exists.

Breathing is also primarily an inclusion phenomenon. It's the way of entering or leaving any situation. If no commitment is desired the breath is cut off along with a tightening of the muscles. This cuts down virtually all vital functions. A full commitment of a person's time and energy involves full breathing, a charged-up body. The Indians and yogis have recognized the importance of breathing control, pranayama, for centuries. It is the key to someone's involvement. Routinely, when I'm giving a lecture or demonstration to a large group, I will begin by doing some activity that requires them to breathe deeply, either screaming, pounding, deep breathing, or anything that gets them pumped up. I find it makes a big difference in the audience's attention and presence.

The same holds for an encounter group. Whenever a member shows a lack of involvement, getting him into some activity requiring deep breathing almost inevitably brings him in. Breathing patterns become ingrained early in life, and a person is usually not aware of his lack of full breathing. Improving the breathing pattern is probably one of the fastest ways to change the feeling of the entire organism. In bioenergetic therapy, the "air or breath is equivalent to the spirit, the pneuma of ancient religions, a symbol of the divine power residing in God, the father figure. Breathing is an aggressive act in that inspiration is an active process. The body sucks in the air. The way one breathes manifests one's feeling about his right to get what he wants from life."

In terms of the body systems, not only are the sense organs and respiration related to inclusion, but so are the digestive and excretory systems, which focus on exchange with the environment and which deal with whether an object will be in or out of the body. These systems express the body's desire to incorporate or reject outside objects. A person with a desire to exclude will reject food and/or excrete readily and, in the extreme, develop vomiting and diarrhea. One who is anxious to include will go in the other direction, namely, overeating and constipation. A well-resolved relation in the inclusion area should result in good digestion and elimination.

If we consider the interaction between a person and his body, the inclusion problem is one of energy. A body excludes itself in the world by being energyless. The difference between living and not living is the difference between having the flows of energy, nerve impulses, blood circulation, breathing, and so on, and not having them. When a body includes itself, it is filled with energy and feeling.

Hence the problem of inclusion is in or out; the interaction centers on encounter, and the physical aspect is that of energy.

Control behavior refers to the decision-making process between people and areas of power, influence, and authority. The need for control varies along a continuum from the desire for authority over others (and therefore over one's future) to the need to be controlled and have responsibility lifted from oneself.

An argument provides the setting for distinguishing the inclusion-seeker from the control-seeker. The one seeking inclusion or prominence wants very much to be one of the participants in the argument, while the control-seeker wants to be the winner, or, if not the winner, on the same side as the winner. If forced to choose, the prominence-seeker would prefer to be the losing participant, while the dominance-seeker would prefer to be a winning nonparticipant.

Control is also manifested in behavior directed toward people who try to control. Expressions of independence and rebellion exemplify lack of willingness to be controlled, while compliance, submission, and taking orders indicate various degrees of accepting control. There is no necessary relation between an individual's behavior toward controlling others and his behavior toward being controlled. The sergeant may domineer his men, for example, and also accept orders from his lieutenant with pleasure and gratefulness, while the neighborhood bully may dominate his peers and also rebel against his parents.

Control behavior differs from inclusion behavior in that it does not require prominence. The power behind the throne is an excellent example of a role that would fill a high-control need and a low need for inclusion. The joker exemplifies a high-inclusion and low need for control. Control behavior differs from affection behavior in that it has to do with power relations rather than emotional closeness. The frequent difficulties between those who want to get down to business and those who want to get to know one another better illustrate a situation in which control behavior is more important for some and affection behavior for others.

Concern about one's competence, especially in the area of masculinity, leads to overmasculine responses. This is often seen in politics, where concern about one's assertiveness often leads to absurd overreaction to physical threats, especially when a government official has police or soldiers at his disposal.

Control problems usually follow those of inclusion in the development of a group or of an interpersonal relationship. Once the group has formed, it begins to differentiate; different people take or seek different roles, and often power struggles, competition, and influence become central issues. In terms of interaction, these issues are matters of confrontation, to use a term now in vogue.

The extreme person who is too low on control, called an abdicrat, is one who tends toward submission and abdication of power and responsibility in his interpersonal behavior. He gravitates toward a subordinate position where he will not have to take responsibility for making decisions, where someone else takes charge. He consciously wants people to relieve him of his obligations. He does not control others even when he should; for example, he would not take charge even during a fire in a children's schoolhouse in which he was the only adult. He never makes a decision if he can refer it to someone else.

For the individual who has successfully resolved his relations in the control area in childhood, power and control present no problem. He feels comfortable giving or not giving orders, taking or not taking orders, whatever is appropriate to the situation. Unlike the abdicrat and autocrat, he is not preoccupied with fears of his own helplessness, stupidity, and incompetence. He feels that other people respect his competence and will be realistic with respect to trusting him with decision-making.

Speculation on the physical concomitants of control behavior begins with control of the muscles through tightening and through intellectual or nervous system activity. The central nervous system, along with the endocrine system, is generally credited with controlling the anatomy.

Ida Rolf has a fascinating concept of the relation of the core of the body, by which she means the head and spinal column, to the envelope, which includes the two girdles, the pelvic and shoulder girdles with attached appendages, legs and arms. Her idea is that the core represents *being* and the envelope *doing*. Some people develop one and not the other, both, or neither.

For a male, a great deal of control is usually expressed in the formation of the upper arms, shoulders, and neck. Attaining masculinity is frequently related to having hulking, heavily developed shoulders and neck and back muscles. Wrestlers and football linemen typify this formation in the extreme, as the large muscle that goes from the middle of the back up into the neck, the trapezius, is so overdeveloped that it appears that they have no necks.

The feeling of being out of control, and thereby vulnerable, was brought home to me personally when a Rolfer working on my neck freed the trapezius muscle that I had held chronically tight so that my head and neck began to rise up out of my shoulders. As I stood there with my head elevated to a place where it felt both unfamiliar and wonderfully free, I felt frightened.

The image that came to mind was of the boy in the circus who sticks his head through the bullseye of a target for people to throw balls at. I felt very exposed, very much in plain sight for everyone to see, with no place to hide. You may capture some of that feeling by standing up straight, putting your chin in and letting your head rise up as if it had a string through the crown, and let your shoulders relax down. When you get as high as you can, look around. When this happened to me I had a clear feeling of why my head had sunk into my shoulders. It was safer, more protected, and less vulnerable.

In general, the pattern of muscle tensions represents the defense pattern of a person. It is the way in which he controls himself so that he can cope with the world. A pattern of no chronic muscle tensions—as opposed to muscle tone—would then represent a nondefensive state, perhaps something like the egolessness of the Eastern mystics.

Intellectual control involves voluntary shaping of the body propensities. Control is exercised over the body's desires by moral codes and in line with parental upbringing so that thought is used to govern action.

In the interaction between a person and his body, the control problem is one of centering. A body undercontrolled is disorganized; a body overcontrolled is rigid. A well-controlled body functions with integration among its parts so that they flow easily and appropriately. Inappropriate movement and coordination result when the body is uncertain of what it is doing. Centering means placing everything in its appropriate place so that one is "hooked-up." Being off center makes all movement slightly disconnected.

In the sexual act, control has to do with the occasion and timing of the orgasms and the direction of movement. Withholding an orgasm is an act of personal control that often has a hostile motive, "you can't satisfy me." Sexual control problems would include difficulty of orgasm, premature ejaculation, and the lack of ability to let go.

Thus the problem of control is top or bottom; the primary interaction is confrontation, and the physical aspect is that of centering.

Affection behavior refers to close personal emotional feelings between two people, especially love and hate in their various degrees. Affection is a dyadic relation, that is, it can occur only between pairs of people at any one time, whereas both inclusion and control relations may occur either in dyads or between one person and a group of persons.

Since affection is based on building emotional ties, it is usually the last phase to emerge in the development of a human relation. In the inclusion phase, people must *encounter* each other and decide to continue their relation; control issues require them to *confront* one another and work out how they will be related. To continue the relation, affection ties must form and people must embrace each other to form a lasting bond, and also to say goodbye.

The person with too little affection, the underpersonal type, tends to avoid close ties with others. He maintains his one-to-one relations on a superficial, distant level and is most comfortable when others do the same with him. He consciously wishes to maintain this emotional distance, and frequently expresses a desire not to get emotionally involved, while unconsciously he seeks a satisfactory affectional relation. His fear is that no one loves him, and in a group situation he is afraid he won't be liked. He has great difficulty in genuinely liking people, and distrusts their feelings toward him.

His attitude could be summarized by, "I find the affection area very painful since I have been rejected, therefore I shall avoid close personal relations in the future." The direct technique of the underpersonal is to avoid emotional closeness or involvement, even to the point of being antagonistic. The subtle technique is to be superficially friendly to everyone. This behavior acts as a safeguard against having to get close to, or become personal with, any one person.

In his self-concept, the underpersonal believes that if people knew him well, they would discover traits that make him unlovable. As opposed to the inclusion anxiety that the self is worthless and empty, and the control anxiety that the self is stupid and irresponsible, the affection anxiety is that the self is nasty and unlovable.

The overpersonal type attempts to become extremely close to others. He definitely wants others to treat him in a very close way. The unconscious feeling on which he operates is, "My first experiences with affection were painful, but perhaps if I try again they will turn out to be better." Being liked is extremely important to him in his attempt to relieve his anxiety about being always rejected and unloved. The direct technique for being liked is an overt attempt to gain approval, be extremely personal, ingratiating, intimate, and confiding. The subtle technique is more manipulative and possessive, to devour friends and subtly punish any attempts by them to establish other friendships.

The basic feelings for the overpersonal are the same as those for the underpersonal. Both responses are extreme, both are motivated by a strong need for affection, both are accompanied by a strong anxiety about ever being loved and basically about being unlovable, and both have considerable hostility behind them stemming from the anticipation of rejection.

For the individual who successfully resolved his affectional relations in childhood, close emotional interaction with another person presents no problem. He is comfortable in such a personal relation as well as in a situation requiring emotional distance. It is important for him to be liked, but if not he can accept the fact that the dislike is the result of the relation between himself and one other person; in other words, the dislike does not mean that his is a totally unlovable person. And he is capable of giving genuine affection.

The primary interaction of the affection area is that of embrace, either literal or symbolic. The expression of appropriate deeper feelings is the major issue, particularly in group situations, where a paradox arises. At the beginning of the group there are many expressions as to how difficult it is to express hostility to people. It often later develops that there is only one thing more difficult—expressing warm, positive feelings.

A difference between inclusion, control, and affection behavior is illustrated by the different feelings a man has in being turned down by a fraternity, failed in a course by a professor, and rejected by his girl. The fraternity excludes him, telling him that as a group they don't have sufficient interest in him. The professor fails him and says, in effect, that he finds him incompetent in his field. His girl rejects him, implying that she doesn't find him lovable.

The affectional aspect of the sexual act is the feeling that follows its completion. This can be anything from a flood of warm, affectionate, loving feelings to a revulsion and thoughts of "what am I doing here?" It depends partly on how well the heart and genitals are connected. The circulatory (heart) and reproductive (genital) systems are most directly related to the area of affection.

In the interaction between a person and his body, the affectional problem is one of *acceptance*. The body may be charged up with energy and coordinated through centering, but the problem of body acceptance remains. An accepted body can allow feeling to flow through it without avoiding any part. Sensation is not blocked. An unaccepted body works against itself, trying to become sickly or dissociated. Thus, the ideal body feels energetic, centered, and acceptable.

With respect to an interpersonal relation, inclusion is concerned primarily with the formation of a relation, whereas control and affection are concerned with relations already formed. Within existent relations, control is the area concerned with who gives orders and makes decisions, whereas affection is concerned with how emotionally close or distant the relation becomes.

In summary, the problem of affection is close or far; the interaction is embrace, and the physical aspect is acceptance.

The Foundations of Interpersonal Influence

Robin N. Widgery and Stewart L. Tubbs

College students usually look with excitement and anticipation to the day when they will begin their chosen careers. Much of their success will depend upon the ways in which they learn to apply what has been learned in the classroom to the day-to-day problems of the workplace. But, they will soon discover that their ultimate success on the job may hinge less on what they know and more on their ability to communicate effectively with others. Surveys of college alumni groups have consistently reported that graduate success has depended importantly on what they learned in their communication classes. The most important skill that they have applied in their professions is the ability to present ideas and objectives so convincingly that others readily see the value of these ideas, and accept and use them. It is no over-statement to say that your ability to learn the principles of persuasive communication, and the ability to apply them, will have a significant impact on your eventual success in your chosen professions. Most of what is achieved in our lives, at home, dorm, community or job, will be accomplished with and through others. The ability to influence the outcomes of groups and their objectives is essentially the definition of leadership (Ellis and Fisher, 1994, p. 47).

The purpose here is to explain some of the principles of persuasion. Toward this end the perspective of attitude change theory offers a rich body of knowledge. When translated to daily experience, these principles can help you stimulate, inspire, and motivate your peers and eventually your fellow workers. For several decades, scholars have found the study of attitude change theory to be relevant to every facet of life: family, college, community and work.

Perhaps the most popular explanations of attitude change can be found among the consistency theories. Although different researchers have proposed various consistency theories (Newcomb, 1953; Festinger, 1957; Osgood, Suci, and Tannenbaum, 1957; and Heider, 1958), the first such theory was developed by Fritz Heider (1946). He explained the concept of *cognitive balance*. The basic premise of his theory is that people prefer to have psychological or cognitive comfort and avoid situations which involve cognitive stress or *"imbalance."*

These terms describe a state of psychological discomfort occurring when an individual's beliefs, feelings, values, perceptions or behaviors are in conflict. For example, a person *(P)* who feels negatively toward an idea *(X)*, but who receives a message in support of the idea from a respected source *(O)*, would suffer some psychological pressure (imbalance) to change his attitudes about the idea and/or the source. The important elements demonstrating this relationship are presented in Diagram A.

DIAGRAM A

An Unbalanced System

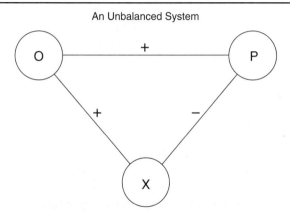

DIAGRAM B

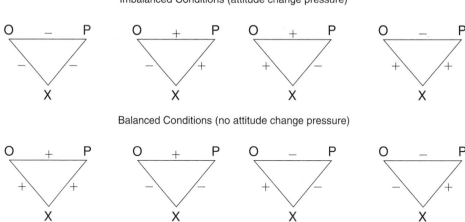

Imbalanced Conditions (attitude change pressure)

Balanced Conditions (no attitude change pressure)

The basic principle of Heider's theory is that if the *algebraic product* of the signs in the triad *(P/O/X)* is positive, your attitude system is balanced. If the product is negative, your attitude system is unbalanced. A positive sign can be considered as a positive relationship, or logical association, between the elements within the triad. The positive sign (+) may also represent respect, liking, trust, or other positive feelings or relationships by you *(P)*, the receiver. A negative sign (–) may be considered a negative relationship, or no association. The negative sign may also represent disrespect, dislike, distrust, or other negative feelings or relationships perceived or felt by you *(P)*.

The practical implication of this is: When the attitude system is unbalanced, the receiver *(P)* is motivated to change his attitude(s) or beliefs in order to restore a state of balance, or psychological comfort. But, if the attitude system is balanced, no psychological pressure exists to motivate a change in attitude. In Diagram B are the eight permutations called *cognitive triads*. These represent all possible balanced and unbalanced relationships between the receiver, source and message *(P, O, and X)*.

If there is an unbalanced condition, there is psychological pressure for the person (receiver) to restore balance, to change his feelings and beliefs. Summarizing considerable research on this issue, Festinger and Aronson (1968) indicate that there are three predictable ways that balance may be restored. First, the receiver's *(P's)* attitude toward the source *(O)* may change. In fact, this is the most likely part of the system to change. If a source *(O)* tries to persuade us of something we don't want to believe, we may discredit that person rather than change our attitude toward the idea *(X)*. This new "balanced" triad is diagrammed below.

A second possibility is that the receiver's perception of the source's attitude toward the idea may change *(O + X to O – X)*. In this instance, the receiver

DIAGRAM C

Person's Attitude Changes toward the Source

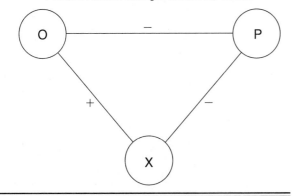

might *rationalize* about the source's attitude toward the idea instead of actually changing his own attitude toward the idea. This change will also result in a
balanced triad, like the one in Diagram D.

A third way for the receiver *(P)* to restore balance is to change his attitude
toward the idea *(X)* itself. This is the outcome preferred by the source,
whose goal is to persuade. However, as we have seen, this change (persuasion) could be the least likely to occur, given the other two alternatives. This
possibility is diagrammed below.

DIAGRAM D

Person's Perception of Source's Attitude toward the Idea

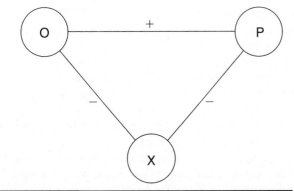

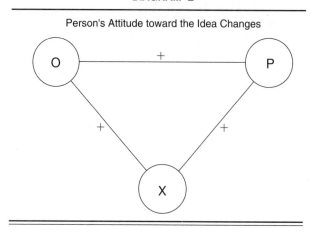

DIAGRAM E

Person's Attitude toward the Idea Changes

Implications for Persuading Others

The source *(O)* should be interested in how the "right" attitude change can be made to occur through appropriate communication behavior. In this section we will explore a method for accomplishing these constructive attitude changes among others. First, if we know that in an unbalanced condition the most likely relationship to change is the source-receiver *(O/P)* link, then the first thing that can be done is to bolster (strengthen) that link. If a friend (the source) wants to increase his credibility to strengthen the *O/P* linkage, he must demonstrate that he has certain key values which you (the receiver) associate with trusted and respected behaviors in others.

For example, Hellriegel, Slocum, and Woodman (1983) argue that the overwhelming bulk of leadership research would support the conclusion that most people value *competence, consistency, fairness, concern, clarity of directions, honesty, and sensitivity* to feelings of others. Covey (1990) writes that if the leader (the source) emphasizes these aspects of behavior consistently toward those who follow, he may then draw on his good image, much like a bank account, when his influence is needed to gain the commitment of others to do an unattractive task. If his image is strong and positive, it becomes more difficult for the follower *(P)* to change this part of the triad *(P + O to P − O)* in order to restore balance in the attitude system. This is illustrated in Diagram F by adding a secondary triad to the primary triad in Heider's model. If the *P*'s attitude toward the *O* changes from + to −, it will create a new imbalance in this *source values triad*. This places pressure on the *P* (the receiver) to maintain a positive attitude toward the *O* (the source).

The second most likely change used to restore balance in the system is for the receiver *(P)* to change (reshape) his perception of, or beliefs about, the source's attitude toward the task *(O + X to O − X)*. This may occur through

DIAGRAM F

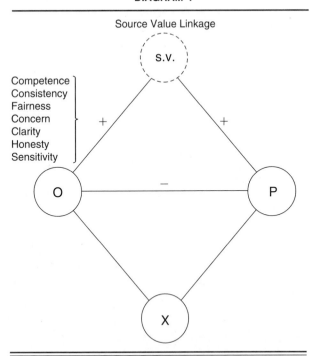

Source Value Linkage

Competence
Consistency
Fairness
Concern
Clarity
Honesty
Sensitivity

a process of rationalization, allowing the receiver's attitude system to restore balance without having to actually change his attitude toward the task itself. The source *(O)* can try to keep this rationalization from occurring by demonstrating his *sincerity, commitment, enthusiasm, excitement, and unambiguous support* for the task (O'Donnel and Kable, 1982; Smith, 1982). When the source demonstrates these behaviors as related to the specific idea *(X)*, it will be harder for the receiver to rationalize that the source does not really believe in what he is saying about the idea. In other words, if the *O/X* relationship is seen by the receiver *(P)* to be negative, he would also have to recognize a new imbalance in the *commitment values triad.* This would place psychological pressure on the receiver to continue to perceive the *O/X* relationship as positive. (See Diagram G.)

The third alternative (and the most desirable) for restoring balance to the attitude system is for the receiver to actually change his attitude toward the idea *(P − X to P + X).* In order for this to happen, he should see which of his own needs will be met by accepting the idea *(X).* For instance, in the workplace you will want to have your influence result in positive outcomes. Extending Maslow and Herzberg's theories, Dubrin (1982) lists twenty-two specific outcomes which most employees would consider as meeting their needs:

DIAGRAM G

Commitment Values Linkage

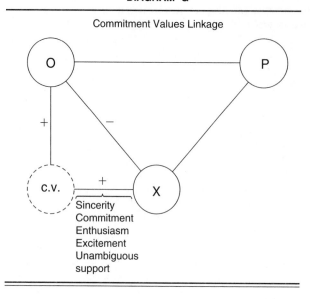

Sincerity
Commitment
Enthusiasm
Excitement
Unambiguous
support

Feedback on desired behavior

Praise, encouragement, and related rewards

Approval

Recognition

Comradeship

Job security

Money

Favorable performance appraisal

Privy to confidential information

Challenging work assignments

Freedom to choose one's own work activity

Opportunity to see oneself become more important, more useful

Seeing results of one's work

Chance to use one's mind

Power to influence coworkers and management

Promotion

Improved working conditions

Capable and congenial coworkers

Business luncheon

Time off from work

Attendance at trade show or convention

Status symbols

The manager in a work environment is more likely to be successful in creating productive attitude change if he/she can show the positive relationships that exist between one or more employee needs and the tasks these employ-

ees are asked to do. Once the *P* (employee/receiver) perceives a positive relationship between need gratification and an unattractive task *(X)*, the pressure is on the *P/X* linkage to change to positive. To resist change leaves the *P*
(receiver) with an unbalanced *needs values triad.* (See Diagram H.) If we put
together the basic *(P/O/X)* triad and the three secondary triads (linkages) we
can see how the entire system looks. (See Diagram I.)

Finally, if we put in the appropriate signs, we can see how the system looks
with all parts balanced. The balanced *source values triad* supports the positive
P/O (receiver-source) linkage. The balanced *commitment values triad* supports
the positive *P/X* (receiver-idea) linkage. And, a balanced *needs values triad*
places psychological pressure on the *P/X* (receiver-idea) linkage to change
from negative to positive. (See Diagram J.)

Balance theory can give an understanding of how commitment to an idea
may be modified by using the receiver's own need for psychological consistency (balance) as a directive force for attitude change. In order to assure the
desired change, however, other more readily modified alternatives may need
to be reinforced so that the receiver changes the desired perception toward
the idea, and not toward the source or the source's attitude toward the idea.
From this model come three important guidelines for those who would persuade and influence others:

DIAGRAM H

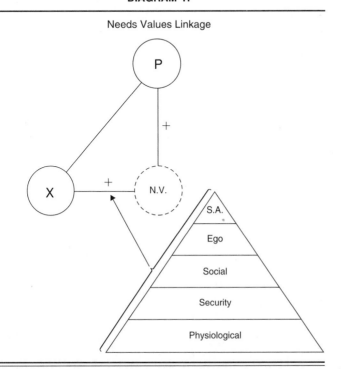

Needs Values Linkage

DIAGRAM I

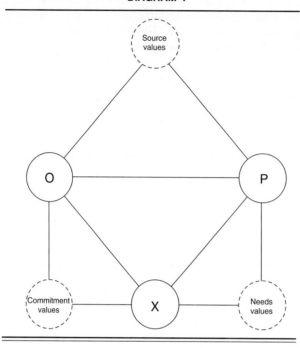

DIAGRAM J

A Balanced System

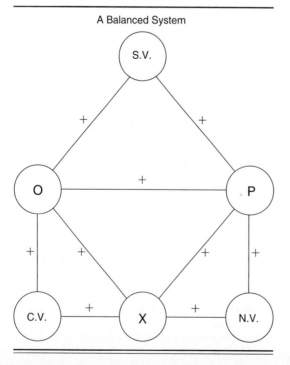

1. *Communicate from a position of credibility.* Without perceived credibility, integrity, competence, and sensitivity to the feelings of others, it is difficult (or impossible) to inspire or gain commitment to your ideas. One may get behavior from others, but not commitment.

2. *Show your own commitment and enthusiasm toward the ideas you propose.* It is not easy for the receiver to rationalize that "even the source isn't excited with the idea" if the source demonstrates unambiguous commitment to the importance of the idea.

3. *Make the receiver aware that the unattractive idea is important in satisfying his various needs.* When the idea is seen to be the avenue through which needs may be attained, the receiver will be more likely to shift toward acceptance of the idea.

There is much value in going beyond the discussion of abstract theoretical models, making behavioral science practical to those who must apply it to the challenges of everyday life. Most people rightly prefer the practical to the theoretical. Commenting on the role of theory in the real world, Kurt Lewin said, "Nothing is more practical than a good theory." The challenge for those who wish to be effective, persuasive communicators is to learn to apply the theory in practical ways to achieve useful and constructive goals.

References

Covey, Stephen. *The 7 Habits of Highly Effective People.* (New York: Simon & Schuster, 1990).

Dubrin, Andrew J. *Contemporary Applied Management.* (Plano, Tex.: Business Publications, Inc., 1982).

Ellis, Donald, and B. Aubrey Fisher. *Small Group Decision Making.* (New York: McGraw-Hill, 1994).

Festinger, Leon. *A Theory of Cognitive Dissonance.* (Evanston, Ill.: Row, Peterson, 1957).

Festinger, Leon, and Elliot Aronson. "Arousal and Reduction of Dissonance in Social Contexts," in Dorwin Cartwright and Alvin Zander (eds.), *Group Dynamics: Research and Theory.* 3rd ed. (New York: Harper & Row, 1968) 125–136.

Fisher, Dalmar. *Communication in Organizations.* (St. Paul: West, 1981).

Geneen, Harold. *Managing.* (New York: Doubleday, 1984).

Heider, Fritz. "Attitudes and Cognitive Organization," *Journal of Psychology,* 1946, 21, 107–112.

Heider, Fritz. *The Psychology of Interpersonal Relations.* (New York: John Wiley, 1958).

Hellriegel, Don, John W. Slocum, and Richard W. Woodman. *Organizational Behavior.* 3rd ed. (St. Paul: West, 1983), Ch. 13.

Newcomb, Theodore. "An Approach to the Study of Communicative Acts," *Psychological Review,* 1953, 60, 393–404.

O'Donnel, Victoria, and June Kable. *Persuasion: An Interactive-Dependency Approach.* (New York: Random House, 1982), Ch. 6.

Osgood, Charles, George J. Suci, and Percy H. Tannenbaum. *The Measurement of Meaning.* (Urbana: University of Illinois Press, 1957).

Smith, Maryann. *Persuasion and Human Action: A Review and Critique of Social Influence Theories.* (Belmont, Cal.: Wadsworth, 1982), Ch. 9.

3

Group Circumstances and Structure

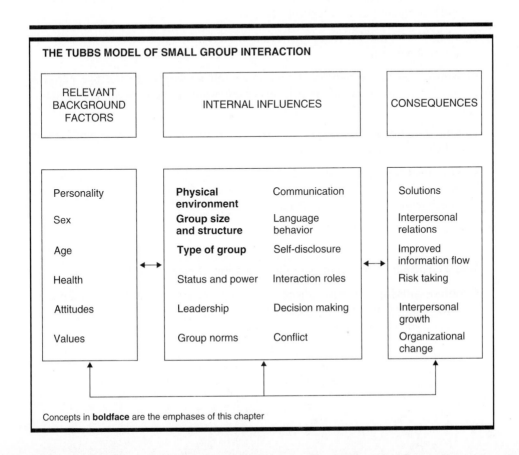

THE TUBBS MODEL OF SMALL GROUP INTERACTION

RELEVANT BACKGROUND FACTORS	INTERNAL INFLUENCES		CONSEQUENCES
Personality	**Physical environment**	Communication	Solutions
Sex	**Group size and structure**	Language behavior	Interpersonal relations
Age	**Type of group**	Self-disclosure	Improved information flow
Health	Status and power	Interaction roles	Risk taking
Attitudes	Leadership	Decision making	Interpersonal growth
Values	Group norms	Conflict	Organizational change

Concepts in **boldface** are the emphases of this chapter

PREVIEW

In Chapter 1, the internal influences of the Tubbs Model of Small Group Interaction were introduced briefly. Chapter 3 includes a more in-depth treatment of physical environment, group structure, and group type. Physical environment is the setting in which small group interaction takes place. Two topics that fit under physical environment are territoriality and seating patterns. Group size and structure are often connected to the notion that people in a group are related in a number of ways. One relationship is characterized by communication networks. The third internal influence is the type of group. It is obvious that groups will interact differently depending on what types of groups they are. Some examples included in Chapter 3 are primary groups, casual and social groups, work groups, and educational groups.

GLOSSARY

Territoriality: The word "territoriality" was coined by Edward Hall and defined as "the tendency for humans and other animals to lay claim to and defend a particular area or territory."

Seating Patterns: Seating patterns often affect the type and volume of interaction of a group.

Communication Networks: Communication networks are the five patterns that demonstrate the different forms of communicating between group members.

Primary Groups: Primary groups are groups that usually include one's family and closest friends.

Casual and Social Groups: Casual and social groups include neighborhood groups, fraternities, and even classmates. The impact of these relationships on behavior is often quite profound.

Educational Groups: Educational groups are groups that interact for the sole purpose of study or instruction.

Work Groups: Work groups are the formation of people on the job.

Problem-solving Groups: Problem-solving groups are groups that form in order to solve one or more problems.

CASE STUDY: Chempure Pharmaceutical Company

Richard E. Weber, M.D.

(A)

Great excitement could be heard echoing from the executive offices of the Chempure Pharmaceutical Company. Chempure, a large midwestern, hundred-year-old pharmaceutical company, had just been informed that the Federal Drug Administration (FDA) had approved Lowerpress, the company's newly developed drug for the treatment of high blood pressure (hypertension). This meant that Chempure was now free to market the product on a national scale. This approval by the FDA represented the successful end result of seven years of developmental work on the compound. It involved the input of many people representing thousands of hours of employee work time and many millions of dollars.

The process of development of Lowerpress began in the chemistry laboratory of Chempure. Once it was decided that the company wanted to develop a drug for the treatment of hypertension, chemists began evaluating known compounds that had the chemical structure that should produce the physiologic effects needed to lower high blood pressure. The chemists developed various modifications of the compounds, and each individual compound that was produced was tested by the biologists to determine its effect on various types of tissue samples to see which compound exerted the greatest physiologic effect. Once the chemists and biologists agreed that a particular compound exerted the desired effect on isolated tissue samples, the compound was then taken over by the pharmacologists, who began testing it in various animal species such as laboratory rats and dogs. Initially the chemists worked as a small team together with a small team of biologists. These teams in turn interacted with a small team of pharmacologists who evaluated the effectiveness of the compound that was developed by the chemists.

This small team of chemists, biologists and pharmacologists was known as the drug discovery team. Once the drug discovery team felt they had a compound worthy of future development, a project team was formed. The project team became the basic organizational unit for the development of Lowerpress. The project team was composed of one or two representatives of the chemistry, pharmacology, pharmacokinetic, toxicology, clinical development, manufacturing, regulatory, and marketing departments. The project team had a chair whose function was to coordinate the activities of the various individual disciplines represented on the team.

In the early stage in the development of the drug the project team met on a monthly basis to review progress reports from the chemistry and pharmacology representatives. At that time the pharmacokinetic department began to evaluate the distribution and metabolism of the compound, first in laboratory animals and later in humans. Also at that time the toxicology department began conducting studies in laboratory animals to be sure there were no cancer-producing or genetic problems with the compound. Once it was determined that the compound had pharmacologic action in laboratory animals and had no apparent harmful effects, the compound was transferred to the clinical development representatives of the project team. The clinical development representatives consisted of a physician who was responsible for the conduct of the studies performed with human subjects and a clinical scientist. A clinical scientist is someone with a degree in a scientific field, usually physiology or biology, who works with the physician to conduct the studies in humans.

Initially the drug was tested in normal healthy human volunteers to be sure that there were no harmful effects. Once it was determined that normal subjects have no adverse reactions to the

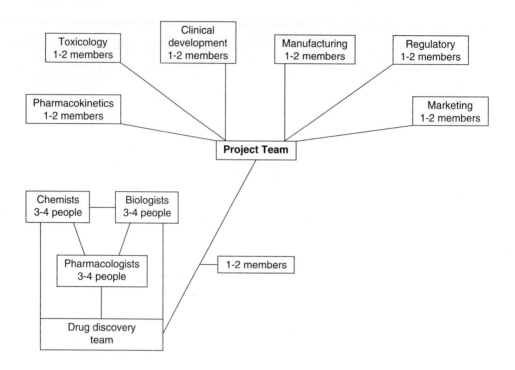

drug, it was tested in patients with known hypertension. At first small numbers of patients were given single doses of the compound to evaluate its blood pressure–lowering effect and to determine if there were any side effects. Once it was determined that single doses were effective and safe, patients were given multiple doses of the drug for up to four weeks. These series of tests were expanded until eventually 1000 patients with hypertension had received the compound for anywhere from one month to up to two years. The clinical trials took three years to perform. During that time the project team continued to meet monthly to discuss the progress of the clinical trials.

In addition, the representatives from the chemistry, pharmacology, pharmacokinetic, and toxicology departments reported on their continued observation of the compound in the animal studies to see if any long-term adverse effects had developed. Also, the regulatory representative of the team tracked the interaction of the company with the FDA. A pharmaceutical company has to periodically report to the FDA on the progress of the development of a compound, including any side effects that may develop during the course of clinical testing. In addition, representatives of the company needed to visit the FDA periodically to update it on the course of the clinical trials and on when they planned to move from small numbers of patients into large numbers of patients and eventually to discuss how the New Drug Application (NDA) was to be presented to the FDA for its approval. The NDA is a series of documents which represent all the essential knowledge that the company has regarding a new compound. At the periodic project team meetings the drug manufacturing representative updated plans to produce supplies of the drug both for the clinical investigation trials and the eventual producing of large amounts of the drug once it was approved for sale.

The project team chair had to ensure that the various activities of the individual departments and units of the company were all progressing at a rate that would eventually result in the NDA's being submitted in a timely manner. If any of the units in the company fell behind their schedule, it affected the overall performance of the entire group. The project team chair met periodically with the representatives on the project team on an individual basis to be sure that their units were making the necessary progress required to meet the NDA submission date and to be sure that they were not experiencing any unexpected difficulties. It was also the project team manager's responsibility to see to it that each unit had the necessary resources required to perform its tasks. It took careful planning to ensure that the various departments finished their work at essentially the same time so that the New Drug Application could be submitted at the designated time. The long-term toxicology studies in animals took three years to determine that there were no long-term cancer and genetic issues. The clinical trials beginning in normal volunteers and progressing to large numbers of hypertensive patients also took three years to perform. These were two steps that needed to be coordinated to ensure that everyone finished on time.

As each clinical trial was completed, a separate report was written to show that the compound was statistically and clinically significantly superior to a placebo (inactive) compound and that there were no clinically significant safety problems. The individual study reports were prepared by a small work team consisting of the physician in charge of the clinical studies, a medical writer, and a statistician. This team met frequently, often once a day, to prepare the reports. Once the reports were prepared for each individual clinical study, the FDA required that an overall summary of the effectiveness and safety of the compound be prepared. These overall reports were summaries of what was found in the individual studies. The two summary documents were also prepared by the same clinical group, working as before with the medical writer and statistician. At the same time that the chemists were preparing a document regarding the chemistry of the compound, the pharmacologists were preparing a document regarding the pharmacological effects of the compound, the pharmacokinetic group was preparing a third document regarding the metabolism and excretion of the drug, and the manufacturing group was preparing a fourth document on the various aspects of the drug as it related to manufacturing and the company's plan to produce the drug once it was approved for marketing. All of these functions were going on simultaneously in small groups, and a representative of each group sat on the project team and made the group's periodic reports.

When all the developmental work on the compound was completed and all of the required documents prepared, the company submitted them to the FDA for its approval. The project team's work did not end at this point because the FDA had frequent questions regarding various aspects of the reports in the NDA. These questions came to the project team, and the project team chairman decided who on the team was best qualified to answer the specific questions of the FDA. The approval process took an additional two years.

The final step before FDA approval of the drug was to present the data to an FDA advisory group. The FDA has a group of 10 to 20 outside consultants who meet periodically to evaluate new compounds. The project team chairman coordinated all of the activities for a presentation to the committee. At the advisory committee meeting a brief summary of the various aspects of the drug from chemistry and pharmacology through the results of the clinical trials was presented. The advisory committee made a recommendation to approve the marketing of the compound. THe FDA followed the recommendation of the advisory committee. At that point the work of the project team was finished.

1. What are your impressions of the processes used to develop new medicines?

2. What do you think of the testing of chemicals on animals?

3. Are there any ways you could suggest to improve the use of teams in the drug development process?

Richard E. Weber, M.D.

(B)

Even though the NDA (New Drug Application) was submitted in a timely manner, things did not always run smoothly. Once Lowerpress went into studies in humans, the work team, which consisted of the physician in charge of the clinical studies, the clinical scientist, the medical writer, and the statistician, met frequently to assess the progress of the study and, as mentioned above, to ultimately prepare the reports of each individual study. There were frequent areas of disagreement among various members of this small group. At times, the physician and the clinical scientist did not agree on various aspects of the study. Such things as study design and the selection of the outside investigators to do the study were areas of conflict. These disagreements were handled by the physician and the clinical scientist meeting in private and discussing in a rational manner their areas of concern and disagreement. By the process of both sides' discussing their concerns, they were always able to reach an acceptable compromise without undo difficulty. These areas of disagreement reflected honest differences of opinion. These differences were resolved because each party respected the other person's professional judgment and was willing to arrive at a compromise that both parties felt was acceptable.

Areas of conflict frequently arose between the physician and/or the clinical scientist versus the statistician. The conflict reached a peak when the clinical scientist and the statistician were at odds over how the data generated from the various studies should be reported in the individual study reports. After a series of confrontations between the clinical scientist and the statistician, the clinical scientist reported to the physician that he worked with on the project that the progress of the work team was at a standstill because he (the clinical scientist) and the statistician could not agree on how to handle specific aspects of the data collection. In order to try to resolve this conflict, the physician asked the clinical scientist and the statistician to meet with him, at which time each of the two parties who were in conflict explained to the physician his side of the issue. The physician heard both sides of the issue and stated his opinion. In this case he tended to side with the clinical scientist. Rather than resolve the area of conflict the statistician refused to change his opinion, and as a result the progress on the project came to a standstill. This resulted in a situation which could not be tolerated, for it would mean that the project would not finish on time.

1. How would you resolve the problem now facing the physician leading the project?

2. What future problems do you anticipate? How would you address them?

3. What practical lessons from this case apply to your life?

Richard E. Weber, M.D.

(C)

The physician, realizing that he and the clinical scientist had reached an impasse with the statistician, went to the supervisor of the work team statistician. The physician explained the problem to this statistician and objectively outlined both the side of the clinical scientist and himself and that of the work team statistician. The supervising statistician listened to the physician

Discussion Group Techniques

In addition to the major formats discussed above, there are a number of subformats or techniques that may be employed in discussion groups. These techniques are often used for short periods of time as *part* of a discussion group format. Popular discussion group techniques include the following:

Phillips 66: Phillips 66 is a specific technique developed by J. D. Phillips. It simply allows all the members of an audience to form groups of about six people to discuss a specific topic for about six minutes and then report the group's conclusion through a spokesperson. Realistically, this technique is more useful if longer time limits are allowed (up to an hour or so). The general term for this, when time and group size are not limited to six, is a *buzz group* or *buzz session.* The technique offers the advantage of allowing a lot of people to participate in a fairly efficient manner. The results from all groups are compiled and used to solve the problem faced by the entire assembly.

Case discussion: A case discussion is an educational discussion centered on a real or hypothetical event. The case problem is presented to the group, and members attempt to solve it as best they can. A case problem is included at the beginning of each chapter in this book to illustrate the way in which small group theory and research apply to real-life problems.

Role playing: Role playing simply allows participants to adopt a new "role" or set of behaviors other than their own. For example, quiet individuals may be assigned the role of leader, or argumentative members may be assigned the role of harmonizer or compromiser. Meek members may be asked to play the role of the "devil's advocate." In each case the individual gets an opportunity to practice a role in an attempt to build his or her group skills. This helps develop role flexibility so that participants can adopt new and different role behaviors as the need arises. Role playing also may be used to demonstrate to the rest of the group what a given role may do to a group discussion. The chronic-nonconformist role can be secretly given to one member to show how the others will react. The typical reaction is that the role player gets a lot of attention from the rest of the group for a while but will be ignored after a time if he or she continues to deviate (see Chapter 4 for more on deviation).

Another version of role playing is role reversal. In this case, participants try to take the part of another person (usually one with whom they have a conflict). Biracial groups, labor-management groups, and others frequently use this technique to develop empathy for the other person's point of view. It often results in funny situations, which also help relieve some of the tension. Try some of the role-playing exercises in this book to help get a feel for what role playing is like—for example, Exercise 1 at the end of Chapter 2.

Fishbowl: In the fishbowl technique one small group attempts to solve a problem for a specified period of time (often thirty minutes), while a second group, seated around the outside of the first group, observes the process. After the discussion, the observer group gives feedback to the first group as to what behaviors they were able to identify as helpful or harmful to the group's progress.

Then the two groups reverse positions and roles: the observers become the observed, and vice versa. This technique may be aided by the use of videotape equipment.

Conference: A conference is a series of meetings on topics of common interest between and among people who represent different groups. For example, representatives from different colleges and universities may gather at a conference to discuss problems of finance, curriculum, community service, and other issues. Conferences often involve hundreds of people and may last several days. For the past several years, different countries have hosted world food conferences in an attempt to plan for the feeding of the world's population. Conferences may also be quite small and last a short period of time. The critical element is that different groups are represented. An example of the latter type of conference is the plant manager's weekly conference in a manufacturing plant where representatives from production, engineering, maintenance, inspection, personnel, and other departments get together to organize their efforts and to solve common problems.

NGT: The Nominal Group Technique (NGT) was developed by Delbecq, Van de Ven, and Gustafson (1975) as a technique to reduce the effects of group conformity pressure. The NGT method has six phases. First is a silent, independent generation of ideas written down on paper. Second is a round-robin listing of ideas on a large sheet of newsprint or blackboard so everyone can see. The third step is a clarification of points without any critique. Fourth, everyone individually ranks the ideas. Fifth is a clarification of the vote. Sixth is a final ranking of the ideas. Jarobe (1988) has found that this method results in better decisions than less structured group discussions. Clearly, this method incorporates the advantages of a group in that several people's ideas are used. At the same time, it minimizes the disadvantage that often occurs when group members' ideas are subject to self-censorship based on one's fear of being rejected by other group members.

Computer-assisted Groups

Small groups can now do computer-supported cooperative work by means of *groupware.* This software uses the same input as regular small group communication but changes the mechanics of the throughput. Individuals each type in their ideas to their own computer, which then puts the ideas on a large screen for everyone to see. The key difference is that nobody knows whose ideas are whose. In computerized interaction, the group members are freer and less constrained by the social influence we usually feel in the presence of others. Small group software may also have built-in mechanisms for managing feedback.

Rash (1989) explains groupware this way:

> Groupware . . . is designed to enhance the functioning of a group in much the same way that individual productivity software helps the individual. The difference is that groupware, to be effective, must enhance the interaction of the people in a group. Be-

cause of the nature of a group of people, groupware faces several challenges. First, people who work together are not necessarily located together. . . . Second, a group consists of individuals who may have their own ideas about what work they need to do and how it should be accomplished. (p. 135)

Much groupware recognizes the problem of group tension. Groupware enables a group of individuals "who have their own ideas" to work together more easily than would be the case if the same people were together in a room.

Group meetings are essential. According to Vickers (1992), 30 to 70 percent of executives spend most of their working time in group meetings. In addition, executives must now absorb more information than in the past, partly because computers contribute more information. The natural response is to use computers to process the information that computers make available. Computers allow the integration of significantly more data and more seamless integration of decisions from group to group. These benefits make computer support particularly attractive to work group participants:

> Those involved in developing or implementing work group support will find more receptive users when they are involved in larger groups, groups with multidepartmental membership, or groups that spend more time in meetings. Additionally, users with positive attitudes toward computers and group work or those who now use some form of support for group work are likely adopters. (Satzinger and Olfman, 1992, p. 105)

Idea Generation and Anonymity

"There is an intuitive appeal to the belief that groups, with the diversity of views and experiences that they can bring to a topic, should be effective at generating ideas" (Valacich et al., 1992, p. 50). Investigations of structured and unstructured idea-generation techniques have compared the performance of "interacting groups" that use computers with that of individuals working separately whose ideas are pooled. To assess whether "process losses" are inhibitors of verbal, face-to-face idea generation, but not of computer-mediated idea generation, *production blocking, free riding,* and *evaluation apprehension* were evaluated by Valicich and his colleagues in a computerized environment. "Production blocking" occurs when "only one member of a group can speak at a time. . . . Free riding refers to the tendency of some group members to rely on other group members to accomplish the task without their contributions. . . . Evaluation apprehension refers to the fear of direct reprisals or negative evaluation of contributions that may cause individuals to withhold ideas." (p. 55) The researchers concluded that prior experience within single groups acted to both stimulate new ideas and reduce redundancies.

This study introduced an element of computer-assisted small groups that is not present without the computer anonymity. It is possible that "reduced inhibitions may encourage greater participation of junior or shy group members and the expression of unpopular, novel, or heretical opinions. Anonymity may also lead to the expression of uninhibited comments and the use of strong language" (Valacich et al., 1992, p. 55). One "investigation studying small groups using a computer-mediated idea-generation system found that anonymous, [i.e., computer] groups generated more unique ideas and had higher levels of participation yet were more critical and less satisfied than nonanonymous groups" (p. 55).

Another study (Sproull and Kiesler, 1991) also looked at the masking of group participants by a computer. The researchers concluded that "the results[of a test with groups containing both high- and low-status members] confirmed that the proportion of talk and influence of higher-status people decreased when group members communicated by electronic mail." The computer created a group of equals: "People who regarded themselves as physically unattractive reported feeling more lively and confident when they expressed themselves over the network. Others who had soft voices or small stature reported that they no longer had to struggle to be taken seriously in a meeting." These networked groups also "generated more proposals for action than did traditional ones" (pp. 119–120).

A study by Raja and Hwang (1992)—measuring the variables of (1) decision time, (2) number of alternatives generated, (3) satisfaction with the decision, and (4) decision quality—found that large groups (of nine members) had higher-quality results, did not use less time, and did not have enhanced decision satisfaction. Raja and Hwang conclude: "It is likely that the face-to-face human interaction without the presence of a computer may increase satisfaction with the final decision due to the human and social aspects associated with such interaction" (p. 17).

Leadership

With the advent of computers in every organization, leaders are often "dealing with new or unique decision-making situations, for which there are no standard processes or precedents. In these types of decision-making situations, [leaders] often do not have the breadth or depth of knowledge to make decisions, causing them to operate under greater uncertainty" (Vickers, 1992, p. 790). In these small group situations, leaders *must* rely on their groups to process the multitude of information. However, they must also be cautious about what they share. Uncertainty can arise from sharing pertinent information, sharing risks, sharing ideas, or sharing commitment. Uncertainty leads to two problems: coping with information complexity and coping with relatively unstructured know-how or knowledge. The solution for these leaders is to improve efficiency and effectiveness of decision groups by saving time and resources and producing a "better quality outcome from the group's activity." Vickers suggests that "to maximize process gain and minimize process loss, a group requires collaborative support, such as that offered by GDSS (group decision support systems)." (p. 790) According to Vickers:

> [If] actual effectiveness = potential effectiveness − process losses + process gains, [then] "decision quality is reduced when unproductive group conflict (process loss) reduces the quality of information output. Ideally, effective communication within a group is maintained by achieving levels of conflict that are appropriate to the problem being tackled—process gain. (p. 791)

For leaders, computer-aided communication can be an important means of influencing a group's methods and capabilities. Sproull and Kiesler (1991) write:

> [Leaders] are often attracted to networks by the promise of faster communication and greater efficiency. [But it could be that] the real potential of network communication has less to do with such matters than with influencing the overall work environment and the capabilities of employees. [Leaders] can use networks to foster new kinds of task structures and reporting relationships. They can use networks to change the conventional patterns of who talks to whom and who knows what." (p. 116)

These computer-aided communication channels could bring out multiple new resources by tapping individuals, who by virtue of their organizational stature, would not otherwise be tapped. And this same environment can also alleviate leaders' workloads as it nurtures growth.

Computer-assisted Groups: Where Are They Going?

What is happening now? Do small group interactions need to be redefined? Some trends are already moving into the mainstream, like intercontinental links, simultaneous work programs, and scientific collaborations. In coming years, computer technology will play an increasing role in group interaction. Opper (1988) writes: "Macro trends in business portend well for the future of groupware. These trends say companies will be trying to do more work faster with fewer people, that the 'time to decision' will be shorter, and that small groups rather than individuals or large committees will be the agents getting things done" (p. 282).

Logistical problems will cease: "The information marketplace will also change how we work with geographically distant partners. An increasing number of conferences are already conducted over video links, but these conferences still require all the participants to be in the right place at the right time. New approaches to such collaborations will free people to take part in delayed and distributed meetings" (Dertouzos, 1991, p. 66). Maybe some day Congress will meet electronically, thereby letting senators and representatives remain in the districts they represent.

As small groups foster democracy, so do computers. Dertouzos (1991) claims: "There is no question . . . that computers and networks will democratize human communication. Nearly everyone would be able to put his or her ideas, concerns and demands before all others. This freedom will undoubtedly bring sociological consequences, including the formation of electronic tribes that can span physical distance. . . . People are neither so naive nor devoid of instincts for self-preservation and control that they will surrender their humanity to their tools." People will use their tools to make themselves more efficient and productive, but they won't forget what is best done "live."

Computer technology will most help those who know what they want to accomplish:

> Investigators say that real gains will come when groups use collaboration technology to reshape the way they work together. . . . [Organizations] employing collabora-

tion technology to "capture and reflect on" how they make decisions will find they have a "learning-curve accelerator" that will hone their competitive edge. (Corcoran, 1988, p. 112)

THE SYSTEMS PERSPECTIVE

In this chapter we have looked at some of the elements that constitute the internal influences section of our model. In systems theory these elements would be called part of the *throughput* of small groups. Early in the chapter we examined territoriality, physical environment, and seating behavior in groups. As suggested by the Vietnam negotiations, different cultures have drastically differing perceptions of how to position furniture or whether to have furniture at all. This illustrates the way in which relevant background factors influence such internal influences as territoriality, physical environment, and seating behavior. For example, in Western culture we typically place furniture along the walls with open space in the middle of the room. The Japanese tend to cluster furniture in the center of the room, leaving the space along the walls open. Also, imagine conducting a group discussion while seated barefoot on the floor around very low tables. This should help you picture the importance of background factors in relation to seating behaviors.

Probably the most important internal influence in the model is the type of group. Obviously, the procedures, norms, expectations, and outcomes of a work group will be radically different from those of a social group. For example, a norm of openness in both self-disclosure and candid feedback to others exists in many social groups. However, you might find that to tell your boss or friend exactly what you do *not* like about him or her is certainly inappropriate. The type of group has an enormous impact on the way in which that group functions.

In this chapter we also looked at the literature on communication networks. We saw that the all-channel network was best for group member satisfaction, whereas the wheel produced the fastest results. As our systems perspective leads us to believe, determining the "best" network depends, among other things, on the demands of the situation.

When we discussed the issue of group size, we began to see the connection between the type of group and the appropriate group size. All other things being equal, five seems to be the optimum size for a problem-solving group. However, the optimum size for a group discussion in a classroom may be radically different from that of a work group on an assembly line or in a large office. Even the idea of the "right" size of family group depends on each of our relevant background factors. Typically, people have quite strong feelings about what the "right" size is for a family. These feelings usually result from a lifetime of attitude formation influenced by parents, friends, and, perhaps, religious affiliation.

Group size is also related to the idea of communication networks. As the size increases, the all-channel network begins to bog down in the confusion, and a more controlled network tends to be more appropriate. Group size is also related to the consequences of group interaction. Larger groups tend to produce lower levels of satisfaction and interpersonal relations among participants. Bostrom's research, cited in this chapter, is very revealing. It showed that most people like to talk far more than they like to listen in groups.

In the preceding section of this chapter we looked at different group formats and techniques (for example, panel, symposium, role playing, fishbowl, conference). Obviously, there is a connection between type of group and appropriate format. Can you imagine the U.S. President's cabinet engaging in role playing and fishbowl simulations? Certainly, educational groups use these formats and techniques with a great deal of success, but work groups would be more likely to use panels, symposiums, and conferences.

The type of group format is also related to the desired group outcome. If personal growth is the goal, then role playing or fishbowls are helpful. On the other hand, if the group goal is to solve a task-oriented problem, such as how to cut energy consumption by 10 percent, the panel discussion or the use of groupware is probably more appropriate. As usual, it all depends.

EXERCISE

1. Case Study Discussion

Divide into five-person groups. Each group should discuss the case below.

AGENCIES TIPTOE AMONG LEGAL MINES—ADMINISTRATION
ASKS COURT TO RERULE ON GAY CADET*
By Jim Abrams, The Associated Press
WASHINGTON—The administration sought a rehearing Thursday of court orders to commission gay midshipman Joseph Steffan, but sidestepped the larger battle over whether banning gays from the military is constitutional.

The Justice Department, filing the petition on behalf of the Defense Department, focused instead on the narrower issue of whether the U.S. Circuit Court of Appeals in Washington exceeded its authority in ruling that Steffan be given his Naval Academy diploma and commissioned as an officer.

The court, it said, raised "the gravest legal questions" in regard to the principle of separation of powers that holds that military officers must be appointed by the president and approved by the Senate.

The three federal judges on Nov. 16 ruled that expelling Steffan solely on the basis of his sexual orientation violated the equal protection guarantee of the Constitution.

*From *The Ann Arbor News,* December 31, 1993, p. A6.

The court considered the old policy banning homosexuals in the military, but its ruling could also raise constitutional questions for the somewhat more liberal policy the Clinton administration has put into effect.

The petition expresses the Pentagon's "profound disagreement" with the opinion that the old policy was unconstitutional. But it states that "it is not necessary to take the extraordinary step of rehearing" the constitutional issue because the court looked only at the old policy.

After one of the most divisive debates of President Clinton's first year in office, the Pentagon earlier this month issued regulations for its new "don't ask, don't tell, don't pursue" policy that forbids homosexual practices but does not necessarily discharge members merely for their sexual orientation.

David Smith, a spokesman for the National Gay and Lesbian Task Force, said the decision not to take up the constitutional question was positive, but said he was angry any appeal was being made.

"Appealing any aspect of this ruling conflicts dramatically with the president's oft-stated position that there should be no discrimination within the services," Smith said.

Steffan's attorney, Evan Wolfson of the Lambda Legal Defense & Education Fund, said they were "disappointed by the government's petty effort to continue denying an outstanding midshipman his commission."

He said Lambda, a gay legal rights organization, and the American Civil Liberties Union will file a court challenge to the Pentagon's new policy on gays within the next few weeks.

Steffan, now 29, is in law school at the University of Connecticut.

After you have arrived at group agreement, each group should share its reaction and the reasoning behind it. Discuss the different reactions among the groups.

READINGS: OVERVIEW

In the first article, Gibson and Hanna offer some practical tips for participation in groups.

In the second article, Hyland and Yost offer some additional sage advice for getting the most out of your group members.

Participating in Groups

James W. Gibson and Michael S. Hanna

The advantages of group decision making cannot have an effect unless individual members make certain commitments to the group. Every member of every group assumes four responsibilities by joining the group. Every time they agree to engage in decision making with other people, they agree to give up some of their individual sovereignty so that the group process can work. They assume an obligation to make decisions by certain ethical standards.

Do Your Best

You have something to offer a group. You have knowledge. You are sensitive and analytical. You think. You feel. You believe. You cannot change your strengths and weaknesses, and you do not need to. You are okay just the way you are, and you can contribute to a group. Give your group the best that you have. Do not hold back.

Sometimes individual group members do hold back. For example, people sometimes decline to take a leadership role because they think someone else might want to do it or because they resent a perceived manipulation by others. If you agree to involve yourself in a decision-making group, commit yourself to help that group to make the best decisions possible. If you give less, you violate a standard of excellence that is widely valued in our society.

Behave Rationally

Keep an open mind, listen to evidence and arguments, and withhold personal decisions until the evidence and the arguments have been presented. Behaving rationally means putting the interests of the group ahead of your own personal interests.

We have all known individuals who were unable to put aside their personal convictions in order to listen to another group member's position. These impatient people bring to the decision-making group their own private truths

From *James W. Gibson and Michael S. Hanna,* Introduction to Human Communication *(Dubuque, Iowa: Wm. C. Brown, 1992).*

and their private agendas. For example, a person once served on a committee appointed by the mayor to make recommendations about how the mayor's office could improve two-way communication between the mayor and the community. A member of that group had a personal interest. The person tried to get the group to advocate the support for the improvement of the city-owned art museum. The person's idea was that the museum provided the best "out-reach" opportunity for the mayor. Unfortunately, the person did not want to talk or listen to any other ideas. A private agenda such as this interferes with a group's ability to choose the *best* alternative from a field of possibilities.

Rational behavior implies critical thinking, such as described in the last chapter. Do not behave irrationally. Your responsibilities to the group require that you listen carefully with an open mind, that you consider all the information, and that you work to evolve the most sensible group decisions.

Rational behavior may sometimes require great personal courage. It may mean setting aside personal animosity. It may mean agreeing to work constructively and positively with someone you do not like. It may require you to face and deal with rejection of your ideas. Even so, rational behavior is absolutely necessary. If the members of the group are not rational and do not cooperate, then the group cannot be productive. You take on an ethical responsibility to rational behavior every time you agree to work in a decision-making group.

Play Fair

Group decision making is a cooperative activity. It is not a competitive event at which you champion your viewpoint. This means that group members have the responsibility to seek and to present all of the ideas and evidence, whether or not the information seems contradictory. Every member of the group has a right to expect you to play fair, just as you have a right to expect every other member to play fair. Do not engage in debate in a group decision-making meeting. As a matter of ethical responsibility, you are constrained from competing with other group members.

Listen and Participate

When you have prepared carefully and have something important to say, you want other people to listen to you. You have a right to expect them to take you seriously, to listen to you carefully, to ask you questions, to give you feedback, and to evaluate your ideas with an open mind. If they did less than that, they would be mistreating you.

**FIGURE 4.1   HYPOTHETICAL RELATIONSHIP BETWEEN
WEIGHT AND LEADERSHIP**

© 1971 Henry R. Martin. Reprinted with permission of Meredith
Corporation and Henry Martin.

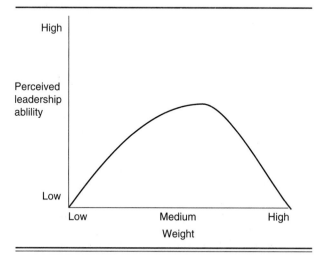

What relationship might there be between weight and leadership? The heavier the better? No, actually the predicted relationship is curvilinear (see Figure 4.1). Thus, people who are too thin or too heavy would be considered either too weak and fragile or too self-indulgent and undisciplined to be good leaders. In one unpublished study conducted in a large company, employees were divided into groups, one whose members weighed within 10 percent of their "desirable" weight (based on a doctor's chart of height and weight) and one whose members deviated more than 10 percent above or below their charted body weight. The percentage of promotions was tabulated for the two groups, and it was found that the medium-weight group had more promotions.

In a study conducted by a Madison Avenue employment agency with branches in forty-three American cities, it was found that overweight persons may be losing as much as $1000 a year for every pound of fat. According to the agency's president, Robert Hall (1974), the survey showed that among executives in the $25,000 to 50,000 salary group, only 9 percent were more than 10 pounds overweight. In the $10,000 to 20,000 group, only 39 percent were more than 10 pounds overweight (according to the standards established by life insurance companies). Hall said that the overweight "are unfairly stereotyped as slow, sloppy, inefficient, and overindulgent. When important, high-paying jobs are at stake and candidates are under close scrutiny, the overweight are less likely to be hired or promoted into them." (p. 1) Hall also stated that companies frequently specify their preference for slim candidates, but only once in twenty-five years did a company request a plump executive; the company was a manufacturer of oversized clothing.

Closely related to body weight is body type. Sheldon (1940, 1942, 1954) identi-fied three different body types, or *somatotypes.* The very thin person is called an *ectomorph,* the very heavy and soft person an *endomorph,* and the medium weight, muscular type is the *mesomorph.* Intuitively, we might expect leaders to come from the mesomorphic body type. Although there are no studies to support or refute this prediction, it is a provocative theory that might someday be tested. For exam-ple, those who are successful in political campaigns and in movie careers seem to be more often than not mesomorphic. We also know from several research studies that more attractive people are perceived as having higher credibility (for example, higher expertise and better character) on the basis of their looks alone (Mills and Aronson, 1965; Widgery and Webster, 1969; Widgery, 1974).

In addition to physical traits, certain personality traits were thought to be associ-ated with leadership. A list of some of these traits includes self-confidence, domi-nance, enthusiasm, assertiveness, responsibility, creativity, originality, dependabili-ty, critical thinking ability, intelligence, and ability to communicate effectively. Although all these traits have some commonsense appeal, Stogdill (1948) surveyed over 200 leadership studies and found that out of all the identified traits, only 5 percent were common to four or more of the studies surveyed. In a recent update, however, Bass (1993, p. 93) has had somewhat greater success in securing a level of agreement among leadership trait studies. His results appear in Figure 4.2.

In summarizing his latest thoughts on the trait theory, Bass (1993) states:

> Although leaders differ from followers with respect to various aspects of personality, ability, and social skills, tests of such traits have been of limited value for selection of leaders. Traits do not act singly but in combination. . . . The leader who acquires leadership status in one group tends to emerge as leader when placed in other groups. Thus, perhaps the best prediction of future leadership is prior success in this role. (p. 413)

On the other side of the coin, Geier (1967) was able to identify five negative traits that consistently prevented group members from emerging as leaders. Such members were (1) uninformed about the problem being discussed, (2) nonpartici-pative, (3) extremely rigid in holding to pet ideas, (4) authoritarian in bossing oth-ers around, and (5) offensive and abusive in language style. Although the trait the-ory has not held as many answers as early philosophers and theorists had hoped, it has provided us with some helpful information and insight.

Bennis and Nanus (1985) interviewed ninety contemporary American leaders, from Ray Kroc, founder of McDonalds, to John H. Johnson, publisher of *Ebony,* to John Robinson, coach of the Los Angeles Rams. They concluded:

> Myth 3. Leaders are Charismatic. Some are, most aren't. Among the ninety there were a few—but damned few—who probably correspond to our fantasies of some "di-vine inspiration," that "grace under stress" we associated with J.F.K. or the beguiling capacity to spellbind for which we remember Churchill. Our leaders were all "too human"; they were short and tall, articulate and inarticulate, dressed for success and dressed for failure, and there was virtually nothing in terms of physical appearance, personality, or style that set them apart from their followers. Our guess is that it oper-

FIGURE 4.2   FACTORS APPEARING IN THREE OR MORE STUDIES

Reprinted with permission of The Free Press, a division of Macmillan, Inc., from *Stogdill's Handbook of Leadership,* rev. ed., by Bernard M Bass. Copyright © 1993 by The Free Press.

Factor No.	Factor Name	Frequency
1	Social and interpersonal skills	16
2	Technical skills	18
3	Administrative skills	12
4	Leadership effectiveness and achievement	15
5	Social nearness, friendliness	18
6	Intellectual skills	11
7	Maintaining cohesive work group	9
8	Maintaining coordination and teamwork	7
9	Task motivation and application	17
10	General impression (halo)	12
11	Group task supportiveness	17
12	Maintaining standards of performance	5
13	Willingness to assume responsibility	10
14	Emotional balance and control	15
15	Informal group control	4
16	Nurturant behavior	4
17	Ethical conduct, personal integrity	10
18	Communication, verbality	6
19	Ascendance, dominance, decisiveness	11
20	Physical energy	6
21	Experience and activity	4
22	Mature, cultured	3
23	Courage, daring	4
24	Aloof, distant	3
25	Creative, independent	5
26	Conforming	5

ates in the other direction; that is, charisma is the result of effective leadership, not the other way around, and that those who are good at it are granted a certain amount of respect and even awe by their followers, which increases the bond of attraction between them (pp. 223–224)

Bennis and Nanus summarize their research this way: "Managers do things right, leaders do the right thing." (p. 3)

Circumstances Theory

Ira Hayes was an American Indian who became famous for having been one of the U.S. marines who lifted the American flag after the battle of Iwo Jima in the South Pacific during World War II. Ira Hayes just happened to be standing nearby when the photographer solicited a group to pose for the picture that later became world-famous. Ira instantly became a national hero and was sent on cross-country U.S. Savings Bond drives to raise money for the American war effort. Ira's pride made him feel so guilty for being a "counterfeit hero" that he began to drink. He eventually died an alcoholic.

Ira Hayes is the classic example of a person being at the right place at the right (or wrong) time. This is sometimes called the *circumstances theory of leadership*. Another facet of this theory is that a person may be an effective leader in one circumstance but perform poorly in a different circumstance. Therefore, some theorists would argue that the circumstances make the leader. A good example of this is the student/faculty softball, football, or basketball teams that are found on some campuses. Although the professors are usually the leaders in the classroom (because of a relatively higher level of expertise in the subject), the students are usually the leaders on the athletic field, where they often know more about the game and are almost always in better physical shape than the professors.

Like trait theory, circumstances theory seems to have some validity. However, there are many exceptions to the rule. Charles Percy was president of Bell and Howell Corporation at age 30 and has also functioned effectively as a U.S. senator. Robert McNamara functioned well as president of Ford Motor Company, U.S. secretary of defense, and head of the World Bank organization. George Schultz and John Glenn are two more individuals who have succeeded in numerous capacities in and out of government. Circumstances theory, although somewhat valid, leaves something to be desired in explaining the complex phenomenon of leadership.

Function Theory

A theory that deviates rather dramatically from the first two is *function theory*. Underlying this theory is the notion that leaders are made, not born. That is, leadership consists of certain behaviors or *functions* that groups must have performed. These functions are identifiable behaviors that can be learned by anybody. We can all improve our potential as leaders by learning to perform these key functions more effectively. Although trait and circumstance theories assume there is little we can do to become leaders if we aren't a certain height or if we never seem to be in the right place at the right time, function theory offers hope for those of us who may not have been born Kennedys or Rockefellers or who are not asked to be in famous photographs.

The two important functions that have been consistently identified are referred to by a variety of terms, but are basically the same concepts. They are (1) task orientation and (2) people orientation.

A negative example of people orientation is provided by Bennis and Nanus (1985) in their book on leaders' strategies. Writing about Jimmy Carter's leadership style, they quote one of his loyal cabinet officers, who said: "Working for him was like looking at the wrong side of a tapestry—blurry and indistinct" (pp. 36–37).

In contrast, Sayles (1993) puts it well when he writes, "Effective leadership requires involvement. . . . Working leadership involves the capacity to make fast-paced trade-offs (each involving embedded people and technology issues)" (p. 13).

With function theory, the emphasis has shifted away from the leader as a person and toward the specific behavioral acts that facilitate group success. Leadership may be "possessed" by any group member who performs these leadership functions. The task-oriented behaviors are those directed toward the group's accomplishing its goal. The people-oriented behaviors are directed toward the maintenance of the interpersonal relationships in the group. It is assumed that people-oriented activities ought to have an indirect effect on helping accomplish the group's task. An analogy would be that of a machine. The machine operates to accomplish a task (producing parts). However, if the machine is not cleaned and lubricated, it will break down sooner or later, thus halting its productivity. Similarly, although task-oriented groups may require a leader who can help them accomplish their goal, they may cease functioning if they become too bogged down in personality conflicts or counterproductive interpersonal friction. Both task-oriented and people-oriented behaviors are required to enable a group to progress. Bales, in Figure 4.3, offers a summary of the twelve types of specific behavioral acts (six task-oriented, six people-oriented) and the average percentage of the interaction in any given group discussion that would probably fall into each category.

FIGURE 4.3

Adapted from *Personality and Interpersonal Behavior* by Robert F. Bales. Copyright © 1970 by Holt, Rinehart & Winston, Inc. Reprinted by permission of Holt, Rinehart & Winston, Inc.

	Category	Percentage	Estimated Norms
People-oriented (positive)	1. Seems friendly	3.5	2.6– 4.8
	2. Dramatizes	7.0	5.7– 7.4
	3. Agrees	18.5	8.0–13.6
Task-oriented	4. Gives suggestions	3.8	3.0– 7.0
	5. Gives opinions	24.5	15.0–22.7
	6. Gives information	8.3	20.7–31.2
	7. Asks for information	10.3	4.0– 7.2
	8. Asks for opinions	12.5	2.0– 3.9
	9. Asks for suggestions	2.3	0.6– 1.4
People-oriented (negative)	10. Disagrees	1.0	3.1– 5.3
	11. Shows tension	7.8	3.4– 6.0
	12. Seems unfriendly	0.5	2.4– 4.4
		Total: 100.0	

Ross summarizes the work of Bales and others in an extended model of the twelve Bales Interaction Process Analysis (IPA) categories (Figure 4.4).

The function theory of leadership seems to hold the most promise for teaching most of us how to improve our own leadership abilities. For example, many students hesitate to participate in discussions for fear of "saying something stupid." Yet several research studies indicate that simply participating at all is one primary requirement of becoming more of a leader. Other studies show that individuals who are able to perform both task- and people-oriented functions in groups are likely to get better results from their groups than those who are less effective in performing these two functions.

Effective leadership on the job emphasizes a high concern for people and a high concern for task in the workplace. Under such conditions the workplace becomes a "worthplace" (Karlins and Hargis, 1988, p. 665). In a worthplace, production and quality of the product are high, and employee satisfaction is high. "Unfortunately a significant number of American managers persist in over-emphasizing 'task' concerns, while ignoring or downplaying the importance of 'people' concerns in the workplace" (p. 665). Managers' perceptions of their own leadership styles have been found to be very different from their employees' perceptions. An investigation of fifty-two large organizations, reported by Karlins and Hargis (1988), found that most managers (88 percent) perceived themselves as striking a balance between task and people concerns, with a high concern for both (9,9 on the Blake-Mouton Grid). However, most subordinates (85 percent) reported that they worked for managers who emphasized a high concern for tasks and a low concern for people.

These skewed perceptions of leadership likely have a detrimental effect on management. When a leader of a group perceives himself or herself as being effective in meeting the needs of the group and the group members do not perceive the same, the system breaks down. In order to transform a workplace into a worthplace, managers must learn to have more accurate perceptions of their leadership styles.

Katzenbach and Smith (1993) emphasize: "Team leaders genuinely believe that they do not have all the answers—so they do not insist on providing them. They believe that they do not need to make all key decisions—so they do not do so. . . . Most important, like all members of the team, team leaders do real work themselves" (p. 131).

The final important implication to grow out of the function theory of leadership is that these functions need not be performed by the one person designated as group leader. In fact, the implication is the reverse. To the extent that all group members learn to perform these two functions, overall group leadership will be improved. This is often referred to as *shared* or *democratic* leadership, which we will examine in the next section.

Leadership Styles

A great deal of attention has been paid to the different types of available leadership styles. Early studies identified three different styles: autocratic, democratic, and laissez-faire.

FIGURE 4.4 INTERACTION PROCESS ANALYSIS, CATEGORIES OF COMMUNICATIVE ACTS

Based on Robert F. Bales, *Interaction Process Analysis* (Reading, Mass.: Addison-Wesley, 1950), p. 9; A. Paul Hare, *Handbook of Small Group Research* (New York: Free Press of Glencoe, 1962), p. 66; and Clovis R. Shepherd, *Small Groups: Some Sociological Perspectives* (San Francisco: Chandler, 1964), p. 30.

Major Categories	Subcategories	Illustrative Statements or Behavior
Social-emotional area — Positive reactions	1. Shows solidarity	Jokes, gives help, rewards others, is friendly
	2. Shows tension release	Laughs, shows satisfaction, is relieved
	3. Shows agreement	Passively accepts, understands, concurs, complies
Task area — Attempted answers	4. Gives suggestion	Directs, suggests, implies autonomy for others
	5. Gives opinion	Evaluates, analyzes, expresses feeling or wish
	6. Gives information	Orients, repeats, clarifies, confirms
Questions	7. Asks for information	Requests orientation, repetition, confirmation
	8. Asks for opinion	Requests evaluation, analysis, expression of feeling
	9. Asks for suggestion	Requests direction, possible ways of action
Social-emotional area — Negative reactions	10. Shows disagreement	Passively rejects, resorts to formality, withholds help
	11. Shows tension	Asks for help, withdraws, daydreams
	12. Shows antagonism	Deflates other's status, defends or asserts self, hostile

Key: a. Problems of communication   b. Problems of evaluation   c. Problems of control
      d. Problems of decision   e. Problems of tension reduction f. Problems of reintegration

The issue in these three leadership styles is the degree and location of control. The *authoritarian,* or *autocratic,* leader has a high need to maintain control of the group himself or herself. Some might even say that the autocratic leader has an obsession for control. When this obsession reaches the extreme, it is manifested in the following types of behaviors (Sattler and Miller, 1968, pp. 250–251):

1. The authoritarian leader usually plans to get to the conference room when everyone else is assembled. He fears getting to the meeting early, for he has no interest in carrying on non-task-related conversation. This does not mean that the leader is a latecomer—he isn't; if the meeting is scheduled to start at 3:10 P.M. , you will be sure that the leader will be present and the meeting will start on the proper split second.

2. Often the leader will present an extended introduction to start a meeting, in part because he wishes others to know how well informed he is.

3. Sometimes the authoritarian will outline precise procedures on how the discussion is to be conducted. Thus, he might tell the group that Mr. A will comment on Item 1, B and C on Item 2, and D on Item 3. Such advice on procedure is not given in order to be helpful to others; largely, it seems, the authoritarian uses rules of order to make his own task easier.

4. Authoritarians, more than other leaders, specialize in questions directed to specific persons such as, "Jones, what are your facts?" and "Now I want to hear from Smith." Such leaders do not frequently use open or "overhead" questions that any person in the group may answer.

5. Authoritarians appear to be unable to withstand pauses in discussion—if such leaders cannot get rapid verbalization from others, they will themselves supply verbal noises.

6. The leader almost invariably maintains strict control over the order and sequence of topics; he appears to love placing group members in a "straitjacket" of restrictions.

7. The authoritarian leader interrupts others often, for at least three reasons: to correct errors whether major or insignificant, to keep persons talking about what he desires, and in general to show who is in command.

8. Clever authoritarians at times encourage group members to discuss irrelevant matters at considerable length. This is true, of course, only when to discuss the irrelevant is in keeping with the leader's designs.

9. When the leader clarifies contributions, he is sometimes guilty of changing the intent of statements to make them more acceptable to himself. (Here, of course, we have both procedural and content control.)

The *laissez-faire* style of leadership goes to the opposite extreme. Not only is there no concern for control, but there is no direction, concern for task accomplishment, or concern for interpersonal relationships. The laissez-faire style is not really a style of leadership at all; it is nonleadership.

The *democratic* leadership style represents an attempt to find a reasonable compromise between the other two extremes. The leader does attempt to provide direction and to perform both task and social leadership functions, but at the same time he or she tries to avoid dominating the group with one person's views. Some would argue that no matter how hard an individual tries, some domination cannot be avoided.

Which leadership style is best? In order to answer this question, we must determine the criteria for judging effectiveness. Some criteria are (1) the quality of the group output, (2) the time taken to accomplish the task, (3) the satisfaction of the group members, (4) the absenteeism of group members, and (5) the independence developed in group members. Manz and Sims (1993) reported (1) that the quality of group output was better under democratic leadership, (2) that democratic leadership took more time than autocratic, (3) that member satisfaction was higher under democratic leadership (in fact, hostility was thirty times as great in the autocratic groups, and nineteen out of twenty preferred the democratic group to the autocratic), (4) that the democratic group had the lowest absenteeism, and (5) that the democratic group fostered more independence, whereas the autocratic style bred dependence and submissiveness among group members.

The democratic style got better results in each case except in time taken to accomplish the task. However, subsequent studies have shown that the autocratic leader gets fast results in the short run but that these results may be of poor quality or may be resisted by others. The net effect is that the solution may not be enacted, and the problem will have to be dealt with again on future occasions. Because this amounts to less efficiency, the democratic style may even prove to be less time-consuming in the long run (see Chapter 7 for more on this). In addition, the hostility bred by autocratic leadership produces counterproductive results. For example, in industrial groups, absenteeism, grievances, work stoppages, and sabotage are all ways in which employees attempt to "get back" at what they consider to be harsh leadership. "Goldbricking" in the military is another typical example. An autocratic leadership style fosters group norms that say, "Do as little as possible to get by, and look busy when the boss is around. However, when the cat's away . . . "

Barrett and Carey (1989) note: "History records that Abraham Lincoln sought input from his cabinet officers regarding the appointment of Ulysses S. Grant as Commander of the Grand Army of the Republic. When each cabinet member spoke against the appointment, Lincoln responded that the vote was seven nays and one aye—and that the ayes had it" (p. 3). Communication is important to the democratic leader because he or she relies so heavily on the input and support of group members.

In a four-year study of problem-solving teams, Larson (1993) found that the most effective leaders were those who created a process in which people have confidence. He describes some of the other requirements of effective team leaders as follows:

> [Successful team leadership] demands great patience. It is accompanied by a willingness to give up control and ego needs and to create ownership by the people involved. . . . It shows itself by a clear focus on the problem and as intense involvement with others in shaping an effective response to the problem. (p. 9)

In summary, leadership is hard work, but it mostly involves sharing the task and allowing others to exert their own leadership too.

SuperLeaders

Manz and Sims (1990) and Sims and Lorenzi (1992) have proposed a type of leadership that seems to be the ultimate extension of democratic leadership *Super-Leadership*. A person who exhibits this type of leadership is called the *SuperLeader.* A SuperLeader who gets a lot of other people involved is said to develop *SuperTeams.* Sims and Lorenzi write, "To bring about successful team development, the leader must first establish the capacity of the . . . group to take on new responsibilities" (p. 212). Listed below are six ways that the SuperLeader can improve a team's environment:

1. Encourage self-reinforcement, such that the team members find ways to identify and administer meaningful performance-[based] . . . outcomes for themselves.

2. Encourage self-criticism, through which team members learn to diagnose inappropriate behaviors and engage in appropriate self-reprimands.

3. Encourage self-set goals for the group, having team members identify and articulate key areas for progress.

4. Encourage self-observation/evaluation, with team members controlling their own consequences only after assessing their own behaviors.

5. Encourage high self-expectations . . . by developing a culture of risk taking and success.

6. Provide opportunities for rehearsal prior to meeting final work demands, so that team members can practice and further develop requisite team skills with less risk to success and self-esteem. (Sims and Lorenzi, 1992, p. 212)

The SuperLeadership approach seems the most closely relevant to small group interaction and seems to be the trend in leadership development of the future.

The SuperLeadership philosophy is well summarized in the famous words of Lao-tzu:

> A leader is best
> When people barely know that he exists,
> Not so good when people obey and acclaim him,
> Worse when they despise him.
> "Fail to honor people,
> They fail to honor you";
> But of a good leader who talks little,
> When his work is done, his aim fulfilled,
> They will say, "We did it ourselves."

FOLLOWERSHIP

Although leadership is written about more than most topics relating to small group interaction, followership is much less frequently discussed. Because leadership is defined as successful attempts to influence, followers are required to make leaders. In fact, leadership and followership go hand in hand. Earlier we saw that one style of leadership (democratic) in many cases seems to be best. What style of followership is best? Let us first look at three alternative followership styles.

Followership Styles

Milgram (1974) summarizes almost fifteen years of research on this topic in his book *Obedience to Authority*. In Milgram's experiments, subjects were told to administer electric shocks to other subjects as part of an experiment in learning associations between word pairs. The victim was strapped in a chair and was unable to escape the shocks. The control panel on the shock generator indicated voltage up to 450 volts, which level was labeled, "Danger: Severe Shock." As the voltage was increased, the victim screamed, "Get me out of here; I can't stand the pain; please, I have a heart condition." These protests were continued for any and all shocks administered above 150 volts. (No actual shocks were given, but the subjects really thought they were shocking the victims.)

A group of psychiatrists was asked to predict how much shock the subject would administer to the victim. They predicted that almost every subject would refuse to obey the experimenter, that those who administered any shocks at all would stop at 150 volts, and that only about one in a thousand would go all the way to 450 volts (the end of the control panel). Out of Milgram's original forty subjects, however, twenty-six (65 percent) obeyed the experimenter's orders and administered the shocks right up to the 450-volt limit. However, Milgram found that as situations were changed (for example, if the victim was brought into the same room with the subject), the subject was less willing to shock the victim. The behavior found in Milgram's experiments illustrates what might be termed a *dependent* style of followership.

Large organizations such as the military, organized religions, and government and industrial organizations frequently produce a higher level of dependence in people. As we saw earlier, autocratic leadership produces a higher level of dependent followership. Most of us are caught up to some degree in the obedience syndrome, but with much less harmful or dramatic results.

A second type of follower is the *counterdependent* person. Counterdependence is a type of behavior that is rebellious and antiauthoritarian. Although the dependent personality is thought to result from overly punitive parents, the counterdependent personality is thought to result from overly permissive parents. People who are used to doing things more or less their own way resent a leader or any authority figure who intervenes. This type of person would be dissatisfied with almost any style of leadership. It may not be too much of an exaggeration to say that this group consists of misfits who are pretty much chronic problems. In the industrial work force they create major problems for leaders wherever they go. Steinmetz (1969) quoted Edward Cole, former president of General Motors, as stating:

A research study found that a relatively few employees—28%—filed 100% of the grievances and accounted for 37% of the occupational hospital visits; 38% of the insurance claims, 40% of the sick leaves, 52% of the garnishments, and 38% of the absenteeism experienced at a certain factory. Thus not only are there a comparatively small proportion of people who are absentee-oriented, but these same people tend also to be the ones who create a significant number of all the other problems generated within the organization. (pp. 10–11)

This type of follower would be hard for any leader to lead. We saw earlier that a democratic leadership style tends to produce higher levels of member satisfaction. However, Runyon (1973) found in an industrial chemical plant that some hourly employees (primarily young workers) did not have high job satisfaction regardless of type of supervisory style. Even a participative (democratic) style did not produce a high level of satisfaction. Perhaps it is fair to say that some people are simply difficult to lead, and that in dealing with them, one leadership style would be about as good (or bad) as any other. The problem then would be to try to bring the followers to a point where they could accept legitimate leadership from others.

The third followership style is the *independent*. The independent is one who can either take over and lead when the situation demands or follow the lead of others when that role is more appropriate. Benjamin Franklin once said, "He that cannot obey cannot command." This implies the role flexibility required of both an effective leader and an effective follower.

Interestingly enough, in a totally different context, Milgram found that when he asked subjects to shock the victims in his studies, psychiatrists (professional group) predicted that they would disobey rather quickly, whereas other middle-class adults (nonprofessional group) predicted that they would obey somewhat longer and give more intense shocks. It appears that, to some extent, education and perhaps the subsequent self-confidence tends to correlate with independence of followership and decision making.

To illustrate the contingency aspects of leadership, one student wrote:

As a second grade instructional aide, I led dependent followers. For these students, who were highly motivated, "gifted" children, I found that a group-centered approach was best, because it forced the students to make decisions which affected them. This improved their academics and matured their thinking processes. As a resident adviser, I led counterdependent followers. The beginning of the year was handled democratically but after about six weeks the autocratic method proved more effective. Those students who became dissatisfied changed their followership style, so that they would be treated more democratically; those students who did not change at least accomplished the basic tasks—to establish a community conducive to study and to obey the rules of the school and the laws of Michigan and the U.S., which they were not doing under a democratic style of leadership. Finally, as the vice-president of a fraternity, I found a democratic style to be most effective. This provides for personal development and satisfaction, while still accomplishing the tasks which are outlined. However, becoming too group-centered can be a detriment because of the physical size of the membership, and the nature of the tasks which are accomplished.

FIGURE 4.5   LEADERSHIP AND FOLLOWERSHIP STYLES

Leadership Styles	Followership Styles
Autocratic	Dependent
Democratic	Independent
Laissez-faire	Counterdependent

This is an excellent example of the systems aspect of small group interaction. In each of the situations described above, several factors were acting in combination to influence and determine the most effective leadership style. "If you believe in people's abilities, they will come to believe in them" (Conger, 1989).

An independent follower requires an empowering leader. Research suggests that the practice of *empowering* employees leads to independent followership styles. Empowerment—instilling a sense of power in subordinates—seeks to strengthen an individual's beliefs in his or her sense of effectiveness. Empowering leaders will provide a positive emotional atmosphere for their employees, reward and encourage their employees in personal ways, express confidence in their employees, and foster responsibility and initiative among their employees (Tubbs, 1993a).

In this section we have looked at three styles of followership. We have labeled them the dependent, the counterdependent, and the independent types. On the basis of this discussion, which followership style seems to describe your predominant style? How does your style change in response to different leaders and different situations? Note the trends shown in Figure 4.5.

CONTINGENCY THEORY

Building on the previous theories, two approaches have been offered that are highly consistent with the systems approach taken in this book. Fiedler (1967) has developed a *situational,* or *contingency,* theory of leadership. Hersey and Blanchard (1993) have developed a somewhat different theory. Although these models are both referred to as situational theories, the term "contingency theories" also seems appropriate, because the leader's effectiveness is contingent, or dependent, upon the combination of his or her behaviors and the situation.

Fiedler and Chemers (1974) and Potter and Fiedler (1993) argue that a combination of three separate factors determines a leader's effectiveness: (1) leader-member relations, (2) task structure, and (3) position power. Leader-member relations are roughly equivalent to what we have come to know as a person's interpersonal skills or people orientation. If a leader is people-oriented, the leader-member relations are likely to be good. If, on the other hand, his or her orientation is that people are a necessary evil in getting something done, then the leader-member relations are likely to be poor.

Task structure is the second variable in Fiedler's theory. If a group's task is highly structured and the leader has a manual of procedures to be followed, it would be harder for group members to challenge the leader's approach. On the other hand, if the task is highly ambiguous, such as trying to determine policy by predicting future events, then the group members might have quite a bit of legitimate input that could be as good as or better than the leader's idea alone.

The third variable is position power. This can be either strong or weak. If the leader heading a work group has the power to hire and fire, to promote or not, and to determine raises or punishment, then the leader has strong position power. If, on the other hand, the group is comprised of volunteers working for a church committee or a student organization, the leader has weak position power to get people to do the task. In the model shown in Figure 4.6, we see the results of Fiedler's research. This model clearly shows that these three variables have a strong influence on the leader's effectiveness; in other words, leadership effectiveness is congruent upon these three variables. If we take the example described above in which a leader is working with a group of volunteers for a student organization and the task is fairly unstructured (without clear guidelines on how to proceed), then the person who is not people-oriented will be very ineffective. In fact, the group members will simply not come back to the next meeting. This theory is fascinating in its implications for leadership, because the same leader acting in the same way would likely be very successful in leading a military group where the operations manual supported "going by the book" and where followers who didn't obey would end up in the guardhouse.

Vroom (1993) has studied leadership and participative decision making for over twenty years and he concludes:

FIGURE 4.6   FIEDLER'S CONTINGENCY LEADERSHIP MODEL

From Fiedler and Chemers, *Leadership and Effective Management* (Glenview, Ill.: Scott, Foresman, 1974), p. 80. Copyright 1974 Scott, Foresman & Co. Reprinted by permission of the author.

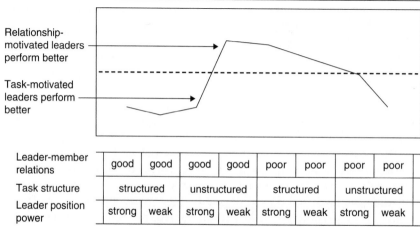

Leader-member relations	good	good	good	good	poor	poor	poor	poor
Task structure	structured		unstructured		structured		unstructured	
Leader position power	strong	weak	strong	weak	strong	weak	strong	weak

We are convinced that the "bedrock" lies in a situational view of participation, i.e., the most appropriate degree of participation must depend on the circumstances surrounding the participative act. . . . It is more meaningful to talk about autocratic or participative situations than autocratic or participative individuals. (pp. 24, 30)

Building on the ideas we presented earlier in the functions theory section, these authors also stress the two leadership functions of (1) task-oriented behavior and (2) people-oriented, or relationship, behavior. To these they add a third important variable, (3) the readiness of the followers. "Readiness level" could be defined in various ways, but Hersey and Blanchard define it in terms of three components. The first is the ability of the group members. If their ability is quite low, the leader has to be more directive than if the group members have high ability. Second, if the followers have high levels of motivation to achieve, they need less direction than followers who are not "self-starters." In fact, one professor gave a motivation test to a group so low in motivation that they would not even fill out the test! They simply didn't care about it.

The third component of follower readiness is the level of education or experience with the particular task. If a follower is totally inexperienced with fixing a malfunctioning car engine, a high level of ability and motivation may not be enough.

For more on determining the readiness level of the followers, see the article by Hersey and Blanchard at the end of this chapter.

As we see in Figure 4.7, when the readiness of followers is lowest (R1), the leadership style most likely to be effective is S1, or *telling*. With an R2 level, the S2 style, *selling*, is best. *Participating* goes best with a higher level of follower readiness, and *delegating* is the recommended leader behavior for the highest level of follower maturity.

Although it is important to develop some flexibility in our approaches to leadership in different situations, it is also important to realize that we all have limitations. As one colleague remarked, "We can't be a chameleon changing drastically for each situation." Hersey and Blanchard recognize that each of us tends to prefer one or two of these leadership patterns (that is, telling, selling, participating, and delegating). In most situations we gravitate toward whichever of these patterns has worked well for us in the past. The difficulty comes when the leadership that is *required* is different from the one we feel comfortable choosing. For example, George Steinbrenner, the owner of the New York Yankees, used a *telling* leadership pattern. However, because he had severely unhappy players and managers, maybe a different pattern (for example, delegating to his manager) would have been more appropriate. Yet it is probably quite hard for Mr. Steinbrenner to move to this other style because of his strong personality. Another factor to keep in mind is that if he had not been the owner of the team and a millionaire, his behavior pattern probably would have been even less tolerated by others in the organization.

FIGURE 4.7   HERSEY AND BLANCHARD'S CONTINGENCY MODEL OF LEADERSHIP

From Hersey and Blanchard, *Management of Organizational Behavior,* 6th ed. (Englewood Cliffs, N.J.: Prentice-Hall, 1993), p. 186.

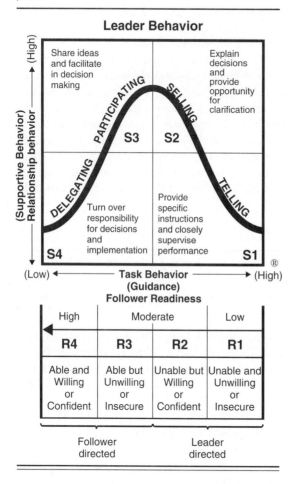

In spite of their limitations, contingency models seem to offer the most promising theories to help guide us in determining the most effective leadership behaviors. They also fit well into the systems approach taken in this book.

GROUP NORMS: SOCIAL INFLUENCE AND CONFORMITY

This entire chapter deals with the process of social influence. In earlier sections we have seen that some people tend more to be the influencers and others the influencees. In this section we will explore some of the results of social influence—namely, conformity pressure.

Like individuals, groups form habits. When people have been together for a time, they develop standardized ways of managing tasks, procedures, and the environment. Wood, Phillips, and Pedersen (1986) define *norms* as "standardized patterns of belief, attitude, communication and behavior within groups. They grow out of member interaction. Then, in systematic fashion, they influence future interaction" (p. 40). Note this example:

> It had to start somewhere. Every third teenager on the street is wearing them—perfectly good blue jeans ripped to shreds.
>
> The most important determinant of a trend, however, is neither merchandisers nor the media. It's the vast, ineffable plasma of intra-teen peer pressure. At some point between the time the media first transmits the image and the time the merchandisers begin to sell it, peer pressure is critical. Ashley Camron, *Teen* magazine editor Roxanne Camron's 13-year-old daughter, is an eighth grader at Colina Intermediate School in Thousand Oaks, Calif. Ashley picked up on ripped jeans about three years ago, cutting holes in some denim shorts after seeing the look on models and actors. But she didn't have the nerve to wear them to school until her friends started wearing them, too: "If you see it on your friends, then you can wear it in public." Now, she says, everyone's wearing them. (Barol, 1990, pp. 40–41)

Every one of us undoubtedly has felt the pressure to conform at one time or another. We notice pressure from the childhood challenges where we are "chicken" if we don't go along with the group, to the high school or college scene where we are labeled "brown-noses" if we appear to be spending more time in the teacher's office than our classmates think is normal.

Although norms can be described in terms of their functional value to the group, this does not imply that members of the group deliberately develop norms with the conscious intention of achieving positive group benefits. According to Thibaut and Kelley (1986):

> The development process underlying the emergence of norms are likely to yield rules that have positive functional values for the relationship. As norms are decided upon, imported from other relationships, and tried out, only the more useful ones are likely to be retained. This is not to say that the norms found in any group will be the best solutions to various problems of control, coordination, and synchronization. (p. 141)

Actually, the term "norms" refers to the written or unwritten laws or codes that identify acceptable behavior. Obviously, norms will vary drastically from one group to another. Ouchi (1981) writes:

> The influence of cultural assumptions is clearly reflected in the contrast between Japanese and American styles of decision making. Typically, the Japanese devote extensive time to defining and analyzing problems, but move with great speed in making final decisions. Americans follow an opposite path in which minimum time is devoted to analysis, while making the final decision consumes substantial time. No wonder international negotiations are often so frustrating for all parties. (p. 28)

The Japanese norms for group productivity have been widely admired and written about in our country. In perhaps the most fascinating spin-off, Japanese companies that have started firms in the United States have brought their norms here. Hatvany and Pucik (1981), in their comprehensive analysis of successful Japanese management policies, write:

> Acknowledging the enormous impact of groups on their members—both directly, through the enforcement of norms, and indirectly, by affecting the beliefs and values of members—Japanese organizations devote far greater attention to structural factors that enhance group motivation and cooperation than to the motivation of individual employees. Tasks are assigned to groups, not to individual employees, and group cohesion is stimulated by delegating responsibility to the group not only for getting the tasks performed, but also for designing the way in which they get performed. (p. 14)

A recent study reported by Mydans (1990) found that poor academic achievement by black students was, in part, because of group norms. He states: "Many black students may perform poorly in high school because of a shared sense that academic success is a sellout to the white world. . . . The study argues that this grows out of the low expectations that white Americans have of blacks, low expectations that have taken root among blacks themselves." The research was conducted in a predominantly black high school in Washington, D.C. Because it was important to the students to maintain a black identity, some black students shunned schoolwork: "They chose to avoid adopting attitudes and putting in enough time and effort in their schoolwork because their peers (and they themselves) would interpret their behavior as 'white'." Other behaviors considered to be acting "white" were, "speaking standard English, . . . going to the opera or ballet, studying in the library, going to the Smithsonian Institution, doing volunteer work, camping or hiking, and being on time" (p. B6). Clearly, group norms serve as a powerful force to inhibit these students' future success.

By now you may have asked yourself, "Why do we even need to have norms?" Actually, norms often serve to reduce ambiguity and to help us feel more at ease. We often feel uncomfortable when we don't know what behaviors are acceptable in a given situation—for example, when moving from elementary school to junior high or middle school, going from junior high to high school, or graduating from high school and going to college. Remember the uneasiness you felt during your first day in each of these new situations. Only after we have learned some of the common practices or norms can we begin to relax and "be ourselves." One student who went to Harvard a few years ago learned that the norm was to buy expensive sweaters and then take scissors to fray the elbows so that the sweaters didn't look like new.

The norms in our society regarding clothing are quite strong. It is interesting to note that even going without clothes involves certain norms. On a nude beach, wearing clothes or even a bathing suit is frowned upon. Jones (1981) writes that at Black's Beach in San Diego, forty to fifty thousand nude bathers gather on a given day. He describes the norms there as follows:

Nude beaches usually are pretty remote. Gawkers aren't interested in walking very far. . . .

If someone is obnoxious, if some guy keeps his clothes on and stares at the women, it's a matter of peer pressure telling him, hey buddy, what's your problem? Why don't you move on now? This isn't a peep show.

Forty years ago, a psychologist named Leon Festinger (1954) hypothesized a theory of social comparison. This theory pointed out the need each of us has to check out our own ideas with those of others. The more ambiguous the situation, the greater is this need. In addition, when we find ourselves at odds with others, we feel pressure to reduce the discrepancies one way or another. The more we are attracted to the group, the more pressure we will feel to change toward the group norms.

On the hunch that this theory might have some relevance in predicting attitude influence on pot smoking, one student (Unger, 1974) conducted a modest study in which he asked, "What has been the most significant source of influence on your views toward pot smoking?" The largest source of influence (43 percent) was peers; the second largest (37 percent) was authoritative written documents; the next (8 percent) was lectures; and the remainder (12 percent) was other sources. These data would seem to confirm Festinger's thesis that we are inclined to look to others to help us determine the guidelines for our own opinions and behaviors. It is also significant to note that, as we saw from the study at Bennington College discussed in Chapter 3, the value changes we undergo in college are likely to last for a lifetime.

Conformity: Research and Applications

In the 1993 movie *The Firm,* Tom Cruise joins a Memphis law firm only to find out that "the firm" doesn't approve of its employees' spouses working, encourages its employees to have children, has never had one of its employees fail the bar exam, and so on. This film depicts the incredible conformity pressure that the new lawyers and their spouses are subjected to. By the way, as you enter into your career, don't be surprised if you find some more subtle but unmistakably similar conformity pressures placed upon you.

One of the earliest conformity studies was conducted by Muzafer Sherif (1936). He showed subjects a pinpoint of light projected onto a wall in a completely darkened room. The light appeared to move even when the subjects knew that it was stationary. This optical illusion is called the *autokinetic effect.* Subjects were tested alone and in groups. Subjects were told to report when the light appeared to move and to judge about how far it moved. When tested individually, subjects estimated the light's range of movement at 3.6 inches. After they had discussed their experiences in groups of two and three, the average range of estimated movement had reduced to 0.4 inches. Clearly, the group discussion provided an influence on each person's judgment of the amount of the light's movement. This resulted in the reduced range of estimates of the light's movement. This clearly fits Kiesler and Kiesler's (1969) definition of conformity as "a change in behavior or belief . . . as a result of real or imagined group pressure" (p. 2).

Solomon Asch (1952) also conducted a classic series of conformity studies. Look at the two cards with vertical lines drawn on them shown in Figure 4.8. Which line on card B is the same length as that on card A? If you had been in Asch's study, you and the other seven subjects would have announced your decisions in order as you were seated in the room. You are the seventh to answer out of eight. For the first two rounds there is unanimous agreement. However, on the third trial, everyone in the group agrees that line 1 is equal in length to line X. You think it is line 2, instead. What do you do? This goes on through eighteen experimental trials. In twelve of the trials you are the only one disagreeing with the others. Actually, the others in the group were Asch's paid stooges, or confederates. The experiment was designed to create pressure on subjects to conform or yield to the others.

In several studies a total of more than 600 people participated as naive subjects. Some of the results are summarized below:

1. Group pressure does, indeed, produce conformity.

2. Yielding can be induced even on attitudes having personal relevance.

3. Yielding is greater on difficult decisions than on easy ones.

4. There are large differences in amounts of yielding for different individuals.

5. When subjects are tested again without the group pressure, a major part of the original yielding disappears.

Some situational factors that were found to be pertinent to the conformity process include group size, perceived competence of group members, group unanimity, extremity of group opinion, and group cohesiveness. The size of the group affects conformity in that group pressure increases to a maximum with four people composing the opposing majority. Numbers larger than four, even up to fifteen, produce only slightly more yielding. Higher perceived group competence produced more conformity pressure. Group unanimity appears to have a highly significant effect on conformity. Asch (1956) found that when at least one other member of the group reinforced the one-member minority, the resistance to group

FIGURE 4.8

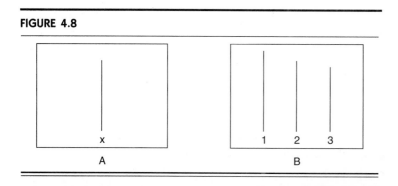

pressure was significantly increased. With regard to extremity of majority opinion, Tuddenham (1961) found that when the majority opinion lies well outside the range of acceptable judgments, yielding occurs among fewer individuals and to a lesser degree. Group cohesiveness caused an increase in conformity, and the second-higher-status group member conformed the most of anyone in the group.

Individual personal factors also have been studied in relation to conformity (see also Chapter 2). Some of the results of the conformity research include the following (Tuddenham, 1961):

1. Conformists are less intelligent.

2. Conformists are lower in ego strength and in their ability to work in stress situations.

3. Conformists tend toward feelings of personal inferiority and inadequacy.

4. Conformists show an intense preoccupation with other people, as opposed to more self-contained, autonomous attitudes of the independent person.

5. Conformists express attitudes and values of a more conventional (conservative) nature than nonyielders.

The pressure to conform is eloquently described by Walker and Heynes (1967) in the following way:

> If one wishes to produce Conformity for good or evil, the formula is clear. Manage to arouse a need or needs that are important to the individual or the group. Offer a goal which is appropriate to the need or needs. Make sure that Conformity is instrumental to the achievement of the goal and that the goal is as large and as certain as possible. Apply the goal or reward at every opportunity. Try to prevent the object of your efforts from obtaining an uncontrolled education. Choose a setting that is ambiguous. Do everything possible to see that the individual has little or no confidence in his own position. Do everything possible to make the norm which you set appear highly valued and attractive. Set it at a level not too far initially from the starting point of the individual or group and move it gradually toward the behavior you wish to produce. Be absolutely certain you know what you want and that you are willing to pay an enormous price in human quality, for whether the individual or the group is aware of it or not, the result will be *Conformity.* (p. 98)

Have you ever noticed what happens to the person who does try to deviate from the group? By definition this person is a *nonconformist.* He or she gets many times more comments directed toward him or her as these variables increase (that is, group cohesion and relevance of topic, as well as acting in a noticeably different way). Think of Suicidal Tendencies and Violent Femmes and others of the "punk rock" genre as examples.

In a quantitative study of the group's reaction to a deviant, Schachter (1951) predicted that the deviant would be talked to the most (frequency of communication) and that the reaction to the deviant would depend upon (1) relevance of the discussion topic, (2) degree of group cohesiveness, and (3) degree to which the person deviated. These predictions are summarized in the chart in Figure 4.9, which is included because the actual data supported virtually all the predictions.

In other words, we are more likely to get hot under the collar when a person deviates from a neighborhood group discussing cross-district busing of our children (high cohesion, high relevance) than when a person deviates from a group of strangers deciding on what color to paint the walls in the school gymnasium (low cohesion, low relevance). Notice that the deviant gets many times more comments directed toward him as these variables increase (that is, group cohesion and relevance of topic, as well as the degree of deviation on the topic). Notice also that in the most extreme case (the solid curved line at the top), the frequency of communication tends to diminish after about two-thirds of the forty-five-minute discussion (thirty minutes). This leads us to believe that a certain amount of rejection or ostracism results if the deviant doesn't come around.

FIGURE 4.9   THEORETICAL CURVES OF COMMUNICATIONS FROM STRONG REJECTORS, MILD REJECTORS, AND FOUR NONREJECTORS TO THE DEVIANT IN THE FOUR EXPERIMENTAL CONDITIONS

From Schacter, 1951, Deviation, rejection, and communication. *Journal of Abnormal and Social Psychology* 46:202. American Psychological Association, © 1951.

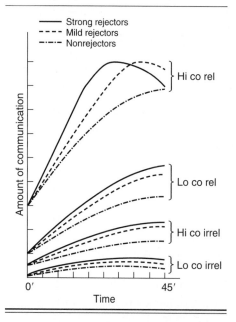

This study represents a quantitative analysis of a group discussion; Leavitt (1964) offers a qualitative analysis of the four stages of conformity pressure. The first stage might be called *reason*. We do not like hearing our ideas disconfirmed, but we are interested in logically convincing the deviant that he or she is wrong. Even at this stage, it is clear we expect the deviant to change to conform to the group and not vice versa. The second stage is *seduction*. During this stage we attempt to appeal to the deviant's social needs. The comments begin to take on the tone of, "Aw, come on, be a sport, we know you don't want to put the whole group on the spot just for the sake of this little issue." It isn't long before the group enters stage three, which is *coercion*. During this stage the group members lose their smiles and good nature. The comments begin to take on the air of threat, something like, "Now look, this has gone far enough. If you won't play ball, then we are going to have to clip your wings but good the next time you want help from us." The fourth and final stage is *isolation*. At this point the group gives up on and ignores the deviant. This tactic may finally bring conformity if the ostracism is prolonged.

Leavitt (1964) summarizes the four stages as follows: "It's as though the members of the group were saying, 'Let's reason with him; if that doesn't work, let's try to tease him by emotional seduction; and if even that doesn't work, let's beat him over the head until he has to give up. Failing that, then we'll excommunicate him; we'll amputate him from the group; we'll disown him'" (pp. 273–274). One student wrote of her experience with this conformity influence:

> As a high school band member I experienced all four of these stages when we were to march in the Apple Blossom Parade.
>
> The band master told everyone to wear saddle shoes. When I explained to him that I had none, he said, "Get some, since everybody needs to be dressed the same" (step 1). I told him I had no money. "Then borrow some," another band member suggested. "Come on, we need you" (step 2). I told them I couldn't borrow any because of an unusual foot size. "Then if you don't get them, you can't march in the parade," said someone else (step 3).
>
> I didn't; I hid when the band came down the street. I never returned to the band again. I felt alone, isolated, and ostracized (step 4), and that ended my musical career. Although it was over twenty years ago, it still hurts when I think about it.

On a more personal level, Williams (1989) reports that in spite of all the publicity regarding the dangers of contracting AIDS from unsafe sex, many young people today continue to engage in risky behaviors. She writes, "Even teen-agers who are not sexually active tend to see the matter as a personal choice, . . . and it seems clear that pressure from peers . . . has more impact on teen-agers generally." On the basis of over 900 surveys and interviews nationwide, she reports: "Teen-agers say that social pressure is the chief reason why so many do not wait to have sexual intercourse until they are older. Both boys and girls say they are pressured by other teen-agers to go further than they wanted to" (p. A1).

Janis (1982) has conducted a thorough investigation of the problems that conformity pressure brought to some major American historical events. He refers to the results as *groupthink*, which he defines as "a quick and easy way to refer to a mode of thinking that people engage in when they are deeply involved in a cohesive in-group, when the members' strivings for unanimity override their motivation to realistically appraise alternative courses of action" (p. 9). Janis cites several major political decisions that were characterized by groupthink, including the escalation of the Vietnam war and the 1961 American invasion of Cuba (the Bay of Pigs). Although not included in his book, Watergate was another example that fits his definition. (The 1987 Iran-Contra arms scandal may also be another example.) Further studies (Whyte, 1989) have cited the Watergate scandal, the decision to launch the space shuttle *Challenger,* and the Iran-Contra arms scandal as disastrous examples of the groupthink phenomenon.

Groupthink tends to occur when several factors are operating at once. These are called the symptoms of groupthink, and they can occur in any group. The eight symptoms are summarized below:

Type I: Overestimations of the group—its power and morality

1. An illusion of invulnerability, shared by most or all of the members, which creates excessive optimism and encourages taking extreme risks.

2. An unquestioned belief in the group's inherent morality, inclining the members to ignore the ethical or moral consequences of their decisions.

Type II: Closed-mindedness

3. Collective efforts to rationalize in order to discount warnings or other information that might lead the members to reconsider their assumptions before they recommit themselves to their past policy decisions.

4. Stereotyped views of enemy leaders as too evil to warrant genuine attempts to negotiate, or as too weak and stupid to counter whatever risky attempts are made to defeat their purposes.

Type III: Pressures toward uniformity

5. Self-censorship of deviations from the apparent group consensus, reflecting each member's inclination to minimize to himself the importance of his doubts and counterarguments.

6. A shared illusion of unanimity concerning judgments conforming to the majority view (partly resulting from self-censorship of deviations, augmented by the false assumption that silence means consent).

7. Direct pressure on any member who expresses strong arguments against any of the group's stereotypes, illusions, or commitments, making clear that this type of dissent is contrary to what is expected of all loyal members.

8. The emergence of self-appointed mindguards—members who protect the group from adverse information that might shatter their shared complacency about the effectiveness and morality of their decisions. (Janis, 1982, pp. 174–175)

For a detailed example of groupthink, see the article by Moorhead, Ference, and Neck at the end of this chapter.

Certain groups are particularly vulnerable to groupthink. Those with members who are high in need for affiliation (see Chapter 2), those that are very cohesive (see Chapter 7), or those that have an autocratic leadership style (see this chapter) are likely candidates. However, there are procedures that can be employed to minimize the possibilities of groupthink (Janis, 1982, pp. 260–276). Some of these precautions are:

- Assign one member to be the "devil's advocate" or critical evaluator to allow disagreements and criticism of the leader.

- Leaders should not reveal their preferences to the group at the beginning of the discussion.

- Several groups with different leaders can work independently on common problems to offer different perspectives.

- Group members should discuss the group's processes with trusted friends and report their reactions to the group.

- Outside experts should be called in periodically as resource persons. They should be encouraged to disagree with the group's assumptions.

- Whenever issues involve relations with rival groups (e.g., labor and management), time should be spent discussing all warning signals from the rivals and hypothesizing alternative "scenarios of the rivals' intentions."

- After preliminary decisions have been reached, the group should adjourn and hold a "second chance" meeting at a later date to let their ideas "incubate."

Although these suggestions may not always be applicable (even if they are, they may not always work), they do offer a constructive alternative to reduce the dangers of groupthink.

In a more recent study, Whyte (1989) argued that the term "groupthink" is an incomplete explanation for such disastrous occurrences (decision fiascoes). Whyte's contention is that the way choices are "framed in a domain of losses" has more to do with risky "groupthink" decisions than actual group dynamics.

Whyte gave consideration to the events surrounding the space shuttle *Challenger* disaster to describe this phenomenon:

> This situation was the product of flawed decisions as much as it was a failure of technology. The pressures on the National Aeronautics and Space Administration (NASA) to launch a space shuttle at the earliest opportunity were intense, despite evidence that this course of action was inadvisable. A decision to delay the launch was undesirable from NASA's perspective because of the impact it would have on political

and public support for the program. In contrast, a successful launch would have appeased the public and politicians alike, and would have amounted to another major achievement. NASA engineers claimed that pressure to launch was so intense that authorities routinely dismissed potentially lethal hazards as acceptable risks.

A choice in the domain of losses was involved on either side of this decision. Had the launch of the *Challenger* been delayed any further, the space shuttle program would have undoubtedly suffered consequences. As it stands, the decision to launch the shuttle amounted in even dearer losses. Considerations in the Whyte study show that the phenomenon of groupthink is not a simple one.

Turner and her colleagues (1992) conducted an ingenious set of experiments with college students in which they found that groupthink did in fact occur. However, the level of groupthink varied along with two other factors. One was the level of cohesiveness (closeness) of the group members. The other factor was the level of outside threat the group experienced. In the high-threat condition, the groups were told that they were being videotaped and that the tapes would be shown in future classes to demonstrate poor group dynamics. The low-threat conditions had no videotaping.

GROUP DEVELOPMENT

A number of writers have been interested in the social influence process as it is manifested in different stages or phases of group development. Group development seems to be partly the result of individual psychological needs and partly the result of the social influences manifested in the group. The various theories on group phases are somewhat incompatible, in that some writers identify three phases and others identify four. Also, some writers identify the phases that occur during the course of one group discussion (Tuckman, 1965; Fisher, 1980), whereas others identify the phases that occur over the course of the life of a group, including several meetings (Bennis and Shepard, 1956; Thelen and Dickerman, 1949). Still another viewpoint is that the phases occur in each meeting and continue to occur throughout the group's life history (Schutz, 1958; Bales and Strodbeck, 1951). This last viewpoint seems the most profound in providing insight into the phenomenon of group development.

With these differing frames of reference in mind, let us look at the four group phases that seem representative of the literature. *Phase 1* (orientation) seems to be a period in which group members simply try to break the ice and begin to find out enough about one another to have some common basis for functioning. It is variously referred to as a period of orientation, inclusion, or group formation. In this phase people ask questions about one another, tell where they are from, reveal what they like and dislike, and generally make small talk. An excerpt from a student paper reveals this:

> Even though we had a task to accomplish for the class, we began by talking about ourselves (one guy and girl found they both liked moto-cross racing, and two others found that they had both been to Daytona Beach last spring break). After we had a chance to "break the ice" we were more willing to throw out ideas on how to go ahead with the group project without being afraid of having our ideas shot down in flames.

Phase 1 seems to be characterized by the establishing of some minimal social relationship before group members feel comfortable getting down to work. However, some executives who have experienced many years of decision-making meetings may begin work with little or no social orientation and only the barest minimum of group orientation. With these exceptions, the vast majority of us feel better having some period to build relationships prior to launching into the group's work.

Phase 2 (conflict) is frequently characterized by conflict of some kind or another. After the orientation phase passes, the pressure to accomplish something sooner or later intensifies whatever differences may exist. One student's description illustrates the transition from Phase 1 to Phase 2:

> We talked about personal interests until some common ground was established, then we found we could talk about the assignment more freely. But after talking about nonsubject things, it was hard to keep the line of talk on the problems at hand. Some wanted to get the assignment accomplished while two guys in the group continually swayed the conversation to things that were easier to talk about, but had nothing to do with the subject (Howard has a big thing for John Deere farm machinery). At first we were constantly trying not to hurt anyone's feelings, so we let the conversation drift. We didn't question or reject each other's ideas, and I feel we often settled for less than we should have. The longer we were in the group together, the more we got to know each other and the more times we voiced our real opinions. That's when the tempers started to flare!

Typically, in Phase 2 the group begins to thrash out decisions for procedures as well as for determining the solution to the group task. Conflict over procedures may be one way in which group members fight for influence or control in the group.

After a period of small talk in one middle-aged encounter group, one member suggested that they go around the group and introduce themselves in some detail, telling what their jobs were, what part of the country they were from, and so on. Just as they were about to begin, another member suggested that they *not* tell these things, to avoid the stereotyping that would inevitably result. A heated argument resulted. Eventually they decided to assume their fantasized identities—that is, they adopted nicknames and behaviors and job titles that represented the type of person they wished they could be. Much later in the course of the group they decided that the new procedure had been much better in helping them to try out behaviors they normally would have been too inhibited to attempt. For example, one female psychiatrist assumed the identity of "Bubbles," a cocktail waitress, because she had always wondered what it would be like to be a sex object and get outside her role as a professional person. The conflict regarding procedures turned out to be very productive for the group in the long run.

Phase 3 (emergence) involves a resolution of the conflict experienced in Phase 2. Group cohesiveness begins to emerge, and the group settles into working more comfortably as a unit. This phase is described by three different sources in the following ways:

> Perhaps the major pitfall to be avoided at this point is that of glossing over significant differences for the sake of harmony. . . . Behavior is essentially a kind of polite behavior which avoids upsetting the group. (Thelen and Dickerman, 1949)

> Resistance is overcome in the third stage in which ingroup feeling and cohesiveness develop, new standards evolve, and new roles are adopted. In the task realm, intimate, personal opinions are expressed. (Tuckman, 1965)

> Social conflict and dissent dissipate during the third phase. Members express fewer unfavorable opinions toward decision proposals. The coalition of individuals who had opposed those proposals which eventually achieve consensus also weakens in the third phase. (Fisher, 1974)

Phase 4 (reinforcement) is the phase of maximum productivity and consensus. Dissent has just about disappeared, and the rule of the moment is to pat each other on the back for having done such a good job. Group members joke and laugh and generally reinforce one another for having contributed to the group's success. Student reactions to a group project in this phase include the following typical comments: "At first I thought this assignment would be a waste of time, but now I think it was the most worthwhile thing we have done in the course so far." "Everybody I have talked to feels like the group exercise was really good. We are looking forward to doing more of these."

Psychologically, we all need to feel that what we do is somehow justified or worthwhile (this is referred to in Chapter 3 as rationalizing or reducing cognitive dissonance). Thus, even if we have had bad experiences with a group, we tend to repress those and remember the good things we have experienced. The various group development theories are summarized in the chart in Figure 4.10 and in the following quotation from the earliest of the group development theorists:

> Beginning with individual needs for finding security and activity in a social environment, we proceed first to emotional involvement of the individuals with each other, and second to the development of a group as a rather limited universe of interaction among individuals and as the source of individual security. We then find that security of position in the group loses its significance except that as the group attempts to solve problems it structures its activities in such a way that each individual can play a role which may be described as successful or not in terms of whether the group successfully solved the problem it had set itself. (Thelen and Dickerman, 1949, p. 316)

FIGURE 4.10   SUMMARY OF LITERATURE ON GROUP PHASES

	Phase 1	Phase 2	Phase 3	Phase 4
Thelen and Dickerman (1949)	Forming	Conflict	Harmony	Productivity
Bennis and Shepard (1956, 1961)	Dependence	Interdependence	Focused work	Productivity
Tuckman (1965)	Forming	Storming	Norming	Performing
Fisher (1980)	Orientation	Conflict	Emergence	Reinforcement
Bales and Strodbeck (1951)	Orientation		Evaluation	Control
Schutz (1958)	Inclusion		Control	Affection

Deadlines and time constraints sometimes offer more initiative than actual accomplishments. In a comprehensive study on models of group development, Gersick (1988) established that a group's progress is triggered more by the group members' awareness of time and deadlines than by completion of an absolute amount of work in a specific developmental stage.

THE SYSTEMS PERSPECTIVE

In this chapter we examined the complicated and fascinating questions of who influences whom and why. In the discussion of status and power we saw that the two go hand in hand; that is, high-status individuals tend to have more power. An obvious extension of this is the notion that because of differing group norms, different characteristics bring about status in different groups. On a football team, the best athlete has the most status. Among college professors, the smartest person usually has the most status. In street gangs, the toughest member typically has the highest status. And so it goes from one group to another.

A major portion of this chapter dealt with the issues of leadership and followership. Although these two are not always discussed together, they are interrelated. Here the systems principle of *equifinality* applies. In other words, the leadership style that would be appropriate in one situation with one set of followers may not be the most appropriate in a different situation with a different set of followers. A great deal of study has led to the belief that the democratic leadership style is the most likely to get the best results in a great many cases. However, our systems perspective reminds us that some situations point to the authoritarian style as the most appropriate. In situations involving life-or-death decisions or in times of crisis requiring rapid decisions, the democratic approach may be too slow or simply impractical. As we saw earlier, two popular theoretical syntheses regarding leadership styles are offered by Fiedler (1967, 1974, 1993) and Hersey and Blanchard (1993). They each suggest a contingency theory of leadership. In other words, the best leadership style is one flexible enough to adapt to the situation. If asked which leadership style is best, they would answer, "It depends."

This chapter also dealt with the topics of social influence and conformity. Systems theory concepts are beautifully illustrated in the literature. Conformity pressure differs depending on the type of group (for example, military versus the commune), the style of leadership (say, authoritarian versus democratic), the personalities of the group members (dominant versus acquiescent), and a number of other factors. We know from the research literature that conformity is more likely (1) in a group in which membership is highly valued by its participants; (2) among members with dependent, obedient, and acquiescent personalities; (3) when the leader is more authoritarian; (4) when the group is unanimously against the deviant member; and (5) to produce public compliance than actual private acceptance. Conformity is clearly dependent on an entire constellation of other variables.

One study analyzed conformity in a systems way (although the authors did not identify their analysis as a systems analysis). Rarick, Soldow, and Geizer (1976) looked at conformity as a result of the combination of the person's personality and the situation in which he or she is placed. The personality variable was self-confidence (they call it self-monitoring), and the situational variable was group size (dyad or three- to six-person group). They found that less confident people conform more in three- to six-person groups than highly confident people. This confirms numerous previous findings. However, they also found that in a dyad, confident people did not conform any more or less than those lacking in confidence. This study very nicely illustrates the systems perspective that all these variables (and others) simultaneously influence one another.

The last section of this chapter dealt with group development. We know that groups go through some fairly common phases, depending on the type of group. As we saw earlier, some writers assume that all the phases occur during the course of one group discussion. Other writers believe that these phases evolve slowly over the group's lifetime. However, the systems theory approach suggests that these phases are simply parts of a recurring *cycle* of events that probably occur during a single meeting and tend to be repeated throughout the group's lifetime as well. This point of view seems to be the most theoretically valid and is supported by other authors who apply the systems approach to the analysis of small group interaction (see, for example, Ellis and Fisher, 1994).

EXERCISES

1. Case Studies Discussion

Break into small groups, and discuss the following case studies. Attempt to reach agreement on each case. Have each group report its decision to the class and the reasons for the choice.

Case A: "Dr. Death" * Dr. Jack Kevorkian (also known as "Dr. Death") has assisted in over a dozen suicides. He is in violation of a Michigan state law prohibiting doctors from assisting in suicides. Thirty four other states have such a law.

All the patients Dr. Kevorkian assisted had requested his help. He videotaped the procedure as evidence that he has done nothing wrong.

On the other hand, physicians around the country argue that his behavior is morally wrong and that it violates the Hippocratic oath, in which doctors pledge to help their patients. Opponents also fear that families could abuse this practice. University of Michigan law professor Yale Kasimar argues: "In a climate in which suicide would often be the 'rational' thing to do, or at least

---

*Based on David Zeman, "A Question of Control," *The Detroit Free Press,* January 2, 1994, pp. 1F, 4F.

a 'reasonable' option, there is a real possibility that it would become the un-reasonable thing *not* to do."

Case B: Jacobs Furniture, Inc.   You are Bev Stone, manager of the Accounting Department of Jacobs Furniture. The entire company has about 1700 employees, 15 of whom are in your department. You have just returned from a meeting held by the general manager, Bill Keppler. In this meeting, Bill explained to all the department heads that there was an important task for them to accomplish. The local United Way drive is currently under way. Each year every organization in the city is asked to do what it can to donate money to the United Way, which supports many worthwhile, nonprofit agencies in the community.

Bill explained that last week the brochures and pledge cards had been sent to everyone in the company and that, to date, only 5 percent had responded. Then, Rick Adams, an engineer on loan to the United Way from a local computer company, gave a short presentation telling of the many worthwhile services the United Way provides. Bill Keppler then said that he wanted each department head to go back to his or her employees and see what could be done to raise the participation rate in each department.

You have mixed feelings about this assignment. On one hand, there is no doubt that the United Way is a deserving organization. On the other hand, because business has been very poor for the past few years, employees have had no raises during that period. Morale is quite low, mostly because of economic pressures. There has been much complaining already about the increases in taxes resulting in less and less take-home pay. Also, with the cost of living on the increase, even the *same* amount of money wouldn't buy as much as it would have five years ago. In this context, you feel awkward about asking people in your work group to donate more of their pay to charitable causes.

Your boss has made it clear that he supports this charity to a very strong degree. Therefore, you must do something. Decide what specific steps you will take in carrying out this task.

2. Interaction Analysis Exercise

Observe a group discussion (perhaps one of the two case discussions from above) and try to use the Bales Interaction Process Analysis scoring sheet (Figure 4.11) to make your observations more systematic. Start by observing and recording only one person in the group. Simply place a check mark in the appropriate row when a person says something in the group. As you gain more experience, record two or three group members. You may also want to try having several people observe the same person to check the reliability of your observations.

FIGURE 4.11   BALES INTERACTION PROCESS ANALYSIS SCORING SHEET

Scoring of Interaction (Bales)	Person 1	Person 2	Person 3	Row Totals
1. *Seems friendly,* raises other's status, gives help, reward				
2. *Dramatizes,* jokes, laughs, shows satisfaction				
3. *Agrees,* shows passive acceptance, understands, concurs, complies				
4. *Gives suggestions,* direction, implying autonomy for other				
5. *Gives opinion,* evaluation, analysis, expresses feeling, wish				
6. *Gives information,* repeats, clarifies, confirms				
7. *Asks for information,* repetition, confirmation				
8. *Asks for opinion,* evaluation, analysis, expresses feeling				
9. *Asks for suggestion,* direction, possible ways of action				
10. *Disagrees,* shows passive rejection, formality, withholds help				
11. *Shows tension,* asks for help, withdraws "out of field"				
12. *Seems unfriendly,* deflates other's status, defends or asserts self				
Column totals				

3. Group Development Exercise

Observe a real-life problem-solving group. Listen carefully for statements that indicate the four phases of group development. You might take notes to record exact statements that illustrate the four phases. Notice also if the group does *not* seem to go through these four phases. Compare your observations with those of others who have observed different groups. Do most of the observations correspond to the research findings?

In the first article, Hersey and Blanchard offer further elaboration on how to identify the maturity of group members, which influences the choice of an appropriate leadership style.

The second article, by Moorhead, Ference, and Neck, describes the group decision difficulties that led to the *Challenger* disaster.

Application of Situational Leadership

Paul Hersey and Kenneth H. Blanchard

In using Situational Leadership, it is useful to keep in mind that there is no "one best way" to influence others. Rather, any leader behavior may be more or less effective depending on the readiness level of the person you are attempting to influence. Shown in Figure 1 is a more comprehensive version of the Situational Leadership Model that brings together our discussion of the past several pages. It will provide you with a quick reference to assist in (1) diagnosing the level of readiness; (2) adapting by selecting high probability leadership styles; and (3) communicating these styles effectively to influence behavior. Implicit in Situational Leadership is the idea that a leader should help followers grow in readiness as far as they are able and willing to go. This development of followers should be done by adjusting leadership behavior through the four styles along the leadership curve in Figure 1.

Situational Leadership contends that strong direction (task behavior) with followers with low readiness is appropriate if they are to become productive. Similarly, it suggests that an increase in readiness on the part of people who are somewhat unready should be rewarded by increased positive reinforcement and socioemotional support (relationship behavior). Finally, as followers reach high levels of readiness, the leader should respond not only by continuing to decrease control over their activities, but also by continuing to decrease relationship behavior as well. With people with high readiness, the need for socioemo-

From Paul Hersey and Kenneth H. Blanchard, Management of Organizational Behavior, *6th ed. (Englewood Cliffs, N.J.: Prentice-Hall, 1993).*

FIGURE 1   EXPANDED SITUATIONAL LEADERSHIP MODEL

Paul Hersey, *Situational Selling* (Escondido, Calif.: Center for Leadership Studies, 1985), p. 32.

Task Behavior–
The extent to which the leader engages in defining roles, i.e., telling what, how, when, where, and if more than one person, who is to do what in:

- Goal-setting
- Organizing
- Establishing time lines
- Directing
- Controlling

Relationship Behavior–
The extent to which a leader engages in two-way (multi-way) communication, listening, facilitating behaviors, socioemotional support:

- Giving support
- Communicating
- Facilitating interactions
- Active listening
- Providing feedback

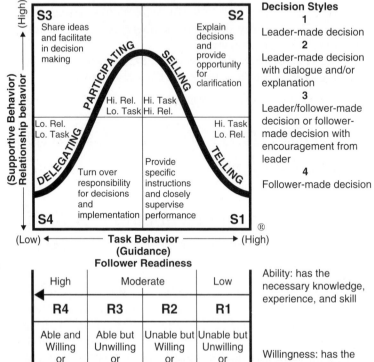

Decision Styles

1
Leader-made decision

2
Leader-made decision with dialogue and/or explanation

3
Leader/follower-made decision or follower-made decision with encouragement from leader

4
Follower-made decision

Ability: has the necessary knowledge, experience, and skill

Willingness: has the necessary confidence, commitment, motivation

When a Leader Behavior is used apppropriately with its coresponding level of readiness, it is termed a High Probability Match. The following are descriptors that can be useful when using Situational Leadership for specific applications:

S1	S2	S3	S4
Telling	Selling	Participating	Delegating
Guiding	Explaining	Encouraging	Observing
Directing	Clarifying	Collaborating	Monitoring
Establishing	Persuading	Committing	Fulfilling

tional support is no longer as important as the need for greater freedom. At this stage, one of the ways leaders can prove their confidence and trust in these people is to leave them more and more on their own. It is not that there is less mutual trust and friendship between leader and follower—in fact, there is more—but it takes less supportive behavior on the leader's part to prove this to them.

Groupthink Symptoms

Janis identified eight symptoms of groupthink. They are presented here along with evidence from the *Report of the Presidential Commission on the Space Shuttle Accident* (1986).

Invulnerability   When groupthink occurs, most or all of the members of the decision-making group have an illusion of invulnerability that reassures them in the face of obvious dangers. This illusion leads the group to become overly optimistic and willing to take extraordinary risks. It may also cause them to ignore clear warnings of danger.

The solid rocket joint problem that destroyed *Challenger* was discussed often at flight readiness review meetings prior to flight. However, Commission member Richard Feynman concluded from the testimony that a mentality of overconfidence existed due to the extraordinary record of success of space flights. Every time we send one up it is successful. Involved members may seem to think that on the next one we can lower our standards or take more risks because it always works.

The invulnerability illusion may have built up over time as a result of NASA's own spectacular history. NASA had not lost an astronaut since 1967 when a flash fire in the capsule of *Apollo 1* killed three. Since that time NASA had a string of 55 successful missions. They had put a man on the moon, built and launched Skylab and the shuttle, and retrieved defective satellites from orbit. In the minds of most Americans and apparently their own, they could do no wrong.

Rationalization   Victims of groupthink collectively construct rationalizations that discount warnings and other forms of negative feedback. If these signals were taken seriously when presented, the group members would be forced to reconsider their assumptions each time they re-commit themselves to their past decisions.

In the Level I flight readiness meeting when the *Challenger* was given final launch approval, MTI engineers presented evidence that the joint would fail. Their argument was based on the fact that in the coldest previous launch (air temperature 30 degrees) the joint in question experienced serious erosion and that no data existed as to how the joint would perform at colder temperatures. Flight center officials put forth numerous technical rationalizations faulting MTI's analysis. One of these rationalizations was that the engineer's data were inconclusive. As Mr. Boisjoly emphasized to the Commission:

> . . . I was asked, yes, at that point in time I was asked to quantify my concerns, and I said I couldn't. I couldn't quantify it. I had no data to quantify it, but I did say I knew that it was away from goodness in the current data base.

> Someone on the net commented that we had soot blow-by on SRM-22 [Flight 61-A, October, 1985] which was launched at 75 degrees. I don't remember who made the comment, but that is where the first comment came in about the disparity between my conclusion and the observed data because SRM-22 [Flight 61-A, October 1985] had blow-by at essentially a room temperature launch. I then said that SRM-15 [Flight 51-C, January, 1985] had much more blow-by indication and that it was indeed telling us that lower temperature was a factor. I was asked again for data to support my claim, and I said I have none other than what is being presented (*Report of the Presidential Commission on the Space Shuttle Accident*, 1986, p. 89).

Discussions became twisted (compared to previous meetings) and no one detected it. Under normal conditions, MTI would have to prove the shuttle boosters readiness for launch, instead they found themselves being forced to prove that the boosters were unsafe. Boisjoly's testimony supports this description of the discussion:

> . . . This was a meeting where the determination was to launch, and it was up to us to prove beyond a shadow of a doubt that it was not safe to do so. This is in total reverse to what the position usually is in a preflight conversation or a flight readiness review. It is usually exactly opposite of that. . . . (*Report of the Presidential Commission on the Space Shuttle Accident*, 1986, p. 93).

Morality   Group members often believe, without question, in the inherent morality of their position. They tend to ignore the ethical or moral consequences of their decision.

In the *Challenger* case, this point was raised by a very high level MTI manager, Allan J. McDonald, who tried to stop the launch and said that he would not want to have to defend the decision to launch. He stated to the Commission:

> . . . I made the statement that if we're wrong and something goes wrong on this flight, I wouldn't want to have to be the person to stand up in front of board in inquiry and say that I went ahead and told them to go ahead and fly this thing outside what the motor was qualified to. . . . (*Report of the Presidential Commission on the Space Shuttle Accident*, 1986, p. 95).

Some members did not hear this statement because it occurred during a break. Three top officials who did hear it ignored it.

Stereotyped Views of Others   Victims of groupthink often have a stereotyped view of the opposition of anyone with a competing opinion. They feel that the opposition is too stupid or too weak to understand or deal effectively with the problem.

Two of the top three NASA officials responsible for the launch displayed this attitude. They felt that they completely understood the nature of the joint problem and never seriously considered the objections raised by the MTI engineers. In fact they denigrated and badgered the opposition and their information and opinions.

Pressure on Dissent   Group members often apply direct pressure to anyone who questions the validity of the arguments supporting a decision or position favored by the majority. These same two officials pressured MTI to change its position after MTI originally recommended that the launch not take place. These two officials pressured MTI personnel to prove that it was not safe to launch, rather than to prove the opposite. As mentioned earlier, this was a total reversal of normal preflight procedures. It was this pressure that top MTI management was responding to when they overruled their engineering staff and recommended launch. As the Commission report states:

> . . . At approximately 11 p.m. Eastern Standard Time, the Thiokol/NASA teleconference resumed, the Thiokol management stating that they had reassessed the problem, that the temperature effects were a concern, but that the data was admittedly inconclusive. . . . (p. 96).

This seems to indicate that NASA's pressure on these Thiokol officials forced them to change their recommendation from delay to execution of the launch.

Self-Censorship   Group members tend to censor themselves when they have opinions or ideas that deviate from the apparent group consensus. Janis feels that this reflects each member's inclination to minimize to himself or herself the importance of his or her own doubts and counterarguments.

The most obvious evidence of self-censorship occurred when a vice president of MTI, who had previously presented information against launch, bowed to pressure from NASA and accepted their rationalizations for launch. He then wrote these up and presented them to NASA as the reasons that MTI had changed its recommendation to launch.

Illusion of Unanimity   Group members falling victim to groupthink share an illusion of unanimity concerning judgments made by members speaking in favor of the majority view. This symptom is caused in part by the preceding one and is aided by the false assumption that any participant who remains silent is in agreement with the majority opinion. The group leader and other members support each other by playing up points of convergence in their thinking at the expense of fully exploring points of divergence that might reveal unsettling problems.

No participant from NASA ever openly agreed with or even took sides with MTI in the discussion. The silence from NASA was probably amplified by the fact that the meeting was a teleconference linking the participants at three different locations. Obviously, body language which might have been evidenced by dissenters was not visible to others who might also have held a dissenting opinion. Thus, silence meant agreement.

Mindguarding   Certain group members assume the role of guarding the minds of others in the group. They attempt to shield the group from adverse information that might destroy the majority view of the facts regarding the appropriateness of the decision.

The top management at Marshall knew that the rocket casings had been ordered redesigned to correct a flaw 5 months previous to this launch. This information and other technical details concerning the history of the joint problem was withheld at the meeting.

Decision-Making Defects

The result of the antecedent conditions and the symptoms of groupthink is a defective decision-making process. Janis discusses several defects in decision making that can result.

Few alternatives: The group considers only a few alternatives, often only two. No initial survey of all possible alternatives occurs. The Flight Readiness Review team had a launch/no-launch decision to make. These were the only two alternatives considered. Other possible alternatives might have been to delay the launch for further testing, or to delay until the temperatures reached an appropriate level.

No re-examination of alternatives: The group fails to re-examine alternatives that may have been initially discarded based on early unfavorable information. Top NASA officials spent time and effort defending and strengthening their position, rather than examining the MTI position.

Rejecting expert opinions: Members make little or no attempt to seek outside experts opinions. NASA did not seek out other experts who might have some expertise in this area. They assumed that they had all the information.

Rejecting negative information: Members tend to focus on supportive information and ignore any data or information that might cast a negative light on their preferred alternative. MTI representatives repeatedly tried to point out errors in the rationale the NASA officials were using to justify the launch. Even after the decision was made, the argument continued until a NASA official told the MTI representative that it was no longer his concern.

No contingency plans: Members spend little time discussing the possible consequences of the decision and, therefore, fail to develop contingency plans. There is no documented evidence in the Rogers Commission Report of any discussion of the possible consequences of an incorrect decision.

Summary of the Evidence

The major categories and key elements of the groupthink hypothesis have been presented (albeit somewhat briefly) along with evidence from the discussions prior to the launching of the *Challenger,* as reported in the President's Commission to investigate the accident. The antecedent conditions were present in the decision-making group, even though the group was in several physical locations. The leaders had a preferred solution and engaged in behaviors designed to promote it rather than critically appraise alternatives. These behaviors were evidence of most of the symptoms leading to a defective decision-making process.

Communication
Processes

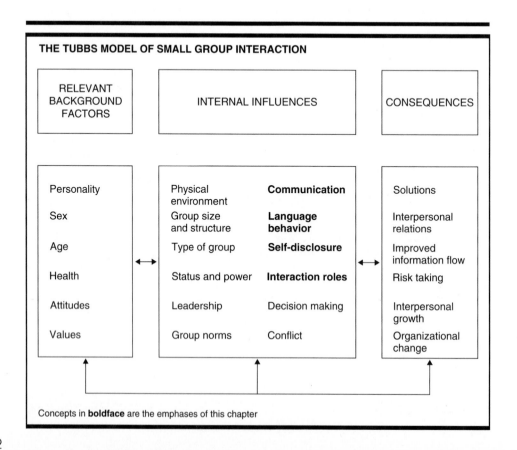

THE TUBBS MODEL OF SMALL GROUP INTERACTION

RELEVANT BACKGROUND FACTORS	INTERNAL INFLUENCES		CONSEQUENCES

RELEVANT BACKGROUND FACTORS	INTERNAL INFLUENCES		CONSEQUENCES
Personality	Physical environment	**Communication**	Solutions
Sex	Group size and structure	**Language behavior**	Interpersonal relations
Age	Type of group	**Self-disclosure**	Improved information flow
Health	Status and power	**Interaction roles**	Risk taking
Attitudes	Leadership	Decision making	Interpersonal growth
Values	Group norms	Conflict	Organizational change

Concepts in **boldface** are the emphases of this chapter

PREVIEW

Chapter 5 continues with four more internal influences. Because communication is one of the most important aspects of group interaction, it is discussed thoroughly. It is first defined and then outlined into several different types. The topic of language behavior is presented, along with four specific problems that groups often confront. These are bypassing, inference making, polarizing, and signal reactions. In a group, one must also decide how much to share or contribute; therefore, self-disclosure is one of the four internal influences found in this chapter. Interaction roles is the last of the internal influences. One often establishes several roles in day-to-day living. Some examples of these are group task, group-building, and group maintenance roles.

GLOSSARY

Intentional-Unintentional Communication: Intentional communication occurs when we communicate what we mean to. Unintentional communication occurs when we communicate something different from what we intend, as when we accidentally offend someone.

Verbal-Nonverbal Communication: Verbal communication is the use of words to get across a message. Nonverbal communication is the use of physical actions, such as facial expression or tone of voice.

Defensive-Supportive Communication: Defensive communication occurs when a psychological barrier is created, known as a *defense mechanism*. This barrier acts to reduce effective communication. Supportive communication minimizes these types of problems.

Content and Process: Content of a group discussion includes comments about the *topic* of the discussion. Process is the *manner* in which the discussion is conducted.

Bypassing: Bypassing is a misunderstanding that occurs when "the sender and receiver miss each other with their meaning."

Inference Making: Inference making refers to going beyond observations and what we know. Inferences represent only some degree of probability of coming true.

Polarizing: Polarizing is the exaggeration that occurs when people attempt to make a point.

Signal Reactions: Signal reactions are learned responses to certain stimuli, such as emotional reactions to really offensive swear words or racial slurs.

Appropriateness: Appropriateness includes several factors that help determine the timing and extent of self-disclosure.

Group Task Roles: Group task roles are identifiable behaviors that are directed toward accomplishing the group's objective.

Group-Building and Maintenance Roles: Group-building and maintenance roles help the interpersonal functioning of the group and alter the way of working by strengthening, regulating, and perpetuating the group.

Individual Roles: Individual roles are roles that are designed to satisfy an *individual's* needs rather than to contribute to the needs of the group.

CASE STUDY: The Faculty Committee

A committee of university faculty members was deciding whom to have vote on an important new policy statement. It had worked for several months to develop and refine this policy statement, and it wanted to send a copy to all people in the university who would be affected by this policy. The committee had not anticipated any difficulty deciding whom to send the memo to. Then this problem occurred:

Prof. Brown: Now that we all have agreed on the final policy to be communicated, let's decide which method should be used to convey the policy.

Prof. Smith: Let's use an interorganization memo. (The group all agreed.) Let's send a ballot to each person through the faculty mail. (Again, general agreement.)

Prof. Brown: OK, the subject of the memo is adoption of the new faculty senate operating procedures, right? (General agreement.) All right, let's address this to all members of the faculty.

Prof. Jones: Whom are you including in the faculty?

Prof. Brown: That's obvious.

Prof. Jones: No, I don't think so. Are department chairmen included as faculty, or are they administrators?

Prof. Brown: Well, they teach, don't they?

Prof. Jones: Yes, but they also serve as administrators.

Prof. Brown: What does it matter what category they go by?

Prof. Jones: OK, let me put it this way. Do the deans and the president qualify as faculty or administrators?

Prof. Thomas: Well, they are listed in the catalog as faculty.

Prof. Jones: OK; however, this policy is the first major step in allowing greater faculty governance at this school. How can we get greater faculty governance if we include members of the administration in our definition of faculty?

Prof. James: Yeh. What if it's a close vote, and all the administrators vote as a block to defeat our new policy?

Prof. Brown: I still think we are making a mountain out of a molehill.

Prof. Jones: (Getting irritated.) We work for almost a year getting a faculty senate organized, and now you think it's a trivial matter whether or not the proposal gets defeated?

Prof. Brown: I didn't say anything of the kind. I only meant that I think it is unlikely that the administration has enough votes to make much difference no matter how we define the term "faculty."

Prof. Jones: Well, I strongly disagree. I think this is a *crucial* point. Are we, the faculty, going to have a hand in running this place once and for all, or are we going to let this little bit of progress be eroded by allowing administrators to vote on our *faculty senate*?

Prof. Smith: I'm afraid our time is running out for today's meeting. Since many of us have classes to go to, I think we should table this discussion until our next meeting. In the meantime, let's all try to rethink our positions on this.

Prof. Jones: I don't have to do any rethinking! If we are going to go back to being dictated to by the administration, I don't want any further part of this committee. I volunteered to be on this committee because I thought we had a chance to improve things around here. I can see now I have wasted my time.

Chairperson: Do I have a motion for adjournment?

Prof. Thomas: So moved.

Chairperson: Is there a second?

Prof. Smith: Second.

Chairperson: Meeting adjourned until next week.

1. What is the major problem for this group?

2. How could they have avoided this outcome?

3. If you could role-play this discussion, what would you say to help resolve this situation?

This group discussion, which actually occurred, illustrates one type of problem groups may encounter: language-related problems and the relationship between language, thought, and behaviors. The committee members could not agree on how to interpret the word "faculty." This disagreement led to emotional reactions and eventually to one member's resignation. This problem is just one type of difficulty related to problems of communication. But before we go any further, let us stop and define *our* terms so we don't run into the same problem this committee did.

COMMUNICATION

Communication Defined

Communication within the small group is both similar to and different from communication in other settings. *Group communication* is defined as "the process of creating meanings in the minds of others." These meanings may or may not correspond to the meanings we intend to create. Group communication involves the sending and receiving of messages between and among the participants. Group communication includes both verbal and nonverbal message stimuli. In all these ways, group communication is similar to communication that occurs in other contexts, such as interpersonal communication (informal communication between two or more people); public communication (between a speaker and an audience); organizational communication (communication in an organizational setting); or

to make decisions about those people. This is reflected in the body of research investigating group members' nonverbal responses to leaders. The data demonstrate the existence of a social mechanism leading to the devaluation of leadership. Butler and Geis (1990) report that when some group members display unfavorable nonverbal responses to a leader, the remaining group members tend to rate that leader's contributions as less valuable. When favorable nonverbal cues are given, the leader's contributions are rated higher. Their study hypothesized and found that competent, assertive women in leadership roles elicit significantly more negative responses than men in the same positions. This is thought to be a result of female leaders' breaking with the stereotypic submissive, "feminine" behaviors. When women served in stereotypic masculine roles (leadership), they received nonverbal disapproval from their peers. This disapproval was passed on to other group members, who assessed the female leaders as making less valuable contributions. This has much to do with the elements of social influence and conformity discussed in Chapter 4.

Hand gestures are another type of visual cue. Barnlund (1968) states, "Next to the face, the hands are probably the most expressive part of the human body." Entire books have been devoted to the study of the hands in oral communication. It was once thought that hand gestures could be taught as a means of developing greater expressiveness. For example, the outstretched hands with the palms up would indicate a request for help, whereas the clenched fist would indicate a threat. The study of gestures today is more descriptive and leans less in the direction of trying to prescribe which gestures should be used in certain situations.

In one company, for example, a union grievance was filed on the basis of a gesture of the employee's boss. The grievance charged: "Animus toward the grievant can be demonstrated by the Department Head's handling of the application. . . . The application was tossed across the desk by the Department Head in the direction of the grievant. The Department Head's manner was offensive, embarrassing and unprofessional to both the grievant and the [union president]" (grievance dated 1986). This grievance went through several steps of the grievance procedure and tied up dozens of hours of managerial time for the better part of a year. There were also threats of legal action.

Axtell (1991) notes that military forces sent to Saudi Arabia during Operation Desert Storm were issued a forty-page booklet on gestures and body language among the Arabs. It offered advice such as the following: Avoid crossing the legs so that the sole of the shoe is pointed at someone, "don't be upset if Arabs stand very close, even touch you, when conversing, . . . [and] the 'O.K.' gesture (thumb and forefinger forming a circle) may be interpreted there as giving a curse" (pp. 12–13).

Physical appearance includes facial attractiveness as well as body shape and size and styles of dress. In one study of physically attractive versus unattractive people, Widgery (1974) found that on the basis of faces alone, more attractive people are consistently assumed to have higher credibility than their homely counterparts. Walster et al. (1966) found that among 752 college students at a freshman dance, physical attractiveness was by far the most important factor in determining the extent to which a date would be liked by his or her partner. B. F. Skinner has argued that beauty is a form of reinforcer, because it encourages us to look once again. Certainly most fashion models of both sexes are reinforcing to look at!

As we saw in Chapter 4, body shape has been described in three basic categories by Sheldon (1954). The mesomorph is muscular and athletic looking and would be considered the most attractive. The ectomorph is tall, thin, and fragile looking. The endomorph is soft, round, and fat. Three representative examples of the respective body types would be Arnold Schwarzenegger, Pee Wee Herman, and John Candy. Our body shapes are usually some mixture of these three types. Jack Lalanne, the famous physical fitness personality, once said on a television show that if you raid the refrigerator every night, even if you are alone, your body itself communicates to everybody every day that you eat too much. So you're not fooling anybody.

Styles of dress also communicate about us. We are often judged as "conservative" or "weird" on the basis of our clothing choices. Lefkowitz, Blake, and Mouton conducted an interesting study of the influence of a person's dress on jaywalking behavior. They collected data on jaywalking on three different days for three different one-hour periods. They wanted to determine if pedestrians (these happened to be in Austin, Texas) would violate the "wait" signal more if they saw someone else violate it than if there were no violator. They were also interested in any differential effects that would result from differences in the violator's dress. The experimenters made use of a confederate who jaywalked while dressed one of two ways. First he dressed in a high-status manner, with a freshly pressed suit, shined shoes, white shirt, tie, and straw hat ("Mr. Clean"). The low-status dress consisted of an unpressed blue denim shirt, soiled and patched pants, well-worn shoes, and no hat ("Mr. Dirty"). Observations were made on 2103 pedestrians who crossed the intersection during the hours of the experiment.

The study revealed several interesting results. Ninety-nine percent of the pedestrians obeyed the "wait" signal when no confederate was present or when the confederate also obeyed. When Mr. Dirty jaywalked, 4 percent of the other pedestrians also violated the signal. When Mr. Clean jaywalked, 14 percent of the other pedestrians also disobeyed.

In addition to clothing, aspects of physical appearance such as hairstyles and jewelry also send visual cues. For instance, a person with multicolored hair or spiked hair and punk appearance would not get very far in a job interview in most companies. In Santa Cruz, California, one food worker at the boardwalk amusement park was not allowed to wear a nose ring at work because doing so was against the law. Originally, the law also prohibited workers with pierced body parts and colorful hairdos. One woman reportedly changed her hair from fire-engine red back to brown. As it is, applicants for jobs have to "tuck their long hair under hats; no dangling earrings are allowed; and tattoos can't show because of possible gang connections" (Associated Press, 1992) What influence do you think factors such as these have on group dynamics?

To summarize, our appearance through facial attractiveness, body shape, and choice of clothing will determine to some extent our influence on others.

Body movements are also an influential type of nonverbal cue. Each of us can probably remember having someone say, "You seem kind of down today," as a reaction to our slumped shoulders and slightly bowed head. Probably one of Peter

Falk's most memorable roles is his slouchy interpretation of the character Columbo. Although there are a wealth of other cues (gestures, raincoat, cigar), his body movements stand out very vividly, as did John Wayne's swagger or Vanna White's walk.

Body orientation is an important factor in small group interaction. Knapp (1972) defines body orientation as "the degree to which a communicator's shoulders and legs are turned in the direction of, rather than away from, the addressee," (p. 97). Mehrabian (1969) found that a seated communicator who leaned forward was perceived as having a more positive attitude than one who leaned backward and away from the person judging. Higher-status persons tend to be more relaxed in staff meetings than lower-status individuals, who sit straighter in their chairs. Body position may also add to our perceiving a person as being "uptight." Schutz (1971) describes this in the context of an encounter group:

> If a person is holding himself tight, I would either move on to someone else and count on the group interaction to loosen him up so that he can work better later, or perhaps choose to try to help him break through that defense. . . . A first step is to ask the person to relax by unlocking his arms and legs if he has them crossed, perhaps to stand up and shake himself loose, jiggle and breathe very deeply for several minutes. (p. 212)

Inclusiveness is another important aspect of body orientation. In a small group discussion, subgroups frequently form that are usually annoying to at least some in the group. Subgroups may be the result of one person directing comments to only one or two others. "Directing comments" refers to body orientation and the direction of eye contact. Those who feel excluded from the discussion will sooner or later begin to withdraw their participation from the group, and the benefit of their contributions will be lost. Thus body orientation can be a potent factor in determining the discussion's outcome.

Vocal Cues

In addition to verbal messages and visual cues, vocal cues affect small group interaction. There is usually some confusion between the terms "vocal cues" and "verbal cues." Perhaps it would be helpful to remember that vocal cues are lost when a verbal (word) message is written down. Vocal cues include regional dialects, methods of pronunciation, and the five major factors of (1) volume, (2) rate and fluency, (3) pitch, (4) quality, and (5) inflection.

Try to imagine the sound of your voice saying, "Now that we are all here, we can get the meeting started." Now think of how it would sound as stated by David Letterman, Eddie Murphy, David Brinkley, Marilyn Monroe, W. C. Fields, Elizabeth Taylor, Mae West, Roseanne Barr, Bart Simpson, or some of your own friends. Each person's voice is unique; sometimes voiceprints are used like fingerprints for identification. This individuality results from the complex combination of vocal cues mentioned above. Speaking with adequate *volume,* or loudness, is the first responsibility of any communicator. Conversely, the first responsibility of listeners is to let speakers know they can't be heard. Speakers should be asked to speak more loudly and to repeat the part that was missed. This requires some tact, however. The intent should be to communicate, "I want to know what you're saying," rather than, "Listen, dummy, I'm important and you're not taking my listening convenience into sufficient account."

Groups tend to have more problems with adequate volume than, say, people involved in personal conversations. As the size of the group increases, the hearing difficulties may also increase, because there are more potential sources of interfering noise and the distance from the speaker to any given member in the group tends to be greater.

A second critical vocal cue is *rate and fluency*. Rate refers to words uttered per minute (WPM), and fluency refers to the lack of interruptions (which may influence the rate). We have all suffered the unpleasantness of listening to a person who injects long pauses in the middle of sentences or who frequently throws in such distracting verbal fillers as "ah," "um," "er," "why I," "and-uh," "like," among others. An average speaking rate is between 125 and 175 words per minute. If the person is able to articulate well—that is, to speak distinctly—a faster rate seems to be more interesting to listen to. Studies in listener comprehension indicate that we can understand rates two and three times the normal speed with little difficulty. In group discussion, the fluent speaker is usually more pleasant to listen to.

Vocal *pitch* refers to the frequency in cycles per second (CPS) of the vocal tones. Melanie Griffith and Dudley Moore have high-pitched (or high-frequency) voices; James Earl Jones and Bea Arthur have lower-pitched voices. There is probably no such thing as the perfectly pitched voice; however, most successful professional announcers seem to have lower-pitched voices (e.g., Merlin Olsen and Dick Enberg).

Vocal *quality* refers to the resonance of the voice. Different examples would include breathiness (Connie Stevens), harshness (George C. Scott), nasality (Sylvester Stallone), and huskiness (Deborah Winger). Vocal quality may determine the extent to which people may want to listen to us for any length of time. Johnny Carson's laugh was once described as being "like the sound of cracking plastic." The voice of comedian Don Adams was once compared to "the sound of scratching your fingernail across a blackboard." On the other hand, some people who try to make their voices sound more deep and resonant come across as phony and artificial.

Inflection refers to the relative emphasis, pitch changes, and duration in uttering different word parts in a sentence. The American southerner's accent is characterized by a drawn-out vowel sound—for example, "Atlanta" (northern pronunciation) versus "Atlaaanta" (southern pronunciation). Inflections also include the rise in vocal pitch at the end of an interrogative sentence:

Are you $^{coming?}$

Probably the most critical thing to remember about vocal inflections is that they may indicate a lot of the emotional tone of a statement. The statement "Oh, great" can be said with true enthusiasm or great disgust. We can use our voices to indicate sarcasm, ridicule, and superiority, and what we convey may be counterproductive to the group's progress.

Leathers (1976) reports that several emotions can be reliably detected in most speakers. He has groups of students rate ten different vocal messages according to the emotions they convey (for example, disgust, happiness, sadness, bewilderment, surprise, anger, etc.). Although Leathers uses this technique for the purpose of research, the practical aspect is that vocal cues do accurately convey emotions. As we become more aware and in control of our nonverbal cues, we may improve our effectiveness in groups. For example, several students complained about a professor who was being quite abusive in his tone of voice to them. They were considering quitting his class because of this. When he was told, he was shocked. He had been unaware of the negative consequences his vocal tone had on his teaching effectiveness.

Clearly, not all the cues are exhibited in the small group setting. However, as we become more aware of our nonverbal behavior overall, we can begin to change some of these cues in situations that appear to need improvement. We can also begin to develop our sensitivities to the nonverbal behaviors of others. For example, if a meeting has been going on for a long time, you can detect tiredness and low levels of energy through bored facial expressions, yawns, or unenthusiastic vocal tones. These cues may indicate that the group needs to take a break in order to continue at peak efficiency. But the person not sensitive to these cues may try to keep pushing a tired group, only to accomplish less and less.

In summarizing this section on verbal and nonverbal cues, we need to point out that all these cues are perceived as a whole. We do not dissect them in reality as we have done in this analysis. For example, it has been found that when we say one thing but nonverbally indicate something else (as with "I really appreciate that" spoken sarcastically), the *nonverbal* message is more likely to be believed. In this same context, subjects in one study who were told to lie showed several nonverbal changes. There were more errors in their speech, they had less direct eye contact, and they talked for shorter durations than they had when they were telling the truth (Mehrabian, 1971). Obviously, nonverbal communication plays a significant role in small groups. Communication experts agree that whether you say anything or not, "you can't not communicate." Thus we need to keep in mind the importance of both verbal and nonverbal messages.

Nonverbal communication takes a different form at the organizational level. Suzyn Ornstein (1989) asserted that people are often unaware of the nonverbal communication that results from the layout and decor of an office. Definite relationships have been established between office design and various organizational behaviors, attitudes, and impressions. An open-office layout, as opposed to the conventional, individual-office design, is often conducive to communication in the workplace and can lead to greater employee satisfaction. If employees are comfortable in their office, they feel that their managers are concerned about their well-being, and they will be more satisfied in their jobs. Other elements of the workplace that affect employee behaviors and attitudes include seating arrangement, lighting, temperature, noise, and the presence of artwork. The decor and layout of corporate offices lead to the impressions that people have about that corporation: "Not only is office configuration important in conveying information about the organization's values, but the physical layout of the offices themselves . . . also serves to reinforce the company's values" (Ornstein, 1989, p. 144).

Ornstein made some suggestions to managers about what they should consider when implementing changes in office layout: (1) Managers should seek input from employees who will be affected by the change. (2) Managers should thoroughly analyze the work to be performed in the space under consideration. (3) Managers should consider the values, goals, and behaviors they want to reinforce by their selection of office design. And (4) managers should consider the influence office design has on outsiders who have cause to visit the facility.

Defensive-Supportive

For several years it has been an established fact that when someone threatens you psychologically, you react by throwing up a barrier against that threat. That barrier is referred to as a *defense mechanism*. Once that defensive barrier has been erected, effective communication is reduced. Thus it is valuable to learn how we can avoid arousing others' protective psychological shields. Gibb (1961) described six differences between what he called defensive and supportive communication climates. These six differences are:

Supportive Climates	Defensive Climates
Description	Evaluation
Problem orientation	Control
Spontaneity	Strategy
Empathy	Neutrality
Equality	Superiority
Provisionalism	Certainty

When we feel we are being evaluated, especially when someone is criticizing us, we are likely to rise to our own defense. However, when we feel that a person is objectively describing us without adding an evaluation, we are not as likely to become defensive. When someone tries to control or coerce us, we become more uncomfortable than when a person seeks to solve a problem without forcing us to go along with the solution. Then, too, a person who has a preset plan usually turns us off, as opposed to one who reacts spontaneously to situations. Strategy often implies a gimmick or some deception. Similarly, when a person is neutral toward us, as opposed to empathic or sympathetic, this usually makes us more defensive. When a person acts in a superior manner instead of treating us as an equal, we say that person is on an ego trip. Such superior behavior is deflating to our self-esteem and arouses our defenses. Finally, when someone acts as a "know-it-all," this attitude of certainty or dogmatism is less pleasant than the attitude of a person who is willing to have an open mind and act with a degree of provisionalism. Gibb found that groups with defensive climates got more bogged down in worthless ego-protecting discussion and accomplished less than those with more supportive climates.

Tjosvold and Tjosvold (1991) offer the following practical advice on how to communicate effectively in a team setting:

1. Express your own ideas clearly and logically, but avoid arguing blindly for them. Consider other viewpoints.

2. Change your mind based on the . . . logical [points] of others. Do not change your mind [only] to avoid conflict.

3. Seek a consensus decision. Avoid majority voting, tossing a coin. . . .

4. Foster opposing views. Encourage people to become involved and speak their minds.

5. Discuss underlying assumptions and ideas. . . .

6. Strive for a win-win solution that incorporates the best of all ideas. . . .

7. Reconsider an earlier decision. (pp. 136–137)

Sometimes it may become necessary to criticize a group member. This is difficult and embarrassing for everyone involved. In fact, Weisinger (1989) described criticism within a group as "one of the most difficult criticism encounters" (p. 245). When one member of the group is criticized, the other members of the group are less likely to contribute, for fear of being put down. Weisinger (pp. 246–248) offered three strategies for criticizing group work or group members while still maintaining a supportive environment for the group:

1. Direct critical comments to the work, and not to the person who performed it.

2. Turn individual criticism into a group criticism by making the statement general.

3. Present the criticism in a way that forces the group members to come up with answers to the problem.

The first strategy depersonalizes the criticism by addressing it to the task rather than the person. It's the difference between saying, "This could use some more work," and "You did this wrong. You must redo it." The latter is more likely to bring about feelings of resentment and defensiveness than the former. The second strategy aims the criticism at the whole group, as a general request for change. Rather than saying, "You are not spending enough time on the project," comment, "We could all stand to commit ourselves more to the project." There is a chance that the person for whom the comment was intended will miss it altogether; however, such a strategy maintains the supportive nature of the group and will help to encourage the other members of the group. The purpose of the third strategy is to involve the group members in the solution process. Instead of laying harsh criticism on the members of the group ("Your sales records are rotten! The company is ready to fold"), invite them to come up with a solution to the problem ("Sales are down throughout the company. Does anyone have any ideas on how to remedy the situation?").

A specific line of research on supportive versus defensive communication has been conducted along the lines of the confirming versus disconfirming aspects of communication. Dance and Larson (1976) define these concepts in the following way: "Confirmation, as used in an interpersonal sense, refers to any behavior that causes another person to value himself more. Its opposite, disconfirmation, refers to any behavior that causes another person to value himself less" (p. 77).

The confirmation-disconfirmation literature has expanded within recent years. Although the basic thrust of the theory remains the same—that is, that communication with others is potentially confirming or disconfirming—the role of such behavior in communication has been continually refined.

Dance and Larson (1976) divide communication patterns into four types:

1. Explicit rejection (disconfirming)

2. Implicit rejection (disconfirming)

3. Explicit acceptance (confirming)

4. Implicit acceptance (confirming)

Explicit rejection involves either a negative evaluation or an overt dismissal of the person or his message. For example:

A: I can't understand how they can just sit on their duffs and not do anything about it. Time is running out.

B: Yeah, well, I don't see you doing anything about it.

Implicit rejection involves four more subtle types of disconfirmation:

a. Interruptions—when a speaker cuts you off in midsentence

b. Imperviousness—when a speaker ignores what you say as if you had never said it

c. Irrelevant response—when the speaker starts off on a totally unrelated topic in response to your initial comment

d. Tangential response—when a person gives some acknowledgment to your initial comment but immediately launches off on a new irrelevant topic

Explicit acceptance involves a positive evaluation of either the person or his communication content. For example:

A: So I just told him straight out that he wasn't going to pull that kind of stuff with me.

B: That took guts.

Implicit acceptance involves either a direct acknowledgment of a person's remark, an attempt to clarify the remark by asking for more information, or an expression of positive feeling. For example:

A: What I meant to say was that I've known him for a long time, and I've never seen him do anything like that.

B: Oh, well, now I understand.

The importance of confirmation-disconfirmation literature lies in the specific identification of communication patterns that seem to help or hinder communication effectiveness in most situations. Cissna (1976), who summarized studies in widely differing situations, found that the only factor that appeared in all these studies was the confirmation-disconfirmation factor. Thus, this factor may be one of the most pervasive dimensions in human communication.

Stephen Covey (1990), in his best-selling book *The Seven Habits of Highly Effective People,* lists as one of the habits: "Seek first to understand, then to be understood." This is excellent advice and is totally consistent with the notion of confirming types of communication. In his follow-up best-seller, *Principle-Centered Leadership,* Covey (1991) states:

> Technique is relatively unimportant compared to trust, which is the result of our trustworthiness over time. When trust is high, we communicate easily, effortlessly, instantaneously. We can make mistakes and others will still capture our meaning. But when trust is low, communication is exhausting, time-consuming, ineffective, and inordinately difficult. (p. 18)

Content and Process

One rather difficult distinction to make about group discussion is the difference between the content of the discussion and the process. Suppose a group is discussing this topic: "How can political corruption in the United States be reduced?" When the discussion is over, the professor asks others in the class to comment on the discussion. Comments concerning the *content* of the discussion might include the following:

- "I think political corruption will always be with us."

- "I think politics are no more dirty now than in the past."

- "The political system has shown its strength by catching its own offenders."

These comments are typical of an untrained observer. They all deal with the topic of the discussion, and the observer frequently gets into the heat of the discussion topic.

Comments regarding the *process* of the same discussion are quite different, as illustrated by the following:

- "Joe dominated the group while the others couldn't get a word in edgewise."

- "Most of your comments were based on opinions. Few actual facts were brought out."

- "I think you got bogged down in defining the problem and never really got to any conclusion as to how to solve the problem."

These comments deal with the process or manner in which the discussion was conducted. This type of observation usually requires more insight into group interaction. Also, this type of comment allows both participants and observers to learn from one sample discussion some principles of group interaction that can be generalized to other discussions. Thus, it is important to be able to distinguish discussion content from the discussion process.

Notice the difference in the following two students' descriptions of a group discussion. They were asked to describe the group processes in their small group. (The topic was the ethics of cloning humans—Exercise 3 in Chapter 1.)

Student 1

I feel a certain resentment toward the idea of *producing* life, which I consider cloning to be. I especially feel a resentment toward producing beings to act as slaves or to be used by us in any way. My group discussed the idea of controlling the traits of cloned human beings for specialized purposes. I do not feel that God appreciates his children tampering with the miracle of life.

Student 2

The group started with the usual "I guess we're supposed to's" and, after only a minimal amount of paper shuffling, got down to the subject at hand.

Of the five-person group, only four participated. It was interesting to note who assumed the leadership role, for how long, for what reasons, how effectively, etc. I feel that the member who occupied this role initially usually does not do so in other groups—that members who seemed to know something about this subject successfully opened the discussion and maintained it by asking others questions. What I looked for but did *not* see was direct eye contact, an authoritative tone of voice (I didn't say authoritarian), and backbone enough to justify occupying the leader's role. I think she was assuming this behavior to get a good grade.

Notice how student 1 discusses only the *topic* of the discussion content. Student 2, however, really discusses the group's *process,* or behavior, and therefore does a much better job of fulfilling the assignment.

Finally, in a very comprehensive study, Insko et al. (1993) found that communication within groups led to significantly greater cooperation and less competition than was the case when individuals worked independently and did not communicate with one another.

LANGUAGE BEHAVIOR

The study of the interaction between verbal symbols and the thought patterns associated with them is referred to as *general semantics.* If you have ever become bogged down in a group discussion because of a difficulty in defining terms or dealing with any problems with language, as in the case study at the beginning of this chapter, you will immediately see the relevance of this topic to the study of small group interaction. In fact, some discussions may even have as their task the problem of choosing the appropriate verbal symbol to represent a concept. New products frequently have several proposed names that may be market-tested for consumer response. The intermediate-size Ford Granada, for example, had several other potential names that apparently were not popular. According to Smith (1974): "Ford tested Eagle, Fairmont, Stallion, Lucerne, Gibraltar, Scandia, and many other monikers before selecting[the name] Granada for its new compact luxury car. Chrysler Corporation's design studies have flirted with special models carrying such names as Boca Raton, Gatsby, Gandy Dancer, Easy Rider and Magnum." Committees spend hours brainstorming possible names and then determining procedures for testing market reaction to the main contenders.

Although few of us will ever make decisions concerning product names, each of us will undoubtedly be involved with language problems of one sort or another in group discussions. Our discussion will focus on four specific problems that frequently plague groups: (1) bypassing, (2) inference making, (3) polarizing, and (4) signal reactions.

Bypassing

In January 1990 an Avianca Airlines passenger plane crashed on Long Island, New York, killing seventy-three people. A subsequent investigation attributed the crash to a miscommunication between the pilots and the air traffic controllers. One report indicated that "Avianca pilots were not trained to use the term 'fuel emergency.' . . . Controllers testified that the plane received no priority to land that night because the term `fuel emergency' was not used" ("Avianca Pilots," 1990).

This case illustrates a situation in which a misunderstanding occurred because of a language problem. This sort of misunderstanding is referred to as *bypassing*. It is defined as "the miscommunication pattern which occurs when the *sender* (speaker, writer, and so on) and the *receiver* (listener, reader, and so forth) *miss each other with their meaning*" (Haney, 1992). In group discussions, the entire focus of the discussion may be diverted by a difference in interpretation of a given word. Note the incredible problems arising in one group as seen by one participant:

> At the start of our meeting I introduced a definition of communication (communication is an expression of ideas). Although the basics were appreciated, Ed and Al requested a revision, as the statement was too simple. They decided to drop the words "an expression of ideas." I didn't believe this was a very good revision and said so. A slight altercation developed lasting about five minutes. It was resolved that other ideas would be considered.
>
> After sufficient waiting (about thirty seconds), I realized no great ideas were forthcoming, so I subtly suggested that my idea be reconsidered. This time Pete and John were on my side. Still, my full idea could not survive Al and Ed, so it was given new form. . . . In the process of getting a communication definition, they had to satisfy me that their changes were justified, while I was attempting to show my original as the best. "Well, you haven't done any better," was surprisingly effective. While I had been using sword points, the best they could muster was a safety pin.
>
> After the mutilation of my last idea, I decided I would not volunteer any more material and thus "watch them squirm."

FIGURE 5.1   THE RELATIONSHIP BETWEEN AN OBJECT AND THE SYMBOL FOR THE OBJECT

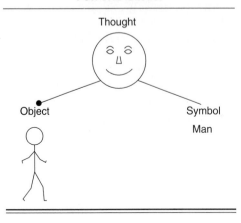

Thought

Object

Symbol

Man

It seems hard to believe that such intense reactions could result from a difference of opinion over the definition of the term "communication." However, this reaction is more typical than atypical.

The diagram in Figure 5.1 helps us understand the relation between an object (or referent) and a symbol used to represent that object. As Figure 5.2 shows, the symbol may vary, but the object remains the same. The object has a word chosen to represent it, but that word and the object have no necessary inherent relation-

FIGURE 5.2   THE SAME OBJECT MAY BE REPRESENTED BY MORE THAN ONE SYMBOL

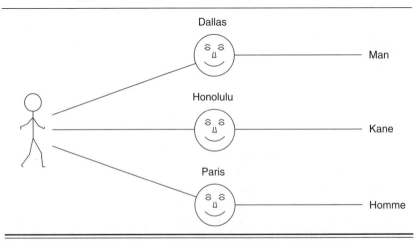

Dallas

Man

Honolulu

Kane

Paris

Homme

ship. It is a little like selecting a name for a newborn baby. At first the choice seems arbitrary, but after a few years it seems impossible to think of that person having a different name. The relationship is indirect between symbol and referent; it exists only in the mind. Because each of us has a different brain and nervous system, the relationship between any given referent and any given word will vary to some extent from person to person.

Part of the bypassing problem is that we frequently assume words contain meaning. A different view is that words are symbols arbitrarily designated to represent concepts or referents. Over time, we begin to associate the word with its referent so strongly that they become inseparable. It is easy enough to say that the word is not the thing and that we should be able to separate the symbol from the referent, but it is difficult in practice not to respond emotionally when another person refers to us as a fascist pig, a nigger, a stupid hillbilly, or a honky. In fact, Ted Danson and Whoopi Goldberg created quite a controversy in October 1993 when they used racial slurs in a comedy skit. Even in comedy, there are limits to what can be said.

Two problems related to bypassing occur when (1) we use the same word to mean different things (dress "casually") or (2) different words are used to express essentially the same idea. For example, we may argue that company employees are not performing properly because of a "communication problem" as opposed to a "lack of motivation." It may be that we are really talking about related problems (that is, employees would be better motivated to perform [motivation problem] if they could suggest some new job procedures to their supervisors [communication problem]), but the issue may be clouded by arguments over the labels used to describe the problem.

Haney (1992) suggests two outcomes that can result from bypassing. On one hand, we may have apparent agreement when, in fact, we are calling different things by the same name (dressing casually). On the other hand, we may have actual agreement but apparent disagreement, as in the employee problem described above. Given these possible outcomes, here are some guidelines (slightly modified) that Haney suggests to remedy the potential difficulties.

- Be person-minded, not word-minded.

- Question and paraphrase.

- Be receptive to feedback.

- Be sensitive to contexts.

McCormack (1984), in his best-selling book *What They Don't Teach You at Harvard Business School,* confirms Haney's advice when he writes: "Insight demands opening up your senses, talking less and listening more. I believe you can learn almost everything you need to know—and more than other people would like you to know—simply by watching and listening, keeping your eyes peeled, your ears open. And your mouth closed. . . . Watch your listen/talk ratio" (pp. 8–9). These points also corroborate the ancient rhetorician who observed, "We have two ears and only one tongue, so that we might listen more than we speak."

In a nutshell, these guidelines focus on the idea that not all of us use words precisely the same way and that all words have the potential for multiple usage and interpretation. When you suspect that there may be a difference in word usage, ask questions, and be willing to try to restate or paraphrase the person's message. Remember to use different words in your restatement to see if the basic intent is understood. Also, be receptive to feedback. If we are too impervious or insensitive to allow for the possibility that we may not have stated something perfectly clearly, then we are unlikely to get much feedback to that effect. However, if we are willing to admit to fallibility, we invite feedback and can benefit from that information. Finally, we can often guess the intended meaning of a given statement on the basis of its use in a given context. For example, one supervisor frequently bade good-bye to his employees with the common phrase, "Well, take it easy now." It was quite obvious from the context that he meant this only as a casual expression. He did *not* intend employees to work less hard. By employing the four techniques mentioned above, we can reduce the frequency of bypassing.

Inference Making

Each of us makes numerous inferences every day. For example, we infer (1) that the sun will rise tomorrow; (2) that a chair won't collapse when we sit down; (3) that the sun is shining on the other side of town, because it is shining at our location; (4) that a car coming at us from a side street will stop at the stop sign and not run into the side of our car; and (5) that a person who consistently fails to show up for a group discussion is not committed to our group task. In each of these five cases, there is some probability that our inference will be borne out by the actual events. However, these five examples illustrate quite a range from most probable (number 1) to least probable (number 5).

Statements of inference go beyond what we know through observations. They represent only some degree of probability of coming true. This idea is illustrated in the diagram in Figure 5.3.

One of the major problems in groups is being able to recognize our own inference making. You can test your own ability on the following sample story. True (T) means that the inference drawn is definitely true on the basis of the information in the story. False (F) means that the inference is definitely wrong on the basis of the information in the story. A question mark (?) means that you cannot be certain of the inference on the basis of the story.

FIGURE 5.3

Observational statements	Inferential statements
←—————————————————————————→	
Approaching certainty	Approaching uncertainty

Sample Story

A customer handed the pharmacist a prescription for birth control pills. "Please fill this quickly. I have someone waiting in the car."

The pharmacist hurried to fill the order.

Statements about the Story

1. A woman was having a prescription filled
   for birth control pills.   T F ?

2. She did not want to become pregnant.   T F ?

3. She was in a hurry to have the order filled.   T F ?

4. The pharmacist did his best to speed up the order.   T F ?

If you answered T to any of the statements, you probably assumed or inferred that the customer and the pharmacist were female and male, respectively. Yet there is no statement in the story to support that assumption. Actually, a man is ordering birth control pills for his wife. The pharmacist, a female, cannot do "his" best to fill the order.

Another way of describing inference making is to say that it involves certain assumptions or conclusion drawing (sometimes jumping to the wrong conclusion). This becomes a problem in groups when we react to each other on the assumption that a person is behaving a certain way for the reason that seems obvious or apparent. However, the person may be acting that way for reasons other than the obvious. For example, a person may aggress against another by saying, "I'm sick and tired of your holding us back in our work." On the surface, this appears to be a comment intended to help the group get more accomplished. Beneath the surface, however, it may be part of an effort to undermine the other person's status in the group and may be a part of the struggle between the two for leadership in the group. These levels can be diagrammed as shown in Figures 5.4 and 5.5. Although it is helpful to recognize that all behaviors are motivated and that they may be motivated by multiple causes, it is also dangerous to attempt to infer too much. Even if we make such an inference, we must recognize the possibility of error.

FIGURE 5.4   SURFACE AND HIDDEN AGENDAS COMPARED

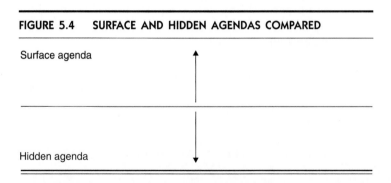

Surface agenda

Hidden agenda

FIGURE 5.5

Levels of Discussion Analysis

Surface agenda	* Perceptive observation
	* Shallow observation
Hidden agenda	* Superficial interpretation of motives
	* Perceptive interpretation of motives

On the other hand, it is often difficult to analyze the group process without making some inferences. For example, one encounter group was having its last meeting, and the discussion somehow got around to the subject of death. After a somewhat extended discussion on this subject, the group leader intervened by saying, "I wonder if this discussion of death is motivated by the reluctance we are all feeling tonight about saying good-bye for the last time." Although this comment was initially rejected by the group, it turned out a lot of people were reluctant to end the friendships that had grown out of this group, and the topic of the discussion shifted to directly expressing and resolving those feelings.

Some inference making may be useful to the group, whereas at other times it may be harmful. A person who tries to read too much into behaviors may become a "psychopest." For example, a person crossing arms across the chest may do this for no reason but increased comfort. An overinterpretation might be that the person is becoming defensive and is trying to put up a barrier between self and others. In attempting to analyze behaviors, it is wise to recognize that analyses often involve inferences that go beyond what we have observed and involve some probability for error.

Polarizing

Perhaps one of the most common problems in groups is polarization. It is difficult to exchange differences in viewpoint without tending to overstate or exaggerate to make our point. When this happens, it encourages the others to exaggerate a bit more in the opposite direction to make their point. Before long the sides are so far apart that constructive discussion of the issues is often discontinued for the time being. Consider the following example:

Kyle: I can't see why a woman should get a job just to avoid the boredom of housework, when a man who needs to support his family goes without a job.

Sue: Just because your masculinity is threatened is no reason to keep women out of work!

Kyle: My masculinity? You women's libbers are always hung up on trying to be the dominant sex!

Sue: You men are all alike. You can't stand being bettered by anyone, especially a woman. You want us to tell you how brilliant you are because you know what day of the week it is.

This exchange actually occurred in a student discussion. The topic was "How can greater job equality be achieved in this country?" The discussion had been progressing well until this polarization occurred. Polarization has three distinct characteristics. First, the statements get more emotionally intense. Second, they go from being specific to being more general ("You men are all alike!"). Third, they tend to move away from the topic at hand (job equality) to other issues ("You can't stand being bettered by anyone").

A simple method usually nips polarization in the bud. It is described by Rogers and Roethlisberger (1952) in the following way:

> The next time you get into an argument with . . . a small group of friends, just stop the discussion for a moment and, for an experiment, institute this rule. "Each person can speak up for himself only *after* he has repeated the ideas and feelings of the speaker accurately and to that speaker's satisfaction." You see what this would mean. It would simply mean that before presenting your own point of view, it would be necessary for you to achieve the other speaker's frame of reference—to understand his thoughts and feelings so well that you could summarize them for him. Sounds simple doesn't it? But if you try it, you will discover that it is one of the most difficult things you have ever tried to do.

After you have tried this restating exercise, notice the effects. First, the tendency for statements to gain emotional intensity is significantly reduced. The calmness is quite dramatic when compared with the interchange between Kyle and Sue above. Second, the discussion tends to stay with manageable specifics rather than move to gross generalities that are quite frequently based on stereotypes (men are not all alike any more than women are all alike). Third, the discussion is more likely to remain focused on the group's discussion topic than to go off on a tangent that may be much less relevant to the group's task. This simple technique actually can be quite potent in reducing the problem of polarization.

Signal Reactions

Signal reactions are learned responses to certain stimuli. Perhaps the best-known example of a signal reaction is the salivation of Pavlov's dogs. Ivan Pavlov was a Nobel prize–winning Russian physiologist. He accidentally stumbled on a very important concept of learning known as *classical conditioning*. He noticed that the carefully calibrated measurements of his test animals' salivation started to break down because his experienced dogs began to salivate in anticipation of the food when he opened the door to the room before he fed them. His coming in the door was the *conditioned stimulus*—the signal that triggered the salivation response. Eventually, he brought the salivation response under stimulus control by associating a bell with food so that the dogs learned to salivate at the sound of the bell even when the food was *not* present.

It is interesting that the founder of general semantics, Alfred Korzybski, wrote that the signal response was an animal-like response. He wrote (1948):

> In Pavlov's experiments a dog is shown food and a bell rung simultaneously. At the sight of food, saliva and gastric juice flow. Associations soon *relate* the ringing of a bell and the food, and, later, simply the ringing of the bell will produce the flow. In another animal some other signal, a whistle, for instance, would produce similar effects. In different people, through experience, associations, relations, meanings, and s.r. [stimulus response] patterns are built around some symbol. Obviously in grown-up humans the identification of the symbol with the thing must be pathological. (p. 249)

Actually, Korzybski was a little extreme in saying that we are pathological to allow such strong connections between signal and response. One study showed that the repetitive sound of a gong produced marked emotional responses in former sailors (as measured by their perspiration levels) but very little emotional reaction among former soldiers. Edwards and Acker (1962) write: "This signal was used as a call to battle stations aboard U.S. Navy ships during the war, and it continued to elicit a strong autonomic response from the Navy veterans. Even though more than fifteen years had elapsed since this stimulus had signaled danger." Although this study did not involve reactions to verbal symbols, it does demonstrate the natural, not pathological, tendency toward strong signal reactions.

A study that directly tested emotional reactions to verbal symbols also proved that strong physiological reactions to symbols are typical rather than pathological. Subjects were exposed to various words on a screen, and their perspiration was measured as an index of their reactions. There were no significant differences between reactions to positive words such as "beauty," "love," and "kiss" and negative words such as "cancer," "hate," and "death." However, some words did cause significant responses. These were referred to as *personal* words and included the person's first and last names, father's and mother's first names, major in school, year in school, and school name. Subjects were significantly aroused by these personal words (Crane, Diecker, and Brown, 1970).

Certainly nobody would argue that these college students were pathological or that they "confused" their own name with themselves as physical beings. Yet these studies collectively indicate that all of us learn to react to certain verbal and nonverbal stimuli in some strong and predictable ways. When the response becomes habitual, it is like a reflex action. At this point, the so-called signal, or automatic response, may create problems.

A recent example of a signal reaction occurred in Sacramento, California. Holes in the pavement used to access utilities are commonly referred to as "manholes." However, because the Sacramento city council has a majority of women, the term "manholes" was thought to be sexist. A major contest was held to come up with a gender-neutral term. Some examples included "sewer viewer," "peopleholes," and "peepholes." The council finally decided on the term "maintenance hole." This appears to be a signal reaction to the term "manhole" (Associated Press, 1990b).

In group discussions, certain phrases may produce signal reactions that are counterproductive. Such phrases have been referred to as *idea killers* (Tubbs, 1993) or communication stoppers. They include, among others:

- "That's ridiculous."
- "We tried that before."
- "That will never work."
- "That's crazy."
- "It's too radical a change."
- "We're too small for it."
- "It's not practical."
- "Let's get back to reality."
- "You can't teach an old dog new tricks."
- "We'll be the laughingstock."
- "You're absolutely wrong."
- "You don't know what you're talking about."
- "It's impossible."
- "There's no way it can be done."

On the other hand, *igniter phrases* that seem to promote group productivity include the following:

- "I agree."
- "That's good!"
- "I made a mistake. I'm sorry."
- "That's a great idea."
- "I'm glad you brought that up."
- "You're on the right track."
- "I know it will work."
- "We're going to try something different today."
- "I never thought of that."
- "We can do a lot with that idea."
- "Real good, anyone else?"
- "I like that!"
- "That would be worth a try."
- "Why don't we assume it would work and go from there."

FIGURE 5.6   SYSTEMATIC NEW ORDER (OF) WORDS

(SNOW Index)

0 external	0 bureaucratic	0 acceptance
1 authoritarian	1 group	1 solutions
2 Machiavellian	2 functional	2 consensus
3 energetic	3 logistical	3 relations
4 situational	4 interpersonal	4 commitment
5 socialized	5 instrumental	5 responsibility
6 systematic	6 managerial	6 development
7 dynamic	7 organizational	7 coordination
8 stagnated	8 executive	8 power
9 transparent	9 homogeneous	9 transactions

Other specific terms that are likely to produce signal reactions are such words as "weirdo," "queer," "honky," "racist," "male chauvinist pig," and many swear words. In fact, even swear words have different levels of offensiveness that vary from culture to culture. Profane words have been classified as (1) religious, (2) excretory, and (3) sexual (Bostrom and Rossiter, 1969). In our culture the sexual words are usually the most offensive; but in Italy, where the Roman Catholic Church is very strong, religious words are considered much more offensive, and in Germany excretory swear words are considered to be the worst. The 2 Live Crew album "As Nasty as They Wanna Be" was declared obscene by a federal court judge in Florida in part because of the use of swear words. This is a vivid example of the emotional impact created by language. One writer expressed her reaction by stating: "But incitement to rape, even if it rhymes and has a rap beat, cannot be defended, whatever its rhythms. . . . Exhortations to sexual violence do not have to be tolerated" (Beck, 1990, p. 7A). Several studies indicate that those who swear may reduce their credibility in the eyes of others (Bauduin, 1971). It also seems advisable to avoid communication stoppers and idea killers whenever possible.

Because we know that words do have a great deal of potential for influencing thought and subsequent action, note the set of terms in Figure 5.6. Just pick any three-digit number at random, and pick the corresponding three words from the lists. These terms all have some relevance to small group interaction. If all else fails, they can be used for fun. For example, 2, 6, 9 would be "Machiavellian managerial transactions." Numbers 8, 4, 3 would be "stagnated interpersonal relations." So if you want to impress your friends with how much you have learned by reading this book, try the "SNOW" index.

SELF-DISCLOSURE

Perhaps one of the greatest dilemmas facing a group member is the choice between openly expressing his or her thoughts and feelings and concealing or distorting inner feelings, thoughts, and perceptions. In a discussion on racial equality, we may not openly reveal our true feelings for fear of sounding like racists or bigots. Nobody wants to be labeled a racist if it can be avoided! On the other hand, if every person in the group conceals his or her thoughts, there will be little said and, therefore, little accomplished. The question is not *whether* to reveal or conceal but *how much* to reveal or conceal. *Self-disclosure* has been defined by Tubbs and Baird (1980) as "a process, whereby an individual voluntarily shares information in a personal way, about his or her 'self' that cannot be discovered through other sources" (p. 15).

You may wonder why a person should bother to let himself or herself be known to others. Experts who studied mentally disturbed individuals concluded that a great deal of human energy is consumed in attempts to keep from being known by others. That energy could be used for other purposes, but neurotic individuals are so "wrapped up in themselves" that they are seldom able to devote sufficient energy to other problems (such as a group problem-solving discussion). All of us are periodically faced with such situations. When we get bad news from home or from a friend, it is much harder to concentrate on such mundane problems as how to budget our study time for tomorrow's exam. However, the mentally unhealthy person is habitually in this state of mind.

Part of returning to mental health involves sharing oneself with others. Jourard (1964) states:

> Self-disclosure, or should I say "real" self-disclosure, is both a symptom of personality health . . . and at the same time a means of ultimately achieving healthy personality. . . . I have known people who would rather die than become known. . . . When I say that self-disclosure is a symptom of personality health, what I mean really is that a person who displays many of the other characteristics that betoken healthy personality . . . *will also display the ability to make himself fully known to at least one other significant human being.* (p. 24)

Perhaps a less self-centered motive for self-disclosure is the desire to improve the quality of communication within a group. Keltner (1970) states:

> We probably do not reveal enough of ourselves in speech-communication to enable our co-communicators to understand us better. The complexities of the world we live in demand better communication than we have known. *To communicate better, we must understand each other better. To understand each other better, we must reveal more of ourselves through speech and speech-communication events.* (p. 54)

Countless students in group discussion feel that they don't know what to contribute to a discussion. They often feel that they have no good or new ideas to add to what has already been said. Yet as we will see in the last section of this chapter, numerous roles may be adopted by group members, several of which involve some degree of self-disclosure. For example, if an idea is initiated by another, you may make a substantial contribution by offering your *reaction* to the idea (opinion giving)—by encouraging or showing agreement or disagreement. Counterproductive role behaviors may also involve self-disclosure (for example, aggressing, reporting a personal achievement, confessing a personal ideology that is irrelevant to the discussion topic, or seeking sympathy from the group).

Self-disclosure is not always desirable. An optimum amount of self-disclosure seems a desirable goal to achieve. Some of us are too closed (concealers); others of us "wear our hearts on our sleeves" (revealers). Culbert (1968) describes the problem of overdisclosing rather vividly:

> The revealer is likely to react by immediately disclosing any self-information to which he has access. The revealer, too, is attempting to master the problem, but for him mastery seems to be attained by explicitly acknowledging and labeling all the relevant elements comprising the situation. While a concealer runs the risk of having insufficient external feedback, a revealer runs the risk of overlabeling the limited number of objective elements present or of labeling them so early that their usefulness in the relationship is nullified. (p. 19)

Encounter groups usually proceed under the assumption that people have learned to be too closed too often. Thus, participants are encouraged to share their feelings and perceptions as openly and honestly as they can. Much of the self-disclosure involves giving feedback to others concerning the ways in which they "come across." This feedback is often useful in reducing the size of the arc of distortion discussed earlier in this chapter.

The Johari Window

Perhaps the most useful model for illustrating self-disclosure in groups is the Johari window (named after its originators, Joe Luft and Harry Ingham) (Luft, 1970). See Figure 5.7 for this model.

This window classifies an individual's relating to others according to four quadrants (or windowpanes). The size of each quadrant represents the person's level of self-awareness. Quadrant 1, the *open quadrant,* represents our willingness to share with others our views on such things as current national or world events, current movies, sports, and what is generally referred to as "cocktail party" conversation.

Quadrant 2 is referred to as the *blind quadrant* or the "bad-breath" area. This area represents the things that others may know about us but that we do unintentionally and unknowingly. We may continually dominate meetings or bore people with long-winded accounts of how good our high school was. Conversely, we may annoy people by our silence, because they may feel that they have opened themselves up to the group while we have "played our cards pretty close to the chest" by revealing little. Group members seem to resent both those who talk too much and those who talk too little.

Quadrant 3 is the *hidden area* that is most likely to be changed (reduced) by self-disclosure. It represents the feelings about ourselves that we know but are unwilling to reveal to others. It may represent our greatest fears, some past experiences we would like to forget, or our secret sexual fantasies, among other things.

Quadrant 4 is called the *area of the unknown.* It represents all the areas of potential growth or self-actualization. This includes almost anything outside our experi-

FIGURE 5.7   THE JOHARI WINDOW

From *Group Processes: An Introduction to Group Dynamics,*
by Joseph Luft, by permission of Mayfield Publishing
Company. Copyright © 1963, 1970 by Joseph Luft.

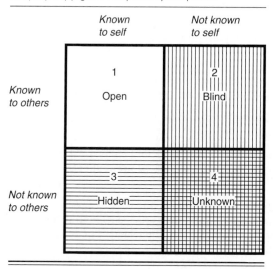

ence, such as the sport we've never played, the places we have never seen, the hobby we haven't taken the time to try, the organization we have never joined, the style of behaving we have never been willing to risk, and others.

Luft advocates changing the shape of the window so that quadrant 1 enlarges while all the others become smaller. I once participated in an encounter group in which we tried to grow interpersonally along the lines suggested by this model. One participant introduced herself as "Mickey" and told us what city she was from, and so on. She was dressed in slacks and a sweater. Only after fifteen weeks did we find out that she was a nun. She had been trying to develop herself as a person without having the rest of us react to her role rather than to her. Thus, her unknown quadrant was diminished by her efforts to try new, less inhibited behaviors. She also reduced her blind quadrant by asking for interpersonal feedback. We might have been more inhibited in our feedback had we known she was a nun. She also destroyed the stereotypes most of us had toward nuns.

More recently, Eisenberg and Witten (1987) have questioned the viability of widespread "open-communication" policies among management and worker groups in a corporation. Open communication for many years has been regarded as the ultimate strategy for improving employee morale and productivity. In an open-communication setting, superiors and subordinates talk with one another freely and openly about company goals, work stressors, and other job-related issues. Eisenberg and Witten, among others, contradict such a blanket statement about open communication. They argue that there are situations when managers and employees have successfully chosen to be more or less open. These decisions stem in part from concern for serving personal goals as well as those of the company.

Appropriateness

Within the above framework questions still arise as to the timing and extent of self-disclosure. Luft (1969) proposes the following guidelines designating situations in which self-disclosure is appropriate:

1. *When it is a function of the ongoing relationship:* What one shares with another belongs in the particular relationship; it is not a random or isolated act.

2. *When it occurs reciprocally:* This implies that there is some degree of interdependence and mutuality involved.

3. *When it is timed to fit what is happening:* The self-disclosure grows out of the experience that is going on between or among the persons involved. The timing and sequence are important.

4. *When it concerns what is going on within and between persons in the present:* Some account is taken of the behavior and feelings of the participants individually and of the persons collectively. There is a recognition of the relationship as an emergent phenomenon in addition to the individual selves.

5. *When it moves by relatively small increments:* What is revealed does not drastically change or restructure the relationship. The implication is that a relationship is built gradually except in rare and special cases.

6. *When it is confirmable by the other person:* Some system is worked out between the persons to validate reception of that which has been disclosed.

7. *When account is taken of the effect disclosure has on the other person(s):* The disclosure has not only been received; there is evidence of its effect on the receiver.

8. *When it creates a reasonable risk:* If the feeling or behavior were really unknown to the other, it may have been withheld for a reason bearing on differences which have yet to be faced by the participants.

9. *When it is speeded up in a crisis:* A serious conflict jeopardizing the structure of the relationship may require that more quadrant 3 material be quickly revealed to heal the breach or help in the reshaping of the relationship.

10. *When the context is mutually shared:* The assumptions underlying the social context suggest that there is enough in common to sustain the disclosure. (pp. 132–133)

Probably the most difficult problem for members of encounter groups to resolve when they go "back home" is knowing how to apply what they have learned without overdoing it. One encounter group graduate said, "How do I use this openness with my boss when he hasn't read the book?" His concern was warranted. It may be quite difficult to put any new behaviors into practice when the others "back home" haven't changed and are still as closed and perhaps as devious as ever.

The most logical advice would be to try to use what you can, when you can. Not all of our learnings will be usable all the time. But certainly some new behaviors (such as increased openness and sensitivity) will be appropriate some, if not most, of the time. Experiences in groups frequently teach us lessons we can't possibly un-learn. Once we have experienced a greater level of personal intimacy with others, day-to-day superficiality may compare rather badly. Schutz (1971) puts it this way:

> Relating to people more honestly is certainly possible. Find someone you have with-held something from and tell it to him. See what happens. Next time you feel like touching someone, do it. Next time you are hurt or frightened, express it. When you catch yourself trying to protect an image, stop, and see if you can be real instead. If you're embarrassed to pay someone a compliment, do it anyway. If you want to know how people respond to you, ask them. (p. 284)

Another way to put it is that the competent communicator has a higher level of rhetorical sensitivity. That is, he or she learns when and with whom to disclose and when and with whom to refrain from disclosure. Total disclosure at all times with all people is obviously not desirable.

INTERACTION ROLES

Each of us is required to enact multiple roles in our everyday living. Usually we are able to function effectively in these different roles, which require or expect certain behaviors. We are, at different times, student, son or daughter, friend, counselor, leader, or follower; some are spouses, parents, and employees as well. It is impor-tant to realize that roles are simply sets of identifiable behaviors. When we say that a person is assuming a role, this does not imply that he or she is faking it or acting in a way that is not within that person's true character. In fact, some writings indi-cate that the more interpersonally sensitive person is one who is able to develop a considerable degree of role flexibility. It is desirable to learn to widen our reper-toire of roles and to discover those roles we most enjoy.

A student relatively new to the small group field indicated an awareness of a few interaction roles:

> This group discussion was a real experience for me. I have never been mixed in with a complete group of strangers and have things work out so smoothly. In most groups you get a few quiet shy ones, who don't say anything, and opposed to them, there's usually one big mouth, normally found in a group, who says everything and has all of the ideas without giving anyone else a chance to give their opinion. It was good to work in a group that was well balanced and one in which everyone participated.

As we mentioned in the discussion of leadership, different functions can be per-formed by any group member. This is another way of saying that individuals as-sume different roles in helping the group move toward its goal. We discussed the task roles and socioemotional functions or roles in Chapter 3. Benne and Sheats (1948) proposed a classification of roles into three broad categories: (1) task roles, (2) group-building and maintenance roles, and (3) individual roles. Although other sets of categories have been developed for research purposes, this time-tested approach is still one of the most useful for learning to identify roles and to develop role flexibility.

Group Task Roles

These behaviors are directed toward accomplishing the group's objective through the facilitation of problem solving:

- *Initiating-contributing:* Proposing new ideas or a changed way of regarding the group goal. This may include a new goal or a new definition of the problem. It may involve suggesting a solution or some way of handling a difficulty the group has encountered. It may also include a new procedure for the group to better organize its efforts.

- *Information seeking:* Asking for clarification, for authoritative information and facts relevant to the problem under discussion.

- *Opinion seeking:* Seeking information related not so much to factual data as to the values underlying the suggestions being considered.

- *Information giving:* Offering facts or generalizations based on experience or authoritative sources.

- *Opinion giving:* Stating beliefs or opinions relevant to a suggestion made. The emphasis is on the proposal of what ought to become the group's values rather than on factors or information.

- *Elaborating:* Expanding on suggestions with examples or restatements, offering a rationale for previously made suggestions, and trying to determine the results if a suggestion were adopted by the group.

- *Coordinating:* Indicating the relationships among various ideas and suggestions, attempting to combine ideas and suggestions, or trying to coordinate the activities of group members.

- *Orienting:* Indicating the position of the group by summarizing progress made and deviations from agreed-upon directions or goals or by raising questions about the direction the group is taking.

- *Evaluating:* Comparing the group's accomplishments to some criterion or standard of group functioning. This may include questioning the practicality, logic, or procedure of a suggestion.

- *Energizing:* Stimulating the group to action or decision, attempting to increase the level or quality of activity.

- *Assisting on procedure:* Helping or facilitating group movement by doing things for the group—for example, performing routine tasks such as distributing materials, rearranging the seating, or running a tape recorder.

- *Recording:* Writing down suggestions, recording group decisions, or recording the outcomes of the discussion. This provides tangible results of the group's effort.

Group-Building and Maintenance Roles

The roles in this category help the interpersonal functioning of the group. They help alter the way of working; they strengthen, regulate, and perpetuate the group. This is analogous to preventive maintenance done to keep a mechanical device such as a car in better working order.

- *Encouraging:* Praising, showing interest in, agreeing with, and accepting the contributions of others; showing warmth toward other group members, listening attentively and seriously to the ideas of others, showing tolerance for ideas different from one's own, conveying the feeling that one feels the contributions of others are important.

- *Harmonizing:* Mediating the differences among the other members, attempting to reconcile disagreements, relieving tension in moments of conflict through the use of humor.

- *Compromising:* Within a conflict situation, yielding status, admitting a mistake, disciplining oneself for the sake of group harmony, or coming halfway toward another position.

- *Gatekeeping and expediting:* Attempting to keep communication channels open by encouraging the participation of some or by curbing the participation of others.

- *Setting standards or ideals:* Expressing standards for the group and/or evaluating the quality of group processes (as opposed to evaluating the content of discussion).

- *Observing:* Keeping a record of various aspects of group process and feeding this information, along with interpretations, into the group's evaluation of its procedures. This contribution is best received when the person has been requested by the group to perform this function. The observer should avoid expressing judgments of approval or disapproval in reporting observations.

- *Following:* Going along with the group, passively accepting the ideas of others, serving as an audience in group discussion.

Individual Roles

These behaviors are designed more to satisfy an individual's needs than to contribute to the needs of the group. These are sometimes referred to as self-centered roles.

- *Aggressing:* Deflating the status of others, disapproving of the ideas or values of others, attacking the group or the problem it is attempting to solve, joking maliciously, resenting the contributions of others and/or trying to take credit for them.

- *Blocking:* Resisting, disagreeing, and opposing beyond reason; bringing up dead issues after they have been rejected or bypassed by the group.

- *Recognition seeking:* Calling attention to oneself through boasting, reporting on personal achievements, acting in inappropriate ways, fighting to keep from being placed in an inferior position.

- *Self-confessing:* Using the group as an opportunity to express personal, non-group-related feelings, insights, ideologies.

- *Acting the playboy:* Showing a lack of involvement in the group's task, displaying nonchalance, cynicism, horseplay, and other kinds of "goofing-off" behaviors.

- *Dominating:* Trying to assert authority or superiority by manipulating others in the group. This may take the form of flattering, asserting a superior status or right to attention, giving directions authoritatively, and/or interrupting others.

- *Help seeking:* Attempting to get sympathy from other group members through expressions of insecurity, personal inadequacy, or self-criticism beyond reason.

- *Special-interest pleading:* Speaking on behalf of some group such as "the oppressed," "labor," "business," usually cloaking one's own prejudices or biases in the stereotype that best fits one's momentary need. (adapted from Schnake, 1990)

It is generally desirable to learn to perform the task roles and the group-building and maintenance roles and to avoid the individual roles. However, even the first and second sets of roles may be misused and abused. For example, there is a fine line between initiating and dominating, between encouraging and flattering, and between opinion giving and recognition seeking. The way in which the role is enacted can make a crucial difference in whether the behavior is viewed as constructive or self-serving. One student attempted to be a gatekeeper by asking silent members if they had any ideas they would like to contribute. After his attempts were rebuked, he wrote the following analysis of his behavior:

> On one occasion, I tried to involve another group member in the discussion against his will. The conflict was resolved in a later discussion, but my bad feelings during the intervening period made me realize that this was an area for attention. . . .
>
> This "expansiveness" and disregard for another person's feelings is an amazing trait to find in myself, because it is something I dislike in other people. It has caused me to resolve that (1) I will not be "overbearing" with quiet people, (2) I will listen more, (3) I will attempt to be more aware of the feelings of others.

Even behaviors motivated by the best intentions may go astray in producing a desired contribution to the group effort.

THE SYSTEMS PERSPECTIVE

In this chapter we examined some issues close to the hearts of many modern communication scholars. The chapter began with an analysis of five critical issues in the study of communication. We looked at the differences between intentional-unintentional, verbal-nonverbal, defensive-supportive, content-process, and therapeutic-pathological communication. Although these issues apply to all communication contexts, our examples and specific applications were focused on the small group context. These issues have considerable overlap with topics discussed in other chapters in this book. For example, how does one express leadership behavior, or establish a group norm, or manifest one's personality, or express one's values? All of these are manifested through behaviors that communicate to others in the group.

The systems perspective fits very well with the emphasis in communication theory on the transactional model of communication. Many authors stress that the participants in any communication event are highly dependent upon one another: they are simultaneously influencing one another and are both senders and receivers at all times. Wilmo (1975) goes so far as to state that "the process of your creating a message may affect you *more* than it does the person receiving it" (p. 402). The transactional point of view can be summarized by stating that a person's communication can be defined only *in relation* to some other or others.

In this chapter we discussed both verbal and nonverbal communication. The systems nature of nonverbal communication is wonderfully illustrated in a recent article about fights breaking out over space in aerobics classes (Wood, 1993). The primary issue develops when one person in the exercise group encroaches on the exercise space of another. One factor in the mix is the territoriality of an individual's personality. Some people are much more territorial than others. A second factor is gender. Men are generally more aggressive than women. A third factor is the person's level of skill and the resulting body shape. As one person states, "If you don't know the routine by heart or if your body fat is higher than 2 percent, it's best not to go [in the front row]" (p. D2). This situation is a perfect example of the systems nature of small group interaction. The type of group, personality, gender, body shape, and ability level all interact to produce the outcome (poor interpersonal relations). "Verbal and nonverbal communication should be treated as a total and inseparable unit." We might add that each of the communication factors discussed in this chapter is, similarly, related to all the others.

In the second section of this chapter we looked at four issues related to language behavior—bypassing, inference making, polarizing, and signal reactions. Each of these factors is related to both the background factors of the individuals and the eventual consequences of group discussion. We saw that background factors were related to signal reactions in the study showing that former sailors experienced a physiological reaction to an alarm bell they had not heard for fifteen years. We also saw that similar reactions can be elicited by such verbal stimuli as our own names or our parents' names. The influence of language on group consequences was shown by the use of "idea killers" such as "It's impossible," "That's crazy," or "That will never work." The net effect of these types of statements is a decrease in potential group productivity in terms of both idea production and interpersonal relations, as we saw in the case study at the beginning of this chapter.

The third section of this chapter dealt with the question, "How much should I reveal and how much should I conceal in a group?" The Johari window was offered as a helpful model for understanding one's relationship to others. Guidelines for appropriate self-disclosure were included. Obviously, appropriate self-disclosure will vary considerably from group to group. High self-disclosure is probably appropriate in an encounter group with a highly supportive atmosphere and a norm of openness and trust. However, social groups, educational groups, work groups, and especially problem-solving groups are hardly the place for a high degree of very personal self-disclosure. Personality also interacts with self-disclosure. If we open up to those who are highly Machiavellian, they will turn around and use our revelations to benefit themselves and possibly to harm us. Appropriate self-disclosure, then, is very much contingent on a number of relevant variables. For this reason, Tubbs and Baird (1980) have developed a contingency model of self-disclosure that suggests how much to disclose and under what circumstances.

The final section discussed the issue of which roles members may adopt in groups. Task and maintenance roles were indicated as useful roles to learn and to use. Individual, or self-centered, roles were identified to help indicate communication behaviors that are typically *not* useful to the group. These roles undoubtedly interact with people's personality traits. For example, the person who is dominant and achievement-oriented will probably adopt the task roles quite comfortably. The affiliators will naturally gravitate toward the group maintenance roles. Finally, the hostile or acquiescent personality types will be tempted to adopt the self-centered roles of aggressing and blocking or help seeking and special-interest pleading, respectively. One of the reasons for studying different types of roles is to increase our ability to adopt different roles in accordance with the demands of the situation.

The readings for this chapter deal with improving management communication skills and with defensive communication.

EXERCISES

1. Case Study:

The following is based on an article by GEORGE F. WILL, the National Endowment for the Arts (NEA).

*WASHINGTON'S WORKS OF ART**

The NEA was created in 1965. By 1993 it was spending $175 million a year of taxpayers' money.

In 1972 the NEA was funding, for example, "Dinner Party," a triangular table with 39 place settings of vaginas on dinner plates. NEA money was involved with the "performance artist" who inserted a speculum into a vagina and invited members of the audience on stage to view her cervix with a flash-

From *Newsweek,* January 10, 1994, pp. 64–65.

light. The NEA funded a Chicago film project that was advertised with a poster announcing "Sister Serpents F___ a Fetus." Recently, NEA funded three Wyoming women for an exhibit of 70 cows painted . . . with feminist thoughts.

New York City spends $87.3 million a year to support 431 arts groups. *The New York Times* reports that plans to increase support for the city's premier art institutions, "possibly by cutting support for lesser ones," was met with "anger and trepidation" by politicians and "members of the arts community."

Any plan for supporting only the best [art] is automatically denounced as "elitist." Finally, it is said that refusal to subsidize the most marginal art is a sin against "diversity."

Mr. Will concludes that "subsidized arts are pork for the articulate, for people nimble and noisy in presenting their employment or entertainment as an entitlement."

Get into groups of five and discuss the pros and cons of taxpayer subsidies for the National Endowment for the Arts. See if you can reach a consensus about this.

2. Self-Disclosure Exercise

Pair off with someone you feel close to. Begin to talk about the topics listed below.★ Feel free to stop if you feel the topics are too close for comfort. Take turns discussing each topic before moving on to the next topic.

a.   Your hobbies and interests

b.   Your attitude toward your body—likes and dislikes

c.   Your family's financial status

d.   Attitudes toward your parents and others in your family

e.   Attitudes toward religion

f.   Your love life, past and present

g.   Personal problems that really concern you

h.   How you react to your partner on the basis of this exercise

---

★The topics are similar to those developed by Sidney Jourard (1964) and published in *Self-Disclosure: An Experimental Analysis of the Transparent Self* (New York: Wiley, 1971), pp. 177–178.

3. Member Roles Exercise

Have a group discussion using the fishbowl format (a group of observers surrounding a group of discussants). Try to identify the roles each member plays by placing a check mark in the appropriate box in the chart shown in Figure 5.8. These observations should be fed back to the group members and discussed in a supportive way. For a variation, some group members can be briefed in advance to act out certain roles to test the observers' abilities to recognize the behavior.

FIGURE 5.8   MEMBER ROLES EXERCISE CHART

Roles / Members	A	B	C	D	E	F	G	H
Group Task Roles:								
1. Initiator-contributor								
2. Information seeker								
3. Information giver								
4. Coordinator								
5. Orientor								
6. Evaluator								
7. Energizer								
8. Opinion giver								
Group-building Roles:								
9. Encourager								
10. Harmonizer								
11. Compromiser								
12. Gatekeeper and exploiter								
13. Standard setter								
14. Follower								
Self-centered Roles:								
15. Aggressor								
16. Blocker								
17. Recognition seeker								
18. Playboy (playgirl)								
19. Dominator								
20. Help seeker								

Much has been written about the importance of developing a supportive style of personal communication in and outside small groups. In the first article, Ellis and Fisher demonstrate the successes that occurred from using certain communication behaviors.

Jack Gibb offers valuable insights in the second article, "Defensive Communication." Many discussions have gone astray because of this problem. Both articles go further into topics discussed in the body of the chapter.

Communication-based Qualities of Effective Groups

Donald G. Ellis and B. Aubrey Fisher

In a series of studies, Hirokawa and his associates set out to identify those qualities of groups that are most associated with effective decision making. They found a number of communication characteristics that separate effective from ineffective groups. The following are the most important characteristics of effective groups:

1. *Groups perform better when their members vigorously evaluate the validity of each other's opinions and assumptions.* Effective groups clarify, modify, and test the opinions of their members; ineffective groups gloss over the opinions of their members. Hirokawa found that whenever a member made a point in an effective group, some other group member would question the point and seek additional specificity and justification. Such communication patterns are quite prevalent in effective groups. Here is an example:

   Bill: The city council will not support the building application because they are concerned about traffic congestion.
   Sue: Really? Why do you say that?

From Donald G. Ellis and B. Aubrey Fisher, Small Group Decision Making: Communication and the Group Process, *4th ed. (New York: McGraw-Hill, 1994), pp. 277–280. Reprinted by permission of McGraw-Hill.*

Bill: Well, they haven't voted on it, but that's what I think.

Jim: Why do you think that? Did you read it somewhere or hear something about it?

Bill: No, not really.

In this example we can see that Sue and Jim challenged the quality of Bill's assertion. They did not let his statement that the city council "will not support the application" enter the group as a fact. Groups that make faulty decisions would not have challenged the statement, but would have proceeded as if Bill's assumptions about the city council were true.

2. *Effective groups provide a thorough and rigorous evaluation of decision alternatives.* Members of effective groups carefully test their decision alternatives. They match the alternatives against the group's preestablished decision criteria and critically evaluate each alternative in the same manner that they evaluate the opinions and assumptions of their fellow members. Forcing themselves to consider all aspects of an alternative, they ask whether or not it is fair, warranted, appropriate, reasonable, etc., to ensure that they have examined it adequately, and they analyze its potential consequences by asking such questions as "What is likely to happen if we implement this decision?" Ineffective groups do not discuss consequences; they go through a superficial discussion of alternatives and tend to settle on one alternative quickly. Here is an example of a superficial evaluation of a decision alternative:

John: Shall we propose the parking lot to the city council?

Ann: Can we justify it?

John: Yeah, we have all the data we have been collecting and it is possible to make the case.

Pete: How about the fairness issue? Do we think that is the best way to use the space?

Al: Yeah, sure.

John: Sounds good to me.

Al: Let's go for it.

This group never really discussed the implications of its decision and therefore never uncovered any problems. The decision was ineffective and unrealistic because the members did not know enough about the problem they were trying to solve.

3. *Decision quality depends on the accuracy of the premises the group uses.* Hirokawa and Pace stated that this is a very important insight that resulted from their work. They found that high-quality groups use facts and inferences that are accurate and reasonable. This is easier to say than it is to do; many people get confused over what constitutes an accurate fact and an intelligent inference. Nevertheless, these skills

can be learned. And the facts and inferences improve when the group is critical and evaluative, practicing the first two characteristics of effective groups discussed above.

4. *The nature of the influential members' influence affects the quality of a group's decision.* All groups have some members who exert considerable influence over the thinking of others by moving the group in certain directions. A group becomes effective when this influence is positive and facilitative, but a negative and inhibitory influence makes a group ineffective.

Positive contributions by influential members include such communicative behaviors as asking appropriate questions, introducing important information, challenging and persuading the group to dismiss unwarranted and questionable information, and keeping the group from digressing. In the group discussing the parking lot proposal, an influential member later asked pertinent questions about the proposal, such as "Where will it be located, what is there now, are there any other planned uses for the space, what will the community think, and are there important aesthetic issues?" These and other such questions forced the group to address many important issues, and this helped it reach a high-quality decision.

Negative contributions by influential members include introducing and supporting erroneous facts and assumptions, getting the group to accept poor information, making ridiculous suggestions, and distracting the group by leading it off in irrelevant directions. An influential member who makes negative contributions is a special problem when he or she is socially attractive. Although the members may like a person who is funny, pleasant, or otherwise appealing, these qualities alone do not make a person an effective task specialist. A group experiences the problems of ineffective groups when a socially attractive member who makes negative contributions exerts too much influence over the group's decision-making process.

Summary

Developing effective communication within a group is not easy. There are no surefire principles for improving communication and group effectiveness. Such improvement ultimately requires a thorough understanding of communication and the group process. Misconceptions to be avoided include the naive assumption of human rationality and an overreliance on agendas.

Improving effectiveness depends on a number of interrelated attitudinal, interpersonal, and group-identity factors. Attitudinal factors involve each members' attitudes toward the group and toward group interaction, along with each individual member's creativity, critical ability, and honesty. Interpersonal factors include active verbal participation, communication skills, the use of supportive communication, and sensitivity when responding to others. When identifying with the group as a whole, effective members develop a sensitivity to the group process, a commitment to the group, and a reasonable attitude toward group slowness. Most important, perhaps, effective group communication often benefits from group members' engaging in interaction that is directed specifically at self-analysis, concentrating specifically on critical episodes from the group's history of past interactions.

Defensive Communication

Jack R. Gibb

One way to understand communication is to view it as a people process rather than as a language process. If one is to make fundamental improvement in communication, he must make changes in interpersonal relationships. One possible type of alteration—and the one with which this paper is concerned—is that of reducing the degree of defensiveness.

Definition and Significance

Defensive behavior is defined as that behavior which occurs when an individual perceives threat or anticipates threat in the group. The person who behaves defensively, even though he also gives some attention to the common task, devotes an appreciable portion of his energy to defending himself. Besides talking about the topic, he thinks about how he appears to others, how he may be seen more favorably, how he may win, dominate, impress, or escape punishment and/or how he may avoid or mitigate a perceived or an anticipated attack.

Such inner feelings and outward acts tend to create similarly defensive postures in others; and, if unchecked, the ensuing circular response becomes increasingly destructive. Defensive behavior, in short, engenders defensive

Reproduced from The Journal of Communication, Vol. 11, No. 3, Copyright, September 1961, pp. 141–148. Reprinted by permission of the International Communication Association.

listening, and this in turn produces postural, facial, and verbal cues which raise the defense level of the original communicator.

Defense arousal prevents the listener from concentrating upon the message. Not only do defensive communicators send off multiple value, motive, and affect cues, but also defensive recipients distort what they receive. As a person becomes more and more defensive, he becomes less and less able to perceive accurately the motives, the values, and the emotions of the sender. The writer's analyses of tape-recorded discussions revealed that increases in defensive behavior were correlated positively with losses in efficiency in communication.[1] Specifically, distortions became greater when defensive states existed in the groups.

The converse, moreover, also is true. The more "supportive" or defense reductive the climate, the less the receiver reads into the communication distorted loadings which arise from projections of his own anxieties, motives, and concerns. As defenses are reduced, the receivers become better able to concentrate upon the structure, the content, and the cognitive meanings of the message.

Categories of Defensive and Supportive Communication

In working over an eight-year period with recordings of discussions occurring in varied settings, the writer developed the six pairs of defensive and supportive categories presented in Table 1. Behavior which a listener perceives as possessing any of the characteristics listed in the left-hand column arouses defensiveness, whereas that which he interprets as having any of the qualities designated as supportive reduces defensive feelings. The degree to which these reactions occur depends upon the personal level of defensiveness and on the general climate in the group at the time.[2]

TABLE 1   CATEGORIES OF BEHAVIOR CHARACTERISTICS OF SUPPORTIVE AND DEFENSIVE CLIMATES IN SMALL GROUPS

Defensive Climates	Supportive Climates
1. Evaluation	1. Description
2. Control	2. Problem orientation
3. Strategy	3. Spontaneity
4. Neutrality	4. Empathy
5. Superiority	5. Equality
6. Certainty	6. Provisionalism

Evaluation and Description

Speech or other behavior which appears evaluative increases defensiveness. If by expression, manner of speech, tone of voice, or verbal content the sender seems to be evaluating or judging the listener, then the receiver goes on guard. Of course, other factors may inhibit the reaction. If the listener thought that the speaker regarded him as an equal and was being open and spontaneous, for example, the evaluativeness in a message would be neutralized and perhaps not even perceived. This same principle applies equally to the other five categories of potentially defense-producing climates. The six sets are interactive.

Because our attitudes toward other persons are frequently evaluative, it is difficult to form expressions which the defensive person will regard as nonjudgmental. Even the simplest question usually conveys the answer that the sender wishes or implies the response that would fit into his value system. A mother, for example, immediately following an earth tremor that shook the house, sought for her small son with the question: "Bobby, where are you?" The timid and plaintive "Mommy, I didn't do it" indicated how Bobby's chronic mild defensiveness predisposed him to react with a projection of his own guilt and in the context of his chronic assumption that questions are full of accusation.

Anyone who has attempted to train professionals to use information-seeking speech with neutral affect appreciates how difficult it is to teach a person to say even the simple "who did that?" without being seen as accusing. Speech is so frequently judgmental that there is a reality base for the defensive interpretations which are so common.

When insecure, group members are particularly likely to place blame, to see others as fitting into categories of good or bad, to make moral judgments of their colleagues, and to question the value, motive, and affect loadings of the speech which they hear. Since value loadings imply a judgment of others, a belief that the standards of the speaker differ from his own causes the listener to become defensive.

Descriptive speech, in contrast to that which is evaluative, tends to arouse a minimum of uneasiness. Speech acts which the listener perceives as genuine requests for information or as material with neutral loadings is descriptive. Specifically, presentations of feelings, events, perceptions, or processes which do not ask or imply that the receiver change behavior or attitude are minimally defense producing. The difficulty in avoiding overtone is illustrated by the problems of news reporters in writing stories about unions, communists, Negroes, and religious activities without tipping off the "party" line of the newspaper. One can often tell from the opening words in a news article which side the newspaper's editorial policy favors.

Control and Problem Orientation

Speech which is used to control the listener evokes resistance. In most of our social intercourse someone is trying to do something else—to change an attitude, to influence behavior, or to restrict the field of activity. The degree to which attempts to control produce defensiveness depends upon the openness of the effort, for a suspicion that hidden motives exist heightens resistance. For this reason, attempts of nondirective therapists and progressive educators to refrain from imposing a set of values, a point of view, or a problem solution upon the receivers meet with many barriers. Since the norm is control, noncontrollers must earn the perceptions that their efforts have no hidden motives. A bombardment of persuasive "messages" in the fields of politics, education, special causes, advertising, religion, medicine, industrial relations, and guidance has bred cynical and paranoidal responses in listeners.

Implicit in all attempts to alter another person is the assumption by the change agent that the person to be altered is inadequate. That the speaker secretly views the listener as ignorant, unable to make his own decisions, uninformed, immature, unwise, or possessed of wrong or inadequate attitudes is a subconscious perception which gives the latter a valid base for defensive reactions.

Methods of control are many and varied. Legalistic insistence on detail, restrictive regulations and policies, conformity norms, and all laws are among the methods. Gestures, facial expression, other forms of nonverbal communication, and even such simple acts as holding a door open in a particular manner are means of imposing one's will upon another and hence are potential sources of resistance.

Problem orientation, on the other hand, is the antithesis of persuasion. When the sender communicates a desire to collaborate in defining a mutual problem and in seeking its solution, he tends to create the same problem orientation in the listener; and, of greater importance, he implies that he has no predetermined solution, attitude, or method to impose. Such behavior is permissive in that it allows the receiver to set his own goals, make his own decisions, and evaluate his own progress or to share with the sender in doing so. The exact methods of attaining permissiveness are not known, but they must involve a constellation of cues and they certainly go beyond mere verbal assurances that the communicator has no hidden desires to exercise control.

Strategy and Spontaneity

When the sender is perceived as engaging in a stratagem involving ambiguous and multiple motivators, the receiver becomes defensive. No one wishes to be a guinea pig, a role player, or an impressed actor, and no one likes to be the victim of some hidden motivation. That which is concealed, also, may appear larger than it really is with the degree of defensiveness of the listener determining the perceived size of the suppressed element. The intense reaction of the reading audience to the material in *The Hidden Persuaders* indicates the prevalence of defensive reactions to multiple motivations behind strategy. Group members who are seen as "taking a role," as feigning emotion, as toying with their colleagues, as withholding information, or as having special sources of data are especially resented. One participant once complained that another was "using a listening technique" on him!

A large part of the adverse reaction to much of the so-called human relations training is a feeling against what are perceived as gimmicks and tricks to fool or to "involve" people, to make a person think he is making his own decision, or to make the listener feel that the sender is genuinely interested in him as a person. Particularly violent reactions occur when it appears that someone is trying to make a stratagem appear spontaneous. One person has reported a boss who incurred resentment by habitually using the gimmick of "spontaneously" looking at his watch and saying, "My gosh, look at the time—I must run to an appointment." The belief was that the boss would create less irritation by honestly asking to be excused.

Similarly, the deliberate assumption of guilelessness and natural simplicity is especially resented. Monitoring the tapes of feedback and evaluation sessions in training groups indicates the surprising extent to which members perceive the strategies of their colleagues. This perceptual clarity may be quite shocking to the strategist, who usually feels that he has cleverly hidden the motivational aura around the "gimmick."

This aversion to deceit may account for one's resistance to politicians who are suspected of behind-the-scenes planning to get his vote, to psychologists whose listening apparently is motivated by more than the manifest or content-level interest in his behavior, or to the sophisticated, smooth, or clever person whose "oneupmanship" is marked with guile. In training groups the role-flexible person frequently is resented because his changes in behavior are perceived as strategic maneuvers.

In contrast, behavior which appears to be spontaneous and free of deception is defense reductive. If the communicator is seen as having a clean id, as having uncomplicated motivations, as being straightforward and honest, and as behaving spontaneously in response to the situation, he is likely to arouse minimal defense.

Neutrality and Empathy

When neutrality in speech appears to the listener to indicate a lack of concern for his welfare, he becomes defensive. Group members usually desire to be perceived as valued persons, as individuals of speech worth, and as objects of concern and affection. The clinical, detached, person-is-an-object-of-study attitude on the part of many psychologist-trainers is resented by group members. Speech with low affect that communicates little warmth or caring is in such contrast with the affect laden speech in social situations that it sometimes communicates rejection.

Communication that conveys empathy for the feelings and respect for the worth of the listener, however, is particularly supportive and defense reductive. Reassurance results when a message indicates that the speaker identifies himself with the listener's problems, shares his feelings, and accepts his emotional reaction at face value. Abortive efforts to deny the legitimacy of the receiver's emotions by assuring the receiver that he need not feel bad, that he should not feel rejected or that he is overly anxious, though often intended as support giving, may impress the listener as lack of acceptance. The combination of understanding and empathizing with other person's emotions with no accompanying effort to change him apparently is supportive at a high level.

The importance of gestural behavior cues in communicating empathy should be mentioned. Apparently spontaneous facial and bodily evidences of concern are often interpreted as especially valid evidence of deep-level acceptance.

Superiority and Equality

When a person communicates to another that he feels superior in position, power, wealth, intellectual ability, physical characteristics, or other ways, he arouses defensiveness. Here, as with the other sources of disturbance, whatever arouses feelings of inadequacy causes the listener to center upon the affect loading of the statement rather than upon the cognitive elements. The receiver then reacts by not hearing the message, by forgetting it, by competing with the sender, or by becoming jealous of him.

The person who is perceived as feeling superior communicates that he is not willing to enter into a shared problem-solving relationship, that he probably does not desire feedback, that he does not require help, and/or that he will be likely to try to reduce the power, the status, or the worth of the receiver.

Many ways exist for creating the atmosphere that the sender feels himself equal to the listener. Defenses are reduced when one perceives the sender as being willing to enter into participative planning with mutual trust and respect. Differences in talent, ability, worth, appearance, status, and power often exist, but the low defense communicator seems to attach little importance to these distinctions.

Certainty and Provisionalism

The effects of dogmatism in producing defensiveness are well known. Those who seem to know the answers, to require no additional data, and to regard themselves as teachers rather than as co-workers tend to put others on guard. Moreover, in the writer's experiment, listeners often perceived manifest expressions of certainty as connoting inward feelings of inferiority. They saw the dogmatic individual as needing to be right, as wanting to win an argument rather than solve a problem, and as seeing his ideas as truths to be defended. This kind of behavior often was associated with acts which others regarded as attempts to exercise control. People who were right seemed to have low tolerance for members who were "wrong"—i.e., who did not agree with the sender.

One reduces the defensiveness of the listener when he communicates that he is willing to experiment with his own behavior, attitudes, and ideas. The person who appears to be taking provisional attitudes, to be investigating issues rather than taking sides on them, to be problem solving rather than debating, and to be willing to experiment and explore tends to communicate that the listener may have some control over the shared quest or the investigation of the ideas. If a person is genuinely searching for information and data, he does not resent help or company along the way.

Conclusion

The implications of the above material for the parent, the teacher, the manager, the administrator, or the therapist are fairly obvious. Arousing defensiveness interferes with communication and thus makes it difficult—and sometimes impossible—for anyone to convey ideas clearly and to move effectively toward the solution of therapeutic, educational, or managerial problems.

Notes

1. J. R. Gibb, "Defense Level and Influence Potential in Small Groups," in L. Petrullo and B. M. Bass (eds.), *Leadership and Interpersonal Behavior* (New York: Holt, Rinehart and Winston, Inc., 1961), pp. 66–81.

2. J. R. Gibb, "Sociopsychological Process of Group Instruction," in N. B. Henry (ed.), *The Dynamics of Instructional Groups* (Fifty-ninth Yearbook of the National Society for the Study of Education, Part II, 1960), pp. 115–135.

6

Conflict Resolution and Decision-Making Processes

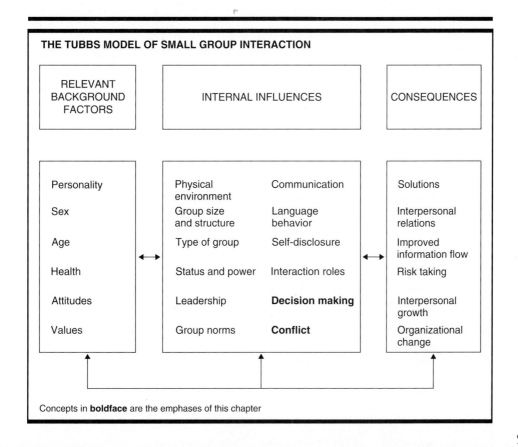

THE TUBBS MODEL OF SMALL GROUP INTERACTION

RELEVANT BACKGROUND FACTORS	INTERNAL INFLUENCES		CONSEQUENCES
Personality	Physical environment	Communication	Solutions
Sex	Group size and structure	Language behavior	Interpersonal relations
Age	Type of group	Self-disclosure	Improved information flow
Health	Status and power	Interaction roles	Risk taking
Attitudes	Leadership	**Decision making**	Interpersonal growth
Values	Group norms	**Conflict**	Organizational change

Concepts in **boldface** are the emphases of this chapter

PREVIEW

The internal influences of the Tubbs Model of Small Group Interaction are concluded in Chapter 6. Several different decision-making processes are presented. The reflective thinking process, which is left-brain-oriented, comprises several phases. The Kepner-Tregoe approach is based mainly on the criteria phase, such as musts and wants. The single question form, brainstorming, incrementalism, mixed scanning, and tacit bargaining are the other methods for decision making discussed in this chapter. The second part of Chapter 6 relates to conflicts, which arise often in groups. Sources and types of conflict are covered along with the undesirability of conflict. The final section places importance on working toward conflict resolution. The conflict grid is used as an illustration.

GLOSSARY

The Reflective Thinking Process: The reflective thinking process is a pattern for small group problem solving that includes six components:
(1) What is the problem?
(2) What are its causes and limits?
(3) What are the criteria for an acceptable solution?
(4) What are the available solutions?
(5) What is the best solution?
(6) How can it be implemented?

The Kepner-Tregoe Approach: This approach is a variation of the reflective thinking sequence. Its most important contribution is the way in which a group works through the criteria phase, differentiating between the musts and the wants of a solution.

The Single Question Form: The single question form is a brief method of group problem solving using the "single question" format.

Brainstorming: Brainstorming is a technique used to *generate* ideas. It emphasizes brain activity. It can be applied as part of the problem-solving process.

Incrementalism: Incrementalism is the process of making decisions that result in change.

Mixed Scanning: Mixed scanning is a decision-making strategy that combines examining a problem comprehensively (the rational approach) and part by part (the incremental approach).

Tacit Bargaining: Tacit bargaining is "bargaining in which communication is incomplete or impossible."

Each of the problem-solving methods described thus far (that is, reflective thinking, the Kepner-Tregoe approach, and the single question form) will probably offer you and your group a way to get better results than if you used no systematic method at all. Try using each of these methods in solving some of the problem exercises in this book. Don't give up—most problems can be solved if we work at them long enough.

Brainstorming

Another popular technique that can be applied to problem-solving is brainstorming (Osborn, 1953). This technique is primarily used to generate ideas and can be applied as *part* of the problem-solving process. It emphasizes right brain activity. For example, groups frequently dwell on one or two proposed solutions to a problem, when many more solutions may be available. Brainstorming would be one way to help generate more alternative solutions for the group to consider.

Brainstorming can be applied to any of the phases of the reflective thinking sequence discussed earlier. The problem identification phase includes the need to determine the factors causing the problem; the criteria phase requires identification of the requirements for an appropriate solution; the solution phase requires some alternatives from which to choose; and the implementation phase requires creative application of the chosen solution. The guidelines (adapted from Osborn, 1953) for using the brainstorming technique are listed below:

Rules for Brainstorming

1. *Put judgment and evaluation temporarily aside.*

   a. Acquire a "try anything" attitude.

   b. No faultfinding is allowed. It stifles ideas, halts association.

   c. Today's criticism may kill future ideas.

   d. All ideas are at least thought starters.

2. *Turn imagination loose, and start offering the results.*

   a. The wilder the ideas, the better.

   b. Ideas are easier to tame down than to think up.

   c. Freewheeling is encouraged; ideas can be brought down to earth later.

   d. A wild idea may be the only way to bring out another really good one.

3. *Think of as many ideas as you can.*

   a. Quantity breeds quality.

   b. The more ideas to choose from, the more chance of a good one.

   c. There is always more than one good solution to any problem.

    d. Try many different approaches.

4. *Seek combination and improvement.*

    a. Your ideas don't all have to be original.

    b. Improve on the ideas of others.

    c. Combine previously mentioned ideas.

    d. Brainstorming is a group activity. Take advantage of group association.

5. *Record all ideas in full view.*

6. *Evaluate at a later session.*

    a. Approach each idea with a positive attitude.

    b. Give each idea a fair trial.

    c. Apply judgment gradually.

Osborn offers a few additional tips to further stimulate the creation of ideas (ideation). After ideas are generated, think of adding, subtracting, multiplying, and dividing as ways of modifying the ideas you already have. Effective toothpaste was improved by adding fluorides. Portable radios were made portable by subtracting size through the use of printed circuits. The common razor blade market was revamped by the creation of a double-edged razor (multiplying). General Motors decided to divide the production of the Oldsmobile Cutlass among several assembly plants, because the single plant at Lansing, Michigan, could not expand fast enough to keep up with demand.

Osborn's ideas have been updated by Sabatine (1989), who suggests the following practical tips for creatively brainstorming solutions:

- The "PMI" method—The next time someone presents a new idea or solution to you, think of all the pluses (P) of the idea, then all of the minuses (M), and finally, what is interesting (I) about the idea.

- Using humorous metaphors and analogies when speaking and writing—"That's like trying to sell anabolic steroids to the Incredible Hulk."

- Engaging in athletic activities, games, and hobbies, especially with children (e.g., "Pictionary").

- Practicing relaxation techniques and simple meditation to reduce stress and anxiety.

- Taking long walks, mowing the grass (incubating).

- Taking notice and discussing your "gut" feelings with others.

- Reviewing your problems or ideas before you fall asleep.

- Carrying a small notebook and recording your insights.

- Daydreaming regularly, engaging in detailed fantasizing and visualizing.

- Drawing and doodling when working on a problem.

Negotiations between union and management are often characterized by each side's making highly publicized statements of extreme positions in order to strengthen its respective bargaining position. Thus the union president will call for a minimum wage increase of 10 percent, and the company's representative will state flatly that 3 percent is all it can afford to give. In reality, both parties exaggerate their public position and privately acknowledge that a 6 or 7 percent agreement is what they are really trying to achieve.

If we assume that in these bargaining situations it would be naive to advise participants to simply "give in," still some reasonable suggestions can be made to increase the effectiveness of communication as well as the quality of decisions made. A good negotiator should learn to master the following abilities:

- Try to gauge your own strength or weakness:

    1. If you're strong, make sure your counterpart knows it.
    2. If you're weak, work hard to keep him from realizing it.

- Try to gauge your counterpart's actual strength or weakness.

- Surmise whether his perception of his strength or weakness accords with your reality:

    1. If your counterpart believes he's stronger than he actually is, educate him to the real facts.
    2. If he thinks he's weaker than he actually is, don't say a word. (Fruend, 1992, p. 46)

In concluding this section on problem solving, we should point out that, to some extent, the situation will affect the strategy of decision making chosen. In some situations one of the rational thinking approaches will be most appropriate; in other, more tentative, situations, the incremental approach may be preferable. The mixed-scanning strategy seems to have application in most situations, and in situations allowing little or no free communication among participants the tacit-bargaining strategy will be most likely. In using any strategy, you should know which one you are using and understand the underlying assumptions and requirements of each. You should also expect some problems with each and realize the communication requirements inherent in each. Also, as you attempt to make decisions, you will undoubtedly encounter many types of conflict, which is the subject of the next section.

CONFLICT AND CONFLICT RESOLUTION

It has been said that conflict is an inevitable part of people's relating to one another. Some would even go as far as to say that a conflict-free relationship is probably a sign that you really have no relationship at all. It has also been said that where there is movement, there is friction, and where there is friction, heat is produced. Certainly many small groups involve movement, especially if their task is to solve and act on problems. It appears obvious that in such cases the heat referred to is the emotional heat that results from conflicts. In fact, Wall et al. (1992) state:

"After 15 years of observation, we have reluctantly come to the conclusion that working together in harmony does not come naturally for human beings" (p. 132).

In our society, conflict is usually considered to be bad, that thing that results in wars, divorces, worker strikes, and bloody noses. However, most experts agree that conflict within and among groups has some *desirable* effects. Both the desirable and undesirable aspects of conflict will be discussed in this section. However, we look first at the sources from which conflicts arise.

Sources of Conflict

Conflict exists whenever incompatible activities occur. An incompatible action prevents, obstructs, interferes with, injures, or in some way reduces the effectiveness of the other action. Incompatible actions may occur within a single person (intrapersonal), a single group (intragroup), between two or more people (interpersonal), or between two or more groups (intergroup). Conflicts may originate from a number of different sources, including (1) differences in information, beliefs, values, interests, or desires; (2) a scarcity of some resource, such as money, power, time, space, or position; and (3) rivalries in which one person or group competes with another. To these sources could be added the difficulty of the task, the pressure to avoid failure, the relative importance of a group's or individual's decision, and differences in skill levels that may cause more skilled individuals to become irritated at the less skilled, which often leads to a reciprocal irritation. In an earlier chapter we discussed personality differences. These differences lead to incompatibilities among certain members of a group. Members may be incompatible because of their differences—or they may be incompatible because of their similarities, such as in the need to achieve or dominate others. All these factors tend to instigate conflict.

Desirability of Conflict

As mentioned above, many writers believe that conflict in a group is desirable. For example, in Chapter 4 we discussed the very real problem of groupthink, which can occur in any group. Conflict helps eliminate or reduce the likelihood of groupthink. Furthermore, Ramundo (1992) argues that conflict has other desirable functions, such as preventing stagnation; stimulating interest and curiosity; providing a medium through which problems can be aired and solutions arrived at; causing personal and social change; being part of the process of testing and assessing oneself and, as such, being highly enjoyable as one experiences the pleasure of full and active use of one's capacities; demarcating groups from one another and thus helping to establish group and personal identities; fostering internal cohesion in groups involved in external conflicts; resolving tension among individuals and thus stabilizing and integrating relationships; eliminating sources of dissatisfaction in social systems by permitting immediate and direct resolution of rival claims; revitalizing existing group norms or helping the emergence of new norms in order to adjust adequately to new conditions; and ascertaining the relative strengths of antagonistic interests within a social system, thereby constituting a mechanism for the maintenance or continual readjustment of the balance of power.

Alfred Sloan was one of the early executives who helped make General Motors successful. He recognized the importance of idea conflict in decision making. Once, Sloan was chairing a meeting of the GM board of directors in which someone presented an idea for buying a small company. After the presentation Sloan asked each member around the table for an opinion. Not one gave an objection to the proposal; they all agreed the company should buy at the earliest possible moment. Finally, Sloan looked at the other board members and said: "Gentlemen, I don't see any reason not to adopt the idea either. Therefore, I suggest we postpone this decision for thirty days while we do some more thinking." Thirty days later the board decided against the plan—after finding out many negatives they had not known earlier (Cosier and Schwenk, 1990, p. 69).

Conflict clearly plays an important role in small group interaction. However, it is a double-edged sword, as we shall see.

Types of Conflict

Many people fail to differentiate between two very different types of conflict— namely, *conflict of ideas* and *conflict of feelings* (often called personality conflict). As we saw in the example above, Alfred Sloan recognized the importance of idea conflict in making a decision. If there is too little conflict of ideas, groupthink can occur, as we saw in Chapter 4. Idea conflict, however, can very easily turn into conflict of feelings. We can call this personal conflict. Notice the difference between the conflicts in these two conversations in a group discussion:

Conversation 1

Judy: Why don't we have our next meeting at my sorority house?

Dave: I think the campus center meeting room might have fewer interruptions. I know how hard it is to have meetings at my fraternity house.

Conversation 2

Judy: Why don't we have our next meeting at my sorority house?

Dave: And have people interrupting us all the time? No, thanks, I'd rather meet in the campus center.

In the first situation there was a conflict of ideas. In the second, the conflict could have escalated to the personal level, depending on Judy's reaction. The personal animosity that may have been created by Dave is the kind that tends to get in the way of group success. As shown in Figure 6.5, our goal in using conflict successfully is to avoid turning idea opponents into personal opponents.

FIGURE 6.5   OPPOSITION AND SUPPORT

	Idea supporter	Idea opponent
Personal supporter	1 + +	2 + −
Personal opponent	3 − +	4 − −

Avoid turning idea opponents
into personal opponents

Undesirability of Conflict

Our society frequently considers conflict to be undesirable. Millions of dollars are lost each year because of work stoppages and strikes. Thousands of divorces result from unchecked marital conflicts. And every once in a while a disaster like the Los Angeles riots following the Rodney King verdict illustrate conflict that has gotten out of control. Even in meetings, discussions, and conferences, conflict may cause reactions similar to that of one student who said, "I don't even want to go to publication council meetings anymore. Every week it is just one hassle after another. Nothing ever gets accomplished because every time we end up arguing."

Conflicts are often hard to keep under control once they have begun. There is a definite trend toward escalation and polarization. Once conflict escalates to a point at which it is no longer under control, it almost always yields negative results. In this same vein, one conflict tends to lay the groundwork for further conflicts at a later time. Part of this is because of defensive reactions. Defensiveness leads us to distort our perceptions so that ambiguous acts are more frequently misconstrued as threatening when they may in fact not be intended that way.

Woolf (1990), in his book *Friendly Persuasion,* offers 101 tactics for negotiating and resolving conflict. Here are a few examples:

- Almost everything is negotiable.

- It doesn't hurt to ask.

- Don't be intimidated just because it's printed.

- Don't take anything personally.

- It never works for one . . . to insult another's intelligence.

- Start high but don't be ridiculous. (pp. 162–187)

Bazerman and Neale (1992) suggest that you ask yourself the following questions to avoid some of the most common mistakes made in negotiating:

FIGURE 6.7   A CONTINUUM OF DECISION-MAKING BEHAVIOR

From Stewart L. Tubbs, *Empowerment* (Ann Arbor, Mich.: U-Train, Inc., 1993), pp. 5–9. Adapted from R. Tannenbaum and H. W. Schmidt, "How to Choose a Leadership Pattern," *Harvard Business Review*, March–April 1958.

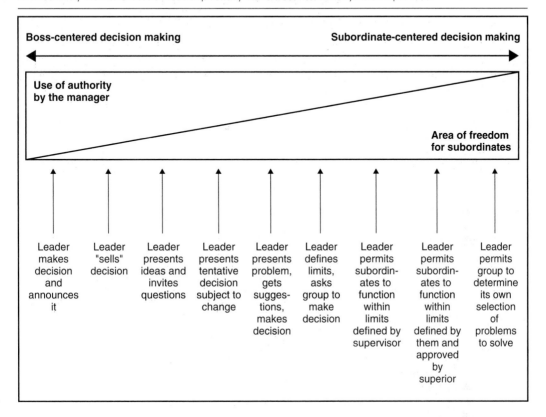

Consensus does not come quickly or easily. Agreement generally results from careful and thoughtful interpersonal communication between group members. If we are to achieve complete group consensus, some individual preferences of group members must be surrendered. The group as a whole must decide if consensus can be achieved. If several members are adamant in their positions and refuse to change their minds in agreement with the others, the group may decide that reaching complete consensus is not worth the effort. In this case it may be better to postpone the group decision—particularly if the group making the decision will also be implementing the decision. If several group members are not in favor of the solution, they will be less anxious to put it into practice.

Conflict resolution seems to improve as we engage in certain types of behaviors. These can be summarized as follows:

1. Focus on the problem, not on personalities.

2. Build on areas of agreement. Most groups have at least some positions or goals that are not mutually exclusive.

3. Attempt to achieve consensus. Try consensus testing by taking a nonbinding straw vote. Then discuss why the minority might be objecting to the decision.

4. Avoid provoking further conflict.

5. Don't overreact to the comments of others. Extreme statements on either side tend to destroy consensus and produce a "boomerang effect."

6. Consider compromise. This is often the best way to go from a win-lose to a win-win situation. (Borisoff and Victor, 1989)

Although these are not hard-and-fast rules, and they may not work in all cases, they should improve a group's chances of keeping conflict at a manageable level so that the group can move forward toward its goal.

Diane Yale (1988), a practicing lawyer and mediator, suggests that the way we think about conflict has a tremendous effect on how we go about trying to resolve it. For instance, if we think about conflict and conflict resolution as a battle to be won or lost, then we go into the situation ready to fight or surrender (depending on our position). She outlines three approaches to conflict that occur in the form of metaphor: the competitive, adversarial metaphor; the problem-solving metaphor; and the creative orientation. In these metaphors, three different ways of thinking about and approaching conflict are presented.

The *competitive, adversarial metaphor* often results in a winner and loser in the resolution process. Yale developed this metaphor as follows: "If your thought . . . is that [conflict] is a battleground, . . . a place where combat or contest is enacted, then someone will be breathing fire, trying to engulf the process in that idiom, and trying to singe and consume us with flame" (p. 18). If group members approach conflict in this way, cohesiveness is likely to suffer. Group members will be at odds with one another.

The *problem-solving metaphor* can lead to frustration among group members. The resolution process can become a burden, and group members are less likely to be satisfied with the results. Yale developed the problem-solving metaphor in the following way: "Something that is problematic is something that is open to doubt, debatable, uncertain, difficult to solve. A problematist is one who is preoccupied with problems. . . . If your [conflict] is focused on problem-solving, everything that comes at you . . . is seen as a problem or a solution. Often your solutions create more problems. . . . In this metaphor, you work hard" (p. 19).

The *creative orientation,* aside from being the preferred model of conflict, brings an innovative quality to group conflict resolution. The emphasis of creative orientation is to design a new reality consistent with the values of the group members and large enough to include the visions of all the parties involved. Yale's own metaphor for this approach to conflict is that of a garden: "If being in a garden were your metaphoric purpose, nurturing would be among the first thoughts that would come to mind—preparing the ground, planting seeds and seedlings, caring for them while they grow, blossom and mature. . . . You may have to prune away or pinch back or thin out so that you get sturdier, healthier lovelier growth. There is a cycle of growth and decay. You do not try to hold on to what is no longer in season, you go on to the next season" (p. 22).

THE SYSTEMS PERSPECTIVE

In this chapter we have examined the very difficult task of improving our ability to make decisions. Most untrained groups do not follow a disciplined path toward a decision. Instead, we frequently find ourselves either off the track or bogged down in conflicts that keep us from accomplishing a task. The focus in this chapter has been biased toward problem-solving groups. However, other types of groups also have to make decisions and deal with conflicts. Certainly these issues arise for families, learning groups (as we saw in the case at the beginning of this chapter), social groups planning events, and work groups solving organizational problems. Conflict, too, is present in each of these types of groups.

It is probably apparent by now that the decision-making process in most groups can be improved. In this chapter we examined seven alternative problem-solving strategies: (1) the reflective thinking process, (2) the Kepner-Tregoe approach, (3) the single question form, (4) brainstorming, (5) incrementalism, (6) mixed scanning, and (7) tacit bargaining. You might want to become familiar enough with all of these methods so that you would be able to use whichever one seems most appropriate for a given problem and a given group. Again, this illustrates the systems principle of *equifinality* in that several alternative methods may be used to reach the same desired end result—namely, the solution to the group's problem.

By now you may have wondered how one *does* decide which of the seven problem-solving strategies to use. Should you use a rational strategy, such as the reflective thinking process or brainstorming, or should you use incrementalism or tacit bargaining? The systems perspective suggests that the appropriateness of any method will depend on the demands of the specific situation. Therefore we need to be familiar with all the alternatives in order to increase our tool kit of behavioral science "tools."

The rational problem-solving methods work well in most cases but seem particularly suited to an autonomous group trying to satisfy its own needs while being allowed to do so by a democratic leader. By comparison, governmental groups are not autonomous and must answer to the taxpayers. Thus incrementalism may be appropriate, because major changes may be demanded without the luxury of enough time to gather exhaustive amounts of data on the problem. It's a little like the old story that when you are up to your hips in a swamp full of alligators, you don't want a systematic estimate of the probability of danger; you want somebody to throw you a rope!

Tacit bargaining seems to be primarily appropriate in the mixed-motive situations we described earlier. Notice the assumptions and viewpoints expressed in the following quotations: Karrass (1993), in his book on negotiating, writes, "In a successful negotiation both parties gain, but more often than not one party wins more than the other" (p. 6).] In a similar vein, Korda (1975) writes, "No matter who you are, the basic truth is that your interests are nobody else's concern, your gain is inevitably someone else's loss, your failure someone else's victory" (p. 4). The viewpoint expressed in these two quotations indicates some of the attitudes and values relevant to the mixed-motive situation. These statements also describe the outcomes or consequences of bargaining types of problem-solving situations. Obviously, such competitive situations suggest very different communication behaviors and skills than would the encounter group, which stresses trust, mutual self-disclosure, and risk taking. Thus the demands of the situation will play a great part in suggesting which problem-solving strategy we will want to employ.

The second part of this chapter dealt with conflict and conflict resolution. It should be emphasized that conflict may have some desirable consequences for the group. However, conflict that gets out of control may be destructive. Also, conflict between ideas is usually more productive than conflict between personalities.

As for personality and its relation to conflict, we would expect more conflict-producing behaviors from those high in aggression, dominance, and need for autonomy. Conversely, we would expect less conflict and more conflict-resolving attempts from those high in need for affiliation and nurturance. Other background factors that would probably relate to conflict include the degree of difference or heterogeneity in group members' ages, sex, values, attitudes, and beliefs. Consistency theories would lead us to believe that the greater and more numerous these differences, the greater the group conflict and the lower the satisfaction level resulting from the discussions.

Perhaps one of the most important factors related to conflict is the style of leadership and the resulting group norms regarding conflict. In this chapter we examined Blake and Mouton's Conflict Grid and Tubbs's (1993a) tells, sells, consults, and joins model. Both models seem to suggest practical methods for developing some leadership expertise in resolving conflicts.

EXERCISES

1. Problem-Solving Discussion Assignment

Each group should decide on a topic and should formulate a discussion question that cannot be answered yes or no. A sample question would be "What can be done about the problem of current marijuana laws?" This form of discussion question is preferable, because it poses a problem to be answered by the group. A less desirable discussion question would be "Should marijuana be decriminalized?" Notice that this question can be answered yes or no and is less open-ended and, therefore, less helpful in prompting discussion.

Each group may want to gather some preliminary information on the topic. (This is optional.) Select a moderator, and work up an agenda for your discussion, including the following:

a. Define the nature and limits of the problem. *Analyze* causes and important aspects of the problem.

b. Determine the criteria by which to judge an acceptable solution to the problem.

FIGURE 6.10   "WIN AS MUCH AS YOU CAN" TALLY SHEET

Round	Strategy Time Allowed	Strategy Confer With	Choice	$ Won	$ Lost	$ Balance	
1	2 min.	Partner					
2	1 min.	Partner					
3	1 min.	Partner					
4	1 min.	Partner					
5	3 min. + 1 min.	Cluster Partner					Bonus round: pay is multiplied by 3
6	1 min.	Partner					
7	1 min.	Partner					
8	3 min. + 1 min.	Cluster Partner					Bonus round: pay is multiplied by 5
9	1 min.	Partner					
10	3 min. + 1 min.	Cluster Partner					Bonus round: pay is multiplied by 10

2 X's:	Win	$2.00 each
2 Y's:	Lose	$2.00 each
1 X:	Win	$3.00
3 Y's:	Lose	$1.00 each
4 Y's:	Win	$1.00 each

4. When all votes are collected, the timekeeper will announce the total vote but *will not* disclose how each individual team voted.

5. As shown on the tally sheet, you will have two minutes to cast your vote for the first round. For all the other rounds, you will have one minute to cast your vote, except for rounds 5, 8, and 10, which are bonus rounds.

6. During each bonus round your team will select as many representatives as it wishes to send to a meeting of the teams. The representa-

tives from all teams will then meet separately for three minutes to discuss their strategy.

7. After the representatives have met, your team will then have one minute to make its final decision about your vote. At the end of each round, when all the votes are in, you will be told the total outcome of the vote (2 X's, 2 Y's; 4 Y's; and so on).

8. There are three key rules to keep in mind:
   a. You are not to talk to the other teams or signal them in any way. You may communicate with them but only during rounds 5, 7, and 10 through your representatives.
   b. All members of your team should agree on your team's vote or at least be willing to go along with it.
   c. Your team's vote must be reported on a small slip of paper when it is called for at the end of each round.

5. Conflict Resolution Exercise: "Gun Control"

Read the following excerpts from an article on gun control.

*POLL FINDS WIDE SUPPORT FOR TIGHTER CONTROL ON GUNS**
By LAWRENCE L. KNUTSON

The *USA Today*-CNN-Gallup Poll found that six out of 10 people oppose an outright ban on handguns, but the reverse was true when questions referred to "cheap" handguns.

The poll comes a day after the *USA Today*, the nation's second-largest daily after the *Wall Street Journal*, devoted a significant portion of the paper to articles focusing on gun violence in America.

. . . 15,377 people were killed in firearms homicides in 1992—12,489 of them with handguns. That is twice the number killed by handguns in 1966. . . . Homicides among Americans under 18 rose by 143 percent over six years, from 602 deaths in 1986 to 1,468 in 1992.

On the other hand, the National Rifle Association argues that every citizen has the right to bear arms. If you add laws limiting these rights, only those who obey the laws will be affected. Those who are criminals will continue to have and use guns.

Get into groups of five and discuss this controversy. See if you can reach consensus in your group. Each group should report the results of its discussion to the class.

From *The Ann Arbor News*, December 30, 1993, p. A1.

READINGS: OVERVIEW

Probably one of the most troublesome issues in small group interaction is how to resolve conflicts. In the first article Martin discusses the application of team concepts from sports to all teams.

The second article, by Acuff, describes several methods for improving conflict-reduction skills. In this article, he shows how conflict can be managed more effectively across cultures. Both articles provide a useful extension of the ideas presented in the chapter.

TeamThink

Don Martin

By conducting only meetings that are necessary, well prepared, and well organized, you set the pattern for business efficiency throughout your organization.

Antony Jay, chairman of London's Video Arts Ltd., says, "Certainly a great many meetings waste a great deal of everyone's time and seem to be held for historical rather than practical reasons; many long-established committees are little more than memorials to dead problems."

Effective meetings serve a number of worthwhile functions. First, they give your staff a chance to be brought up to date, as a group, on what's happening. Second, meetings can become a main focal point for decision-making where consensus is necessary. Finally, meetings can create a commitment to decisions which become binding on the group.

But too often meetings are unproductive and waste valuable time for everyone. A survey of 200 executives conducted by Accountemps indicated that executives waste an average of 288 hours a year attending unnecessary meetings. Here are some suggestions on meetings that can help you use time more effectively and productively.

- *Start every meeting on time.* If all your staffers aren't present, they will be for the next one. Notre Dame's Lou Holtz says, "I normally will walk into a meeting at precisely the proper time. The first thing we do on a

From Don Martin, TeamThink *(New York: Dutton, 1993).*

continuous basis is set our watches. We go by LLH time. This stands for 'Louis Leo Holtz' time."

When Vince Lombardi coached Green Bay, he instituted "Lombardi time," which meant fifteen minutes early. Often when the team bus was scheduled to leave at 10:00, he would direct the driver to pull out at 9:45. If you missed the bus, you had to find your own way of catching up with the team.

General Electric's Medical Health Group in Milwaukee always has one less chair in the room than people invited to the meeting. The purpose is to get people to the meetings on time.

The CEO of Southland Corp., which operates the 7-Eleven stores, starts every meeting at seven or eleven minutes *after* the hour. The CEO figures the odd starting time ups the chances of punctual attendance.

- *Clearly define the purpose of the meeting.* If you can't state the purpose, don't have the meeting. Recognize that there are two types of meetings—the kind where ideas are generated and the kind where decisions are made. It's difficult to mix the two successfully.

- *Always have an agenda.* The agenda should be completed and distributed enough in advance that all participants can prepare for the meeting.

  High-priority items should appear first on the agenda. The early part of a meeting tends to be livelier and more energetic. The top of the meeting is also the place to approach the tough problems—you'll have the time to deal with them.

  The more detailed the agenda, the better everyone can prepare. Terms such as "discuss new venture" are too vague.

- *Control the timing of the meeting.* Besides setting the starting time, it's important to fix the ending time. *You* control the meeting so that it ends on schedule. The participants will appreciate this; they have their own schedules to maintain. Set a time limit beforehand on discussion of less important items on the agenda.

  If meetings have gone on too long in the past, try scheduling them one hour before lunch or one hour before the end of the day. Everyone will develop a strong motivation to see them end.

- *Limit the number of meetings within a certain period.* Don't schedule several meetings consecutively. People need mental breaks, time to deal with their own pressing issues and return important phone calls. If possible, limit your normal meetings to one hour.

  Check the meeting schedules of your key managers. Holding too many meetings in a short time makes it difficult for them to prepare and may disrupt their own work patterns.

- *Never leave a meeting without writing a list that defines all actions agreed upon.* Send it to all attendees, asking for additions or corrections. This way, everyone essentially signs off on the list and acknowledges the actions and deadlines.

- *All potential interruptions should be eliminated.* Telephone calls to participants, papers to be signed, or people walking in with questions should only be allowed if the situation absolutely cannot wait until the end of the meeting.

- *Use breakfast and lunch for meetings with people in your firm.* Breakfast meetings have a built-in deadline, as most people are anxious to get back to their offices. Since it's the first meeting of the day, people are fresh and focused. I've found breakfasts seem to be more oriented to specific business problems, while lunches seem to focus on more general topics and building personal and social relationships. In both cases, the no-interruption rule must hold.

    Our boardroom often functions as a lunch-meeting room. My own office has a table and chairs that accommodate lunch for four. Lunch meetings there eliminate travel time and waiting in restaurants.

- *Schedule a meeting with yourself.* Create "discretionary" or "disposable" free time. This allows you to sit down and *think.* Management consultants McKinsey & Company, in a recent study titled "Leveraging CEO Time," recommended blocking out at least two "CEO Time Alone" sessions a week, each two hours long.

World-Class Negotiating Strategies

Frank L. Acuff

If I listen, I have the advantage: if I speak, others have it.

—From the Arabic

There are many negotiating strategies that tend to work very well in one culture but are ineffective in other cultures. A case in point is the Miami-based project manager who put together a very detailed, thorough, research-oriented proposal and presentation for his Brazilian client. "I felt good that we had done our homework," he later noted. "I was very disappointed,

From Frank L. Acuff, How to Negotiate Anything with Anyone Anywhere around the World *(New York: American Management Association, 1993).*

however, to find that the Brazilian representatives were flatly uninterested in the details I was prepared to explain. A similar approach worked extremely well in Germany only four months earlier."

In spite of the many different negotiating approaches required among cultures, there are five strategies that tend to be effective anywhere in the world. While there may be local variations in how these strategies are applied, their basic premises remain viable. . . .

Negotiating Strategies That Will Work Anywhere

The strategies that tend to be effective in negotiations throughout the world are as follows:

1. Plan the negotiation.

2. Adopt a win-win approach.

3. Maintain high aspirations.

4. Use language that is simple and accessible.

5. Ask lots of questions, then listen with your eyes and ears. . . .

Strategy 1: Plan the Negotiation

Everybody wants to get a good deal, to get a sizable share of the pie, and to feel good about the negotiation. Everybody wants to be a winner. Yet not everyone is willing to do the homework necessary to achieve these ends. . . . The essential steps necessary to plan your negotiation [are]: (1) identify all the issues; (2) prioritize the issues; (3) establish a settlement range; and (4) develop strategies and tactics. Make this preparation a habit and you will set the stage for getting what you want.

There are other factors to consider prior to global negotiations. You can use the Tune-Up Checklist to ensure that you put yourself in the strongest possible position before the negotiation.

THE TUNE-UP CHECKLIST: PRIOR TO THE NEGOTIATION

This is the data-gathering stage where you should get background information related to the other side (TOS), to his or her culture and its effects on the negotiating process, to TOS's organization and other potential players in the negotiation, and to the history of any past negotiations. *What do you know about:*

TOS
- [ ] Family status (e.g., married, single, children)?
- [ ] Leisure or recreational activities?
- [ ] Work habits (e.g., long hours, early to work)?
- [ ] Behavior style (e.g., perfectionist, "big picture"–oriented, task-oriented, people-oriented)?
- [ ] Number of years with current organization?
- [ ] Stability in current position?
- [ ] Overall reputation as a negotiator?
- [ ] What special interest groups might affect the negotiator?

TOS's Culture and Its Effects on Negotiations
- [ ] Are meetings likely to be punctual?
- [ ] What can you expect the pace of the negotiations to be?
- [ ] How important is "saving face" likely to be?
- [ ] Are differences of opinion likely to be emotional or argumentative?
- [ ] Will TOS bring a large team?
- [ ] Will you need an agent or interpreter?
- [ ] Should you prepare a formal agenda?

TOS's Organization
- [ ] What is the organization's main product or service?
- [ ] What is its past, present, and projected financial status?
- [ ] What organizational problems exist (e.g., downsizing, tough competition)?
- [ ] Who is TOS's boss, and what do you know about him or her?
- [ ] Is the organization under any time pressures?

Past Negotiations
- [ ] What were the subjects of past negotiations?
- [ ] What were the main obstacles and outcomes of the negotiations?
- [ ] What objections were raised?
- [ ] What strategies and tactics were used by TOS?
- [ ] How high were the initial offers compared with the eventual settlement?
- [ ] How was the outcome achieved, and over what period of time?

There are many ways to plan negotiations. One study identified five approaches skilled negotiators share when planning their negotiations:

1. They consider twice as wide a range of action options and outcomes as do less skilled negotiators.

2. They spend over three times as much attention on trying to find common ground with TOS.

3. They spend more than twice as much time on long-term issues.

4. They set range objectives (such as a target price of $50 to $60 per unit), rather than single-point objectives (e.g., $55). Ranges give negotiators flexibility.

5. They use "issue planning" rather than "sequence planning." That is, skilled negotiators discuss each issue independently rather than in a predetermined sequence or order of issues.[1]

Strategy 2: Adopt a Win-Win Approach

We don't adopt the win-win approach simply because we are wonderful human beings. It helps us get what we want. There is a difference between how skilled and unskilled negotiators prepare for the win-win approach. Skilled negotiators, for example, tend to spend less time on defense/attack behavior and in disagreement. They also tend to give more information about their feelings and have fewer arguments to back up their position.[2] This last point may seem odd. It might seem that the more arguments one has for one's position, the better. Skilled negotiators know, however, that having only a few strong arguments is more effective than having too many arguments. With too many arguments, weak arguments tend to dilute strong arguments, and TOS often feels pressured or manipulated into settlement.

To achieve a win-win situation, you must tune in to the frequency with which TOS can identify: WIIFT ("What's In It For Them"). This means different things in different cultures. For example, in Saudi Arabia a certain amount of haggling back and forth on terms may indicate your sincerity about striking a deal. To refuse a somewhat expressive give-and-take would be an insult to many Saudi negotiators. A Dallas-based, commercial building contractor now experienced in Saudi Arabia discovered this on his first trip there. "I really got off-base in our early discussions in Riyadh. I felt we were being extremely polite as we patiently explained the reasonableness of our proposal. We fell flat on our faces. The Saudis felt we were inflexible and not serious about doing business. The next project we bid had a lot of fat built into it. We haggled back and forth for four meetings, and they ended up loving us. That's what they wanted—someone to bargain with back and forth. It showed them we cared." This negotiator adds, "I still get a knot in my stomach sometimes when I go through a Saudi negotiation, but at least I know what works now."

Fortunately for this negotiator, he quickly learned the win-win approach for his Saudi client. Yet the very idea of haggling would be a sure win-lose proposition in many parts of the world. In England, for example, it would be hard to come up with a worse idea than to engage TOS in an emotional afternoon of haggling back and forth. The British idea of win-win is a somewhat formal, procedural, and detailed discussion of the facts.

Achieving a win-win result also requires careful scrutiny of both parties' overall goals. You may be seeking short-term profit and cash flow, while your Japanese counterparts may be more interested in long-term viability. In many cases, different goals *can* lead to overall win-win results. Consider the company president negotiating a joint venture in Hungary in order to take advantage of a skilled, inexpensive work force, while her TOS is motivated to find business linkages outside Eastern Europe.

Wherever you negotiate, focusing on win-win results sharply increases your chances for success, particularly in the long term.

Strategy 3: Maintain High Aspirations

In the spring of 1978, the International Air Transport Association (IATA) discontinued its policy of airline ticket price compliance. IATA had been for many years a powerful enforcer that had maintained a firm grip on the airline ticket prices of the world's domestic and international airlines. Immediately after this announcement was made, Leroy Black, my boss, suggested I contact the airlines to determine what, if any, ticket price concessions we might extract as a result of this policy change. The Middle East Division where we worked was located in Dubai, United Arab Emirates, a small oil sheikdom adjoining Saudi Arabia. Our 3,500 workers and many of their family members collectively logged millions of air miles per year.

"That's a good idea," I remember telling Leroy. Shaving 5 or 10 percent—perhaps even 15 percent—would amount to substantial savings on our $4 million annual airline expenses. I was stunned, though, when Leroy suggested we ask for a 50 percent price decrease in ticket costs.

"Are you kidding?" I asked, quite shocked.

"I think that 50 percent is about right," Leroy said serenely.

Our first appointment was with representatives from British Airways. They told us, in a reserved, nice kind of way, to take a hike.

Then KLM, in a *not* particularly nice kind of way, suggested the same recourse as British Airways. The same with Lufthansa. "We really are being a bit chintzy on this thing," I thought to myself.

"Leroy, let's try asking for a little less and see what happens," I suggested.

"I don't know. Let's hang in there awhile longer," Leroy insisted.

Next was Alitalia. As in our appointments with the other airlines, I went through a short prologue explaining the company's position, and assertively put forth that we would like to see a 50 percent reduction in future fares. This caused quite a commotion with the Alitalia representatives, who waved their arms and with great conviction gave us several reasons why this was not possible.

"This is really a little embarrassing," I thought.

They then asked if they could privately telephone their regional headquarters staff. They returned in about ten minutes in a solemn mood.

"Mr. Acuff," one of the representatives said with a grave look on his face. "What you ask is quite impossible. The very most we can offer you is a 40 percent reduction," he said apologetically.

"Excuse me?" I asked. He repeated his offer.

"Unbelievable," I thought to myself. "Give us some time to think about it," I replied.

As soon as they were out of earshot, Leroy and I almost jumped for joy. As it turned out, this was the first of several key concessions we received from the various airlines, ranging from 15 to 45 percent discounts. British Airways, KLM, Sabena, and Lufthansa all soon after reduced their rates well beyond my initial expectations.

This situation was a valuable lesson with regard to aspiration levels in negotiations. What at first seemed like a brash, overbearing approach to business turned out to be very positive. But was it win-win?, you ask. Didn't you just bleed the airlines at a time when they were vulnerable? Not at all. We later found out that the airlines were quite pleased with the new arrangements. They thought discounts might be greater than they were, and, of course, some of the airlines were delighted that they had negotiated better terms than their competitors.

We have all kinds of negative fantasies about high initial demands (HIDs):

"They won't like me anymore. I'll make them really mad and it will hurt the relationship."

"I'll price myself out of the market."

"Maybe we aren't being reasonable."

"This is embarrassing."

In spite of these concerns, there are compelling reasons to go for it, which are summarized in the following World-Class Tips.

World-Class Tips: Seven Reasons Why You Should Have High Initial Demands

1. Don't take away your own power. TOS may do it to you, but don't do it to yourself.

2. HIDs teach people how to treat you.

3. They lower the expectations of TOS.

4. HIDs demonstrate your persistence and conviction.

5. You can always reduce your asking offer or demand. HIDs give you room to make concessions.

6. Remember that time is on your side. Making HIDs gives you more time to learn about your counterpart, and time heals many wounds.

7. There is an emotional imperative for TOS to beat you down. It's important for TOS to feel that they've "won."[3]

World-Class Tip 7 is especially important. Many negotiators find it hard to accept that there is an emotional imperative for TOS to beat you down. To illustrate this point, let's get in the other person's shoes to see how the TOS might feel. You are in Germany to negotiate the purchase of the Drillenzebit, a precision tool-making machine from a Munich-based firm. You say to yourself, "This time won't be like the other times. This time I'm going to do my homework—I will read appropriate industry periodicals and talk to consultants, clients, suppliers, and others who know a lot about the Germans, the German business environment, and the competitive market for precision tool-making machines." So you do your homework and begin to negotiate with the Germans for the Drillenzebit machine. When the subject of price arises, you are ready. You've got the facts, figures, and some *savoir-faire* about German negotiating practices. So you say, "Mr. Dietrich, today I'm going to offer you one price and one price only for this fine Drillenzebit machine. That final price is $74,000—that's U.S. dollars.

Dietrich looks at you for a moment and says, "Let me see if I have this right. That's $74,000—in U.S. dollars?"

"That's right," you repeat, proud that you're sticking by your guns.

"Seventy-four thousand dollars. You've got it. The machine is yours!" he beams.

How would you feel in this situation? Wonderful? Exuberant? If you are like most people, you would have a morbid, sinking feeling that you had just been taken. Your first thought would probably be. "Damn. I should have offered less." Is this reaction logical? No. You did, after all, get what you asked for. You reacted as you did because only part of your needs were met—the logical part—while the emotional part was not.

There are cultural differences as to how high our aspiration level should be with our foreign counterparts, but as a rule thumb, go for it! If you really want $30,000 for your widget machine, don't ask for $30,500. Ask for $60,000. Put TOS in the position of saying to his or her boss, "You know, this woman came in asking $60,000. This price was completely off-the-wall. Excellent negotiator that I am, I got her down to $38,000. I saved us $22,000." And if you are in a competitive bidding situation, stress the quality, service, and other aspects that make your price an excellent value.

Strategy 4: Use Language That Is Simple and Accessible

American English is filled with thousands of clichés and colloquialisms that make it very hard for others to understand. Phrases such as "getting down to brass tacks," "getting down to the nitty gritty," wanting to "zero in on problems," or "finding out where the rubber meets the road" only clog communication channels.

Don't assume that because your foreign counterpart speaks English, he or she fully understands it. This individual may know English as it was taught in school but may not be able to speak it or understand it in conversation with an American. An American executive who regularly travels to Taiwan makes this point. "When I first asked my Taiwanese client if he spoke English, he told me yes. I found out the hard way that his understanding was very elementary and that I used way too many slang expressions. We still do business together, but now I speak more slowly and simply, and I'm learning some Chinese."

This doesn't apply only to slang. Make sure you use the simplest, most basic words possible. Exhibit 1 provides examples of simplified words and terms you should use, even if you're speaking English.

EXHIBIT 1   SIMPLIFYING ENGLISH WORDS AND TERMS

Don't use this . . .	when this will do.
annual premium	annual payment
accrued interest	unpaid interest
maturity date	final payment date
commence	start
utilize	use
acquaint	tell
demonstrate	show
endeavor	try
modification	change
proceed	go
per diem	daily

Strategy 5: Ask Lots of Questions, Then Listen with Your Eyes and Ears

Asking good questions is vital throughout the negotiation, but particularly in the early stages. Your main goal is receiving information. Making a brilliant speech to TOS about your proposal may make you feel good, but it does far less in helping you achieve your ends than asking questions that give you data about content and the emotional needs of TOS.

Exhibit 2 illustrates the importance of asking questions. Skilled negotiators ask more than twice the number of questions as unskilled negotiators. They also engage in much more active listening than those who are less skilled.

EXHIBIT 2   QUESTIONING AND LISTENING IN SKILLED AND AVERAGE NEGOTIATORS

Negotiating Behavior	Skilled Negotiators	Average Negotiators
Questions, as a percentage of all negotiating behavior	21.3%	9.6%
Active listening		
■ Testing for understanding	9.7	4.1
■ Summarizing	7.5	4.2

Source: Neil Rackham, "The Behavior of Successful Negotiators" (Reston, Va.: Huthwaite Research Group, 1976), as reported in Ellen Raider International, Inc. (Brooklyn, N.Y.) and Situation Management Systems, Inc. (Plymouth, Mass.), *International Negotiations: A Training Program for Corporate Executives and Diplomats (1982).*

There is one important consideration when asking questions: Don't do anything that would embarrass your international counterpart. Questions can be much more direct and open in cultures such as the United States, Canada, Australia, Switzerland, Sweden, and Germany than in Japan, Taiwan, Brazil, or Colombia, where indirectness is prized.

> Judge a man by his questions rather than by his answers.
>
> Voltaire

Effective listening is especially challenging when different cultures are involved. This can be the case even when English is the first language of TOS. Mike Apple, in American engineering and construction executive, found this to be the case in England and Scotland. Apple notes that even though English is spoken, one must listen very carefully to English and Scottish negotiators because of their dialects. "When I first got to Scotland, I wondered if some kind of challenge was in the making when a union negotiator told me he was going to 'mark my card.' I asked a colleague about it. As it turned out, the term is one used by Scottish golfers to explain the best approach to the course for those who haven't played there before. The union negotiator was only trying to be helpful," Apple notes. "The lesson learned here? When in doubt, ask for clarification."

If the communication pattern is from low-context countries, such as Japan, China, Saudi Arabia, Greece, or Spain, listening is even more challenging for Americans. In these cultures the message is embedded in the context of what is being said. Mike McMahon, a former managing director for National Semiconductor's Singapore plant, found Singaporeans reluctant to respond directly to questions. He notes, "I had to listen very carefully to figure out what was really on their minds."[4]

Here are some additional tips for effective listening:

- Limit your own talking.

- Concentrate on what TOS is saying.

- Maintain eye contact (but don't stare).

- Paraphrase and summarize TOS's remarks.

- Avoid jumping to conclusions. Be postjudicial, not prejudicial, regarding what TOS is saying.

- Watch for nonverbal cues.

- Listen for emotions.

- Ask for clarification: Assume differences, not similarities, if you are unsure of meaning.

- Don't interrupt.

- Pause for understanding; don't immediately fill the voids of silence.

Some of the rituals of international negotiating serve dual purposes of entertainment and information gathering. Foster Lin, director of the Taiwanese Far East Trade Service Office in Chicago, considers formal Taiwanese banquets and other entertainment as a prime opportunity to gain information on one's negotiating counterpart. Says Lin, "Entertainment demonstrates courtesy toward our foreign guests. It also helps us find out more about the individual person. Is this someone we can trust and want to do business with?" Such occasions can help you as well. Careful listening in this "offstage" time, away from the formal negotiating sessions, can give you another side to the negotiators. Use this time to gather additional data on your counterpart.

A key part of listening relates to body language. TOS may encode messages, making sophisticated, cogent arguments. However, one thing almost always happens during a moment of insecurity or deception: body movements change (e.g., the person literally squirms in his or her seat or blinks more rapidly). Also, be aware of the impact of your own nonverbal behavior. For example, if your gestures are quite expressive and TOS is from Sweden and quite reserved, tone it down a bit. Alternatively, if your facial and arm gestures are unexpressive and you are meeting a Brazilian who is very expressive, loosen up a bit—smile and use expressive hand and arm gestures.

World-Class Tips: Five Positive Things You Can Do without Saying a Word

1. *Smile!* It's a universal lubricant that can help you open the content of the negotiation. A genuine smile says very loudly, "I'd appreciate doing business with you."

2. *Dress appropriately and groom well.* Shined shoes, combed hair, clean nails, and clothes appropriate for the occasion show that you respect yourself and your counterpart. It also communicates that you are worthy of your counterpart's business.

3. *Lean forward.* This communicates interest and attention in almost every culture.

4. *Use open gestures.* Crossed arms in front of your chest may be viewed as disinterest or resistance on your part. More open gestures send a signal that you are open to your counterpart's ideas.

5. *Take every opportunity to nod your head.* Don't you like it when people agree with you? Let TOS know that you are listening by this simple action.

Notes

1. Neil Rackham, "The Behavior of Successful Negotiators" (Reston, Va.: Huthwaite Research Group, 1976), as reported in Ellen Raider International, Inc. (Brooklyn, N.Y.) and Situation Management Systems, Inc. (Plymouth, Mass.), *International Negotiations: A Training Program for Corporate Executives and Diplomats* (1982).

2. Ibid.

3. See Phil Sperber, *Fail-Safe Business Negotiating: Strategies and Tactics for Success* (Englewood Cliffs, N.J.: Prentice-Hall, 1983), pp. 40–41; and Roy J. Lewicki and Joseph A. Litterer, *Negotiation* (Homewood, Ill.: Richard D. Irwin, 1985), pp. 75–79.

4. Frank L. Acuff, "What It Takes to Succeed in Overseas Assignment," *National Business Employment Weekly* (August 25, 1991): 17–18.

Consequences

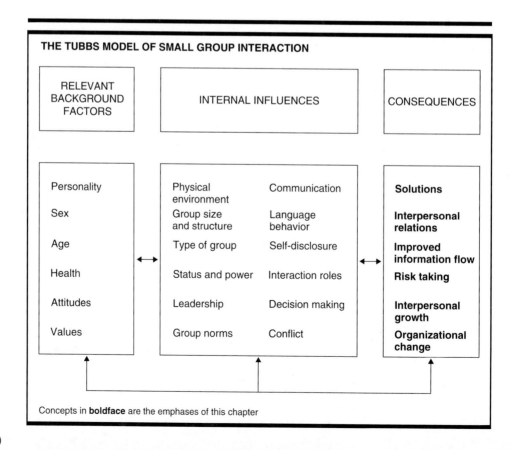

THE TUBBS MODEL OF SMALL GROUP INTERACTION

RELEVANT BACKGROUND FACTORS	INTERNAL INFLUENCES		CONSEQUENCES
Personality	Physical environment	Communication	**Solutions**
Sex	Group size and structure	Language behavior	**Interpersonal relations**
Age	Type of group	Self-disclosure	**Improved information flow**
Health	Status and power	Interaction roles	**Risk taking**
Attitudes	Leadership	Decision making	**Interpersonal growth**
Values	Group norms	Conflict	**Organizational change**

Concepts in **boldface** are the emphases of this chapter

PREVIEW

Chapter 7 is devoted entirely to the consequences section of the Tubbs Model of Small Group Interaction. These consequences are potential outcomes or end results. One consequence (solutions to problems) is discussed, along with the quality and acceptance of solutions. Another end result of group communication is the improvement of intergroup relations. This is often a way of clearing up and reducing misunderstandings. An improvement in information flow often results from group discussion. A great deal of organizational change can also be found under the consequences section. Each of these consequences has several different methods to enhance its values.

GLOSSARY

Acceptance of Solutions: There are three different types of solutions for problem situations: (1) high quality, low acceptance; (2) high acceptance, high quality; (3) high acceptance, low quality.

Quality of Solutions: Groups have the potential to make better-quality decisions than the same individuals would make if working alone.

CASE STUDY: Working at County Pool

Lifeguarding often is seen as a glamorous and ideal job by high school and college students because it involves showing up very casually dressed to work, getting a great tan, being outside at a pool or beach, and engaging in a great deal of swimming and other water sports. But this view omits the daily realities of lifeguarding: the risk that a visitor will be injured or drowned, the tedium of sitting in the hot sun hour after hour, and the nearly constant need to caution children about running and/or breaking other pool rules. It also overlooks other activities lifeguards perform.

County Pool is a junior Olympic-size pool built in the 1970s to provide a safe, quality recreational facility for area children and adults. The pool board (a group of individuals from across the county who oversee operations) and elected county officials are not interested in having the pool make a profit. Rather, their focus is on making the pool available at relatively low cost, charging only enough to cover repairs and associated bills (water, electric).

The pool's summer staff includes a manager, an assistant manager for concessions, and an assistant manager for pool operations. These individuals are paid a weekly salary from the pool's profits. In addition, high school and college students are hired as lifeguards and concession workers. Nearly exclusively during the 1970s and 1980s, such workers were hired through the Manpower Services' Comprehensive Employment and Training Act (CETA) program. To participate in the CETA program, applicants had to demonstrate financial need. Salaries were certainly not grand, not inflated; but for summer work they were comparatively good pay. Association with the CETA program provided several advantages to County Pool. The pool's payroll remained relatively small because a large portion of the salaries was paid through CETA. With repair and equipment costs high, County Pool needed this opportunity to sustain itself independently.

Each year, candidates for pool positions applied to and were screened by CETA personnel; thus, pool management's time and expense were considerably lowered. However, because CETA approved not only the students to be hired but also the salaries, it was to the pool's benefit to keep workers, even poor ones, and to allow them to work all of their hours. Additionally, the pool provided several advantages to the CETA program and to the students it employed. Placements at the swimming pool were highly sought after because of the pool's reputation as a fun place to work. The pool also provided a safe work environment, one where CETA officials could easily do their periodic checks (because so many workers were there at once).

Early Summer—Orientation

The summers began with a staff meeting led by the manager and the assistant managers. The primary purpose of the staff meeting was to let everyone get acquainted and to discuss the general operating procedures and rules of the pool. For example, lifeguards almost always worked half-hour rotations (i.e., if you guarded the deep end of the pool for half an hour, you would shift to a different location—the shallow end or possibly the gate to check admissions or the basket room, where you would provide people with baskets in which to store their personal belongings and then retrieve them when necessary); to provide some heat relief after two half-hour rotations in the sun, lifeguards typically would move to a shaded location (basket room, gate, or concessions) for the next half hour rotation.

At this meeting the managers explained the staff responsibilities. While employees had general job descriptions (e.g., concession worker, lifeguard), all staffers did a variety of jobs. For example, the lifeguards cared for the grounds and were responsible for cleaning activities (daily cleaning of the pool deck and restroom facilities; periodic cleaning of the diving boards and adjacent pavilion). They also performed repairs that didn't require expert technicians and maintained the appropriate water chemistry balance. On busy days at the pool lifeguards were required to fill in at the concessions stand.

From the Beginning—On the Job

In practice, lifeguarding was not glamorous. It was hard work—and sweat. Lifeguards had to say, "Slow down" and "Don't run" seemingly a million times a day. And somehow, at the busiest, hottest times of the summer when the pool was the most crowded, there were more lawn chores, more repairs, and more cleaning that needed to be done. Such times were made easier by staff members willing to "jump in and help." When times were slower, usually because of rain or cooler weather (and typically near the end of the day), staffers could take more breaks, swim, lay out, occasionally run at a nearby track, or leisurely eat concessions. These days led to bonding among staff members as they worked together on a special cleaning projects that could not be completed while the pool was in heavy use, or as they relaxed in the water. All workers hoped for such days to add some variety to the hot, hot days when the pool was overused.

Late June—Teaching Swimming Lessons

Many members of the lifeguarding staff taught swimming lessons before or after work to make extra money. Lucy, a second-year employee, especially enjoyed teaching and she was frequently selected for it because the children responded especially well to her. However, recently she had missed several classes. Missing because one is sick cannot be helped and is easily excusable. But some of her absences were not for illness, and the managers had begun to worry about these. Missing swimming lessons posed a special problem because the children usually became quite attached to their teacher and could be disturbed by her absence and the process of working with someone new.

On Friday evening, before the final class of the week, Lucy called Cary Loomis, the assistant manager of pool operations.

"Cary, I just can't make lessons tonight. Roger somehow got tickets to see Bryan Adams, and I've just got to go with him. I can't miss this concert."

Cary responded, "But Lucy, this is a very important night for the lessons. You know how the children count on you for the last night. Especially this group."

"Really, Cary," Lucy said, "I've been working hard. I deserve a break, and I'm going to go. Just get a fill-in."

Cary got a fill-in—luckily one of the most experienced, most popular swimming instructors. Cary introduced Carmen, the fill-in instructor, to the children; explained to the parents that Lucy apologized for missing the evening (but did not reveal the reason for the absence); and sat poolside facilitating Carmen's group.

All of the children adapted well to Carmen, except five-year-old Michelle Dargan. This shy child had refused to even get into the water until the previous evening and now cried silently because she wanted Lucy. Despite considerable coaxing from Carmen and Cary, Michelle still refused to get into the water. Observing the efforts, Michelle's father walked into the pool area and over to the child. He said, "We've paid for these lessons, and you're going to get in there and swim." With this, the child's silent crying erupted into loud wails, and she ran out of the pool area to her mother.

Mr. Dargan turned to Cary and said, "All of this is your fault. I can't believe that you let this happen. I bet she'll never learn to swim after this letdown. I want my money back."

Cary explained that she was very sorry about the absence and the child's disappointment. She also explained that while she was encouraged by the child's performance the previous evening,

Michelle really needed more lessons to be a swimmer even if she had gotten in and worked hard that evening. Cary invited the father to bring the child back for another week of free lessons.

But Mr. Dargan continued to loudly demand his money. This time he was so loud Cary was certain that even those parents waiting outside the gate who hadn't heard him the first time heard him this time.

Now, really beginning to be embarrassed, and more than a bit angry, once again Cary started to apologize but was interrupted by Mr. Dargan's demands for his money. So she returned his $7.50 paid at the week's beginning for five hour-long group lessons. She didn't really believe that the refund was justified, but in a service industry one works to keep the public happy.

All through the rest of that evening, Cary was upset with the father for his behavior, but she was angry also with Lucy for bailing out at the last minute. Cary thought about how to approach Lucy.

Mid-July—One Busy Day

The temperature hit 101 degrees, the intense sun beat down, and pool attendance peaked. Cary had been assisting with a rush in concessions; but when she returned to the main pool area, she noticed that Micki was still in the deep-end guard chair. She walked over and asked Micki why she was still in this part of the rotation.

Micki replied, "I'm not exactly sure, but Bill or Lance was supposed to be up next. They just never came to relieve me."

Cary located Lance first, asleep on the sun deck above the pool. She woke him and asked if he was scheduled to relieve Micki.

"Nope, I don't think so," Lance responded. "Today I'm following Sheila."

"Do you know where she is now?" Cary asked.

"Probably in baskets. I'm going to relieve her there at 2:30," he said.

"Lance, it is 2:50 now," Cary said.

"OK, I'll go, but I just feel really tired today and I needed to rest. You know, with teaching morning and evening lessons, I'm kinda wiped out. Besides I've only had two half-hour breaks today. After baskets, can I get another break?" Lance asked.

What Lance didn't say, but what Cary remembered hearing earlier, was that he had been out at a party until the early morning.

Cary found Bill in the water, playing tag, and waved him over. "Bill, are you following Micki in the rotation today?"

Bill answered, "Well, yes, I guess."

"I just noticed that Micki's been up there well past her scheduled half hour," Cary said.

Bill countered, "I'll get there sometime. I was just hot and decided that I needed to cool down for awhile."

"Actually, Bill, we really need you up there now. Micki, no doubt, is also quite hot by this time. She probably needs to cool down, too. And she needs to continue through her part of the rotation system, or everyone will get behind," said Cary.

Reluctantly, and with a few gripes to his friends, Bill left the water and headed for the deep-end guard chair.

Late August—The Persistent Dilemma

By the summer's end, two distinct types of pool workers had emerged. The first type loved the children, loved the sun, and were very motivated to pitch in and do whatever needed to be

lems are best solved by persons with a high level of technical knowledge and expertise. They might include important financial decisions involving setting prices, determining expenditures, and so on.

Second, some solutions require *high acceptance but low quality*. These might include fair ways of distributing new equipment, vacation schedules, undesirable work assignments, new offices or office equipment, or a new vehicle such as a truck. Decisions such as these may include all individuals who may be affected by the results of the decision.

Third, some decisions require both *high quality and high acceptance*. It would appear that the majority of problems fall into this category. Because this is the case, Maier recommends that problem-solving groups rather than isolated individuals be used, because the acceptance of the solution is likely to be higher when people are involved in formulating a solution and because we have already seen that groups tend to produce better-quality solutions than individuals.

Participative decision making (PDM) not only can result in high-quality decisions and increased acceptance of the solutions but also may result in increased levels of satisfaction, commitment, and loyalty to the solution and to the group. Let us return to the pen replacement problem. The chances are that if the foremen were made aware of the problem and were asked to help find a way to reduce it, several things would occur. First, they might suggest a good solution. Second, they would be more likely to accept the new solution. Third, they probably would use peer pressure on one another to see that the new solution was followed. In each case, the result might have been better than what actually happened.

See the article at the end of this chapter in which Norman Maier more fully explains the use of the $ED = Q \times A$ *formula. This article also shows the relevance of small group interaction to organizations and their effectiveness.*

Literally thousands of modern organizations are learning a lesson from group theory and research. Lawler (1992) found, through a national survey, that the vast majority of American companies have begun using some form of work teams to improve their organizational performance. Fisher (1993) offers the following explanation for the superiority of group decision making:

> Competitive advantage comes from fully utilizing the *discretionary effort* of the work force, not from buying the latest gadget or using the latest management fad. Voluntary effort comes from employees' commitment, and commitment comes from empowerment. It is simple human nature. Why? In the words of Weyerhaeuser Human Resources manager Doug King, "It's hard to resist your own ideas." (p. 13)

In addition, Moskal (1990) reported that employee decision making was part of a major turnaround at Buick City. The Japanese Andon system was used, which gives the line worker the responsibility and authority to stop the assembly line when a problem occurs. Workers were able to stop production whenever they thought the product wasn't perfect. However, this happened so often that productivity was not maintained. According to a company spokesperson: "The word perfect was the problem. . . . we redefined 'perfect' to mean 'meeting customer expectations and engineering specifications.' Plant brass also modified the 'Stop' concept to include a yellow cord at many operations that now alerts a team coordinator to a potential problem without actually stopping the assembly line" (p. 26). The results are that Buick LeSabre in 1994 was rated second highest in quality out of 154 makes of cars. Ten years earlier, it was second from the bottom (p. 22).

These studies indicate two things. First, people generally are resistant to changes that affect their lives, especially if these changes are initiated by others. Second, group decision making and "people involvement" can be powerful assets in increasing satisfaction and overcoming resistance to change. Let us look at each of these in more detail.

Resistance to change is a phenomenon that some would argue begins with the so-called birth trauma in which the fetus resists being plucked from the warm, dark security of the womb only to be exposed to the shock of the cold, bright, noisy world outside. Over time and experience, most of us develop a "separation anxiety" when we are forced to leave (or be separated from) any place or set of circumstances in which we feel comfortable. Each time we move or change schools or jobs, a certain amount of this is experienced. Try to remember how threatening your first day of high school (or college) was compared to the comfortable security of your immediate past. Resistance to change is normal and tends to increase when we do not understand the need for change or if we are not instrumental in bringing about the change.

Beebe (1986) cites three of the hundreds of companies that are successfully using teams to overcome resistance to change:*

> *Problem:* A mountain of paperwork was building on desks at CH2M Hills Boise office last year. Employees were slow to file reports and other documents in loose-leaf binders favored by the consulting engineering firm. The forms were not pre-punched.
>
> *Solution:* A volunteer group of workers suggested to the company that it switch to pre-punched forms. Doing so would relieve employees of an annoying chore and speed filing, they said.
>
> *Savings:* Pre-punched forms save the Boise office 60 man-days a year, Edward Sloan, CH2M Hill's district coordinator of construction management services said. Companywide it probably saves 2,400 man-days, he said.
>
> *Problem:* It took 15 to 20 minutes to unload each potato truck that entered the Ore-Ida Foods Inc. processing plant at Ontario, Ore. Employees estimated hundreds of hours were being wasted as potatoes moved down truck-mounted conveyors into the building.
>
> *Solution:* A group of Ore-Ida workers in Ontario last year recommended to managers that belly-dump trucks should be used to haul potatoes to the plant. Potatoes could be unloaded into bays in only a few minutes.

---

*By Paul Beebe; reprinted with permission of *The Idaho Statesman.*

Savings: Within one year, Ore-Ida realized $130,000 in labor savings and lost time, said John Walhof, the company's productivity manager.

Problem: Could the error rate of machines that place electrical components on printed circuit boards at Hewlett-Packard Co.'s disc memory division in Boise be improved?

Solution: The employees who operate the machines thought so. One group suggested a series of modifications that improved the manufacturer's error rating of its machines from 3,000 improperly mounted components per million to 500 parts per million, a sixfold improvement.

Benefit: Far fewer components are being mounted incorrectly. Board rejection rates are down and employee morale is up, said Jim Stinehelfer, manufacturing manager in H-P's disc memory division. (p. A3)

Ore-Ida and CH2M Hill teams consist of six to ten people who meet once a week. Hewlett-Packard teams contain up to thirty people. Most of the groups are composed of workers from the same area of the company. "We wanted to create an environment where employees are free to offer suggestions about their working environment, ideas on ways our products are produced, new products," said Ore-Ida's productivity manager of the company's People-Excellence-Products (PEP) program. Ore-Ida has organized 138 PEP teams in all of its U.S. operations, including 35 at its Ontario plant and 35 at its Burley plant. Teams tackle everything from safety issues to product quality. Hewlett-Packard spokesmen have said their company has seen big increases in morale and productivity that can be related to quality teams. Line inspectors have been eliminated in many areas, because employees now monitor the quality of their work. The manufacturing manager of Hewlett-Packard stated that the fundamental reason for the quality teams was to "make the people on the lines feel responsible for the quality of the product. The best way to have them feel that responsibility is to give it to them."

There are several important factors to remember in *overcoming resistance to change.* First, people will accept changes that they have a part in planning. Obviously, it is much easier to live through the trauma of going to college if we choose to go and if we like the college or university than if we are forced by our parents to go or to go someplace we don't like. Second, changes will be accepted if they do not threaten our security. Many office work groups resist innovations such as computer systems for fear that the computer will eventually take away some of their jobs. Third, changes will be more readily accepted when people are involved in gathering facts that indicate the need for change. Farmers who notice decreasing crop yields will be more receptive to farming innovations than those who are prospering. Finally, greater acceptance and commitment will result when the changes are kept open to further revision based on the success or failure of the new procedures. None of us is very enthusiastic about adopting changes for a lifetime. However, if we feel the changes are on a trial basis, subject to modification, we are usually more willing to give them a try. Obviously, to the extent that these conditions are *not* met, resistance to change will be increased.

Many firms are beginning to take a major step toward participation with self-directed work teams. Wellins et al. (1991) define a *self-directed work team* as "an intact group of employees who are responsible for a 'whole' work process or segment that delivers a product or service to an internal or external customer" (p. 3). This organizational innovation has as its fundamental theme the attempt to place a remarkably high degree of decision-making responsibility and behavior control in the hands of the work group itself.

A self-managing team usually elects its own leader, and often management appoints an external leader who acts as a coordinator-facilitator rather than a supervisor. Teams frequently take on responsibilities that have not traditionally been the topic for work groups in the past. Some of these include (1) preparation of the annual budget, (2) timekeeping functions, (3) recording of quality control statistics, (4) solving technically related problems, (5) adjusting production schedules, (6) modifying or redesigning production processes, and (7) setting team goals and assessing internal performance.

For long-term success, teams must function in a responsible manner, and management must possess a high degree of trust and confidence in the system. To help ensure successful teams, organizations typically design them with "well defined physical and task boundaries, sometimes using socio-technical design concepts to ensure an appropriate match between technical systems and the conventions, rules, and norms governing interaction. Task interdependence within teams is usually higher than between teams" (Wellins et al., 1991, p. 5). Sophisticated computerized information systems are frequently used in measuring inputs and outputs across team boundaries. This provides extensive and rapid feedback about the quantity and quality of team performance while reducing secrecy between teams. Teams are provided with as much information as possible.

Management typically initiates the self-managing work concept while striving for additional productivity, improving quality, reducing overhead, and reducing conflict. For the employee, the concept provides the opportunity to exercise more control over aspects of daily work life. Are these teams successful? There is no single conclusive answer to this question, but according to Zenger et al. (1994), there are literally thousands of organizations that have instituted self-directed teams because of the success of this approach. (See also Tubbs, 1993b.) Many other benefits of the team approach seem to manifest themselves. Teams become very flexible and adapt well to changing conditions and new start-ups. Also, organizations with the team concept generally have very high responses to job satisfaction and attitude surveys.

Katzenbach and Smith (1993) put it well: "Unbridled enthusiasm is the raw motivating power for teams" (p. 265). They also write, "Teams will be the primary building blocks of company performance in the organization of the future" (p. 173). It is a high probability that you will find it very useful to learn more about teams and teamwork as you progress in your career.

CHANGES IN INTERPERSONAL RELATIONS

Probably the most notable difference between a television interview with a professional golfer who has just won a major tournament and a baseball team that has won the World Series (or a football team that has won the Super Bowl) is the tremendous amount of energy, enthusiasm, and esprit de corps of the group versus the low-keyed response of the lone golfer. The backslapping, hugging, and champagne splashing of the group are some of the most obvious signs that interpersonal relations are an important by-product of group activity.

In Chapter 6 we examined the positive and negative aspects of conflict. Group discussion may improve interpersonal relations through the successful resolution of conflict. Conflict may be intragroup or intergroup. In either case, resolving conflict tends to affect interpersonal relations favorably.

A common technique for improving intergroup relations is to have members of each group get together and write down their perceptions of (1) themselves, (2) the others, and (3) how they think the others view them. Production and service groups in manufacturing plants frequently need to have such meetings to coordinate their activities more effectively. The production groups often feel that a service department (such as maintenance) does not act quickly enough to get defective machinery working. On the other hand, maintenance people feel as if they are always put under unreasonable pressures, because every time a piece of machinery breaks down, each production supervisor wants immediate attention to his or her problems, even though several machines require repair simultaneously.

Meetings designed to share perceptions of one another and to inform each other of particular problems can potentially clear up and reduce areas of misperception and misunderstanding. After one such meeting, one man said to another from a different department, "After drinking coffee with you and hearing your side of the story, it's going to be hard for me to cuss you out tomorrow the way I usually do." This comment is typical of the increased quality of interpersonal relations that can come out of group problem solving conducted in an atmosphere of support and mutual gain. However, if the meetings are conducted in an atmosphere of blame placing and faultfinding, the relations are likely to be even worse than if the meetings had not been held. In other words, the intermediate influences discussed in Chapters 5 and 6 have a significant influence on the end results.

A subset of interpersonal relations is group cohesion. *Cohesiveness* has been defined as morale or feelings of belongingness. Group cohesion can also be a byproduct or end result of group activity. Generally, a prestigious or successful group is more attractive to belong to and results in higher levels of cohesion. The Chicago Bulls basketball team and the Dallas Cowboys football team are two examples of successful groups that could be expected to have high levels of cohesion.

Cohesion is a result of group interaction, but it in turn influences other things. As we saw in Chapter 4, cohesive groups tend to have stricter norms and tolerate smaller amounts of deviance from the group values. Cohesive groups may have high or low productivity, depending on the group norm regarding productivity. Cohesiveness increases the loyalty of each member to that particular group but frequently breeds deeper cleavages *between* groups. This may become a problem if the groups happen to be part of a single organization in which integration of several groups is necessary. In a study on predictors of performance in project groups (Keller, 1986), group cohesiveness was found to be the strongest predictor of the project groups' performance both initially and over time. The findings suggested that "cohesive project groups were able to achieve high project quality and meet their goals on budgets and schedules." Similarly, Barnard et al. (1992) found that the higher the cohesion among group members, the more likely they were to stick together in their attitudes.

In a two-year study, Tubbs (1993d) measured satisfaction before and after introducing a program to develop employee work teams in a company of about 100 people. The results showed that people's satisfaction with their peers was significantly increased after the program. In addition, the company's productivity and profitability more than doubled. It is clear that working together in teams can dramatically increase people's feeling of closeness and, at the same time, increase their group output.

In summary, it is important to note that small group interaction has the potential of increasing interpersonal relations and cohesiveness. The great emphasis on team building in management training illustrates the usefulness of this concept. In terms of learning theory, the behaviors of talking and cooperating rather than avoiding and competing with one another have been reinforced, and the cooperating behaviors are, therefore, more likely to occur again. Thibaut and Kelley (1986) put it this way: "The selectivity observed in interaction reflects the tendency for more satisfactory interactions to recur and for less satisfactory ones to disappear. The consequences of interaction can be described in many different terms, but we have found it useful to distinguish only between the rewards that a person receives and the costs he incurs" (p. 12). The critical element in improving interpersonal relations through group interaction is to make the experience as rewarding as possible. (See also Varney, 1989.)

Team Building

Note the following analogy between a typewriter and a team:

Xvxn though this typxwritxr is old, it works wxll xxcxpt for onx kxy. I havx wishxd many timxs that it workxd pxrfxctly. It is trux that thxrx arx forty-onx kxys that function wxll xnough. But just onx kxy not working makxs thx diffxrxncx.

Somxtimxs an organization or community is likx this typxwritxr—all thx pxoplx but onx arx working propxrly. You may say to yoursxlf, "Wxll, only onx won't makx or brakx a projxct." But it doxs makx a diffxrxncx. Any projxct, to bx xffxctivx, nxxds thx participation of xvxry mxmbxr.

So thx nxxt timx you think you arx thx "only onx" and that your xfforts arxn't nxxdxd, rxmxmbxr this typxwritxr and say to yoursxlf, "I am an important pxrson in thx organization and community, and I am nxxdxd vxry much" (source unknown).

The analogy above touches on a special case of group interpersonal relations referred to as *team building*. Larson and LaFasto (1989) report the results of their research investigating over thirty leaders of such high-performance teams as:

The Boeing 747 project team

The IBM PC team

The Rogers Commission (*Challenger* Disaster Investigation)

Cardiac surgical teams

The 1986 Mt. Everest expedition

The Centers for Disease Control epidemiology teams

New York stage production teams

The McDonald's Chicken McNuggets team

Championship football teams

On the basis of their fascinating research, eight dimensions of team excellence emerged:

1. *Clear, elevating goal:* For example, the purpose of the Rogers Commission was to determine the causes of the *Challenger* disaster within 120 days. Paul Lazarus, a Broadway producer, is quoted as saying, "It is better to have a clear idea and have it fail than to be unclear in conception, because you can learn from a failure and go on to the next clear idea" (p. 29).

2. *Results-driven structure:* The Mt. Everest team had as its objective getting one or two team members to the top of the mountain. The group's structure was to use the other members strictly as support for getting the one or two strongest members to the summit. The McDonald's Chicken McNuggets team was purposely structured as a separate entity from the rest of the company and reported directly to Bud Sweeney, the project director. The purpose was to cut through the corporate bureaucracy.

3. *Competent team members:* The team members for the Centers for Disease Control are selected for their outstanding talent along the following dimensions: (1) technically competent, (2) friendly and outgoing, (3) politically astute, (4) willing to subordinate his or her own interests in favor of the group goal, (5) willing to spend a lot of time on the task, (6) imaginative, (7) honest, and (8) interested in challenge (p. 60).

4. *Unified commitment:* Dr. Don Wukasch, a member of both the famous Michael DeBakey and Denton Cooley cardiac surgical teams, described his level of dedication to his teams: "Nothing was as important for me as being on that team and making it through the 10 years to get there. It was total commitment, and when I got married, that was part of the deal with my marriage. We looked at it and never had any questions as to what came first. It was the job" (p. 74).

5. *Collaborative climate:* Working well together is the basic building block of teamwork. Trust turns out to be the main ingredient. Anthony Rucci, a Baxter-Travenol Corporation team leader, states, "You need to clearly define the expectations, leaving people with the sense that you trust them enough to do things on their own, that you trust their judgment enough to

let them take some personal initiative, that you are not looking over their shoulder. That is the quickest way that I know of for a manager of a team to demonstrate trust and to build a climate of trust" (p. 87).

6. *Standards of excellence:* Director Paul Lazarus describes the level of excellence exemplified by one Broadway star: "Angela Lansbury did one song, and yet she requested more rehearsal time than anybody else simply because she would not go out on the stage unless she was prepared within an inch of her life. . . . She rehearsed 'Send in the Clowns' . . . once a week for 10 weeks. We could have done it in one rehearsal, but that's the kind of perfectionism that someone like that strives for, and that's why Angela Lansbury is a major star" (p. 102).

7. *External support and recognition:* Emotional support from top leaders above the team followed by financial incentives are the strongest combination to ensure that the team continues to give its best.

8. *Principled leadership:* Although leadership has been discussed in Chapter 4, suffice it to say that Larson and LaFasto (1989) identify effective leaders as those who, (1) establish a vision, (2) create change, and (3) unleash talent (p. 121).

In case you are wondering how to develop this high level of team spirit, Huszczo (1990) identifies the ten pitfalls common to team building.

1. Confusing team building with teamwork

2. Viewing teams as if they are "closed systems"

3. Not using a systematic model to plan the team development

4. Starting team training without assessing team needs

5. Sending team members to team training individually rather than collectively

6. Treating team building as a Japanese management technique

7. Assuming that teams are all basically alike

8. Counting on training alone to develop effective teams

9. Treating team training as a program rather than a process

10. Not holding teams accountable for using what they learn in team training

Although all of these are important misconceptions to consider when examining a group-building communication process, I think it important to emphasize one particular misconception—that of viewing the group as if it were a closed system. A group's performance is a function of its collective abilities, motivations, and opportunities. It is important for group members to improve how they relate with each other, the roles they play, the relationships between these roles, and the norms that help the group members work effectively.

Quite often, group members forget that they are part of a larger system (an organization), which itself can define roles, goals, and norms for the group. At times, changes in an organization will create changes in a group that make it difficult for the group to work effectively. An effective group will create constructive external relationships with its broader system. Group members will have an understanding of the group's role in the organization and learn to recognize threats and opportunities from the larger system.

IMPROVED INFORMATION FLOW

Communication in small groups also can result in an increased knowledge level and increased coordination among group members based on the sharing of information. Information may be distorted severely if passed along serially from one person to the next through ten people. However, the distortion will be significantly decreased if the same ten people hear the information simultaneously in a meeting. In addition, active discussion by participants will help them remember the information better than if they heard it in an announcement or read it in a memo.

Another factor is the tendency for subgroups to form so that information that passes *between* groups is restricted. This is especially true in complex organizations. Lawrence and Lorsch (1969) have referred to problems of this nature as *differentiation-integration* problems. Organizations require specialization (differentiation) in order to operate effectively. Thus, different groups become specialists in such departments as production, finance, legal, research and development, data-processing inspection, master mechanics, engineering, accounting, sales, or personnel. At the same time, these groups must cooperate and coordinate their efforts to keep from working at cross-purposes and generally harming organizational success.

Hammer and Champy (1993) have argued persuasively that the barriers created by the high degree of differentiation in organizations have created the need to, in their terms, "reengineer the corporation." This involves breaking down traditional ways of doing things and reexamining every way in which things have traditionally been done. They use the example of Taco Bell. Before 1983, the chain's typical restaurant was 70 percent kitchen and 30 percent eating area. By 1993 those percentages had reversed (p. 177). Changes like these come directly from greater teamwork and communication across functional areas of the company.

Coordination problems certainly occur among members of a single group as well as among multiple groups in an organization. Almost invariably, groups of students assigned to work on class projects have at least some difficulty in finding (1) each other, (2) a free hour in common in which to meet, (3) the materials necessary to conduct the research for their assignments, and sometimes (4) a suitable place in which to conduct their discussion. In addition, group members may forget that they were supposed to meet, or they may get too busy to prepare for the meeting. A host of other tangential problems may add to the coordination difficulties. Not all of these problems will be solved by group discussions, but they will probably at least be reduced. In some circles this is known as "letting the right hand know what the left hand is doing."

Zenger et al. (1994) point out that group decision making tends to lead to a different type of solution than does person-to-person decision making. In the one-on-one setting, the focus of the solution is on the person perceiving an individual problem. In an organization, this approach frequently solves one person's problem while *creating* new problems for others. Suppose that five supervisors all want to take their vacations in June and July. Assuming that all of them cannot be absent at once, any decision regarding one person's vacation will potentially influence the vacation plans of the others. It may be that one person's plan is flexible and could be modified in light of the situations of the others in the group. The group method then focuses on coordinating the best solution for all, considering the limitations of the job demands.

In addition to offering better decisions for more people, the group decision-making method reduces the jealousy and hostility that frequently accompany the person-to-person method. When individuals are awarded decisions in their favor without others knowing the circumstances surrounding the decision, the others frequently feel that "special deals" have been made, and the superior is accused of playing favorites. However, this reaction is drastically reduced when all interested parties are witness to the decision and the surrounding circumstances. Although the group method may be time-consuming, the end results of increased knowledge level and increased coordination are frequently worth the time spent. In fact, the total time expenditure may be less, because the related problems of jealousy and resentment do not occur as much and do not have to be solved as offshoots of the original problem.

ORGANIZATIONAL CHANGE

It has been said that the only person who likes change is a baby with a wet diaper. Changes that are initiated by someone else are particularly hard for us to accept. In this regard, Tichy and Sherman (1993) quote Jack Welch, the CEO of General Electric, as saying: "Change has no constituency. People like the status quo. They like the way it was. When you start changing things, the good old days look better and better" (p. 245).

On the basis of a rapidly increasing rate of change, modern organizations have been put under greater and greater pressure to adapt or go under. Certainly the policies and practices of colleges and universities have to be different today than they were five years ago. Numerous attempts have been made to help "ease the squeeze" felt by organizations. These attempts usually fall under the general label *organization development* (OD), which is another name for planned organizational change.

Over forty years ago, Kurt Lewin (1951) wrote about the problem of trying to get people to change. He called his analysis *force field analysis*, and it states basically that any situation occurs as a result of the combination of various competing forces. If you have ever tried to live up to your New Year's resolutions, you have experienced this. Figure 7.1 illustrates the concept further. Your motivation to live up to your New Year's resolutions represents one of the arrows labeled "driving

FIGURE 7.1

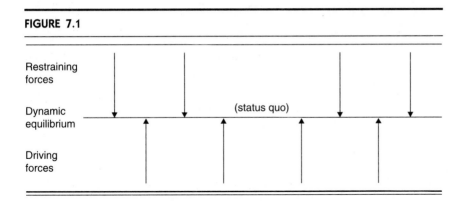

Restraining
forces

Dynamic
equilibrium

(status quo)

Driving
forces

forces." If you are thinking about exercising more or losing some weight, several arguments can add to your motivation (better-fitting clothes, more dates, better health). The restraining forces would be all the reasons why you don't live up to your resolutions (it's fun to eat, it's too cold to exercise, you hate to exercise alone).

Just as this force field analysis can be applied to individuals, it can be applied to groups and to organizations. In groups, some members may want to get the job accomplished (task-oriented behavior), whereas others may be much more interested in socializing with an attractive group member of the opposite sex. In fact, they may have joined the group just to meet that person. How much work actually gets accomplished is the status quo where these competing sets of forces meet. If the socializing couple leaves, the restraining forces will go up. Change can occur through either a reduction in the restraining forces or an increase in the driving forces, or both. Various methods of organizational development are designed to move the status quo in the more positive direction.

Let's say that you have been elected to an office in your sorority, fraternity, or church group or in some other organization. If you have identified things that you think need to be changed, then you are faced with the challenge of creating and implementing organizational change. Now what do you do? Jick (1993) offers helpful advice with the following:

The Ten Commandments of Implementing Change

1. Analyze the organization and its need for change.

2. Create a shared vision and common direction.

3. Separate from the past.

4. Create a sense of urgency.

5. Support a strong leader role.

6. Line up political sponsorship.

7. Craft an implementation plan.

8. Develop enabling structures.

9. Communicate, involve people, and be honest.

10. Reinforce and institutionalize change. (p. 195)

Okay, now how do you go about doing this? Sherman (1994) gives a wonderful example in his book *In the Rings of Saturn,* in which he explains just how the Saturn Corporation was created. As it turns out, a lot of what was done closely follows Jick's ten commandments. Here's a brief summary:

1. General Motors *analyzed itself* and found that it had lost significant market share to the Japanese auto companies. In fact, as Sherman (1994) puts it, "Market share continued to plummet like a Cadillac tossed from a high building" (p. 90).

2. The top leaders created a common direction by establishing what they called the "Group of 99," which consisted of ninety-nine people from GM representing fifty-five plants in seventeen divisions. Forty-two were from the United Auto Workers (UAW) union, thirty-five were from GM plant management, and the remainder came from staffs of both the corporation and the union (p. 81).

3. They *separated from the past* by forming the new Saturn Corporation as opposed to a new division of General Motors Corporation (such as Chevrolet).

4. They *created a sense of urgency* by analyzing the entire process of creating a new car. Alex Maier, a top executive, declared that the current system "is a mess."

5. They *supported a strong leader role* on the part of Roger Smith, GM's chairman of the board, thereby protecting the new company from several attempts to end the project.

6. They *lined up political sponsorship* by involving key opinion leaders from throughout the corporation. In fact, creating the Group of 99 itself was an attempt to build widespread political support through the diversity of its members. Particularly important and unusual was the strong union involvement.

7. They *crafted an implementation plan,* and it was presented to the UAW's leadership and to the GM Executive Committee. According to Sherman, "The committee went along with the recommendations that Saturn be a wholly owned subsidiary of GM but reshaped beyond the parent's recognition" (p. 83).

8. The *enabling structure* was hammered out in the 1984 GM-UAW labor negotiations, during which both parties agreed that the Saturn plant would be built in the United States and that a labor agreement would be worked out consistent with the recommendations of the Group of 99.

9. *Communication and openness* were at an unprecedented level throughout the planning. Owen Bieber, the UAW president, announced: "We have made vast strides here. The agreement is innovative, it's new." For the first time in UAW history, workers are "going to have a great deal of input into how that plant is operated" (p. 86).

10. The changes have been continually *reinforced and institutionalized* in many ways. For example, each employee was trained for 300 to 350 hours. Sherman states, "Operators had to learn not only their assigned tasks, but how to be familiar enough with those of the entire team in order to see the bigger picture and be able to step in and take over another job" (p. 196).

The result is that the Saturn automobile is one of the highest-rated cars on the basis of customer satisfaction. Although there are hundreds of examples of companies moving to a higher level of teamwork to create change, the Saturn story stands out as one of the most dramatic in history.

Excellence comes in all sizes. Not only giant corporations such as Xerox can benefit from using principles of group dynamics. Fernco, Inc., of Davison, Michigan, is an example of a small company that is also benefiting from these innovations (Tubbs, 1993d). Fernco manufactures plastic pipe products and employs 100 people. Several years ago the company began to implement an employee involvement program based on the principles in this book. Your author was asked to design and conduct the program. We began by measuring employee attitudes with a survey to diagnose the strengths and weaknesses in the organization. Several offsite training programs were held with all the company management and the employees who volunteered to join the TAG Teams, as they became known. A set of company guidelines was developed in collaboration with an advisory committee made up of managers and employees. Four TAG Teams were formed to work on problems of their choice. After one year, employee attitudes showed significant improvement, and the teams had proposed numerous innovations that management strongly supported and quickly implemented. The company is the leader in its industry and is widely recognized in the region as an outstanding organization for which to work. Fernco has almost no turnover, and there is a long waiting list to get a job there. This is but one more example of the use of groups to improve an already excellent organization.

See the article by Schlesinger, Sathe, Schlesinger, and Kotter at the end of this chapter for a comprehensive discussion of the methods for accomplishing organizational change.

THE SYSTEMS PERSPECTIVE

This chapter dealt with the consequences of group interaction. In Chapter 1 our model indicated that all the other variables tend to culminate in these consequences. However, in ongoing groups, the outcomes or consequences of earlier group interactions tend to have a continuing influence on subsequent activities. Take the County Pool case study at the beginning of this chapter. As a result of conflict, two types of lifeguards emerged. The type of background of the guards interacted with the lack of rewards to produce poor results. This example illustrates the systems concepts of *input* and *throughput* resulting in *output* that is fed back into the group as new *inputs,* because many groups represent ongoing *cycles* of events.

In this chapter we looked at four potential consequences of group interaction: (1) solutions to problems, (2) changes in interpersonal relations, (3) improved information flow, and (4) organizational change. Each of these potential consequences may vary considerably depending on the particular combination of the other variables depicted in the model. For example, the quality and acceptance of solutions will vary depending on the degree of group member participation.

A great deal of material has been written about member acceptance of group-derived solutions. The term "consensus" is typically used in this context. Consensus means unanimous agreement with the solution. Conceptually, consensus and acceptance of the solution appear to be roughly equivalent.

All the studies cited in this chapter confirm our thesis that small group interaction must be viewed as a system of interrelated variables in which a change in any one variable creates changes in the other variables in the system.

The second section of this chapter dealt with interpersonal relations. We saw that group member relations may be improved as a result of group interaction. However, groups composed of members with highly incompatible personalities or value systems may, in fact, become even more polarized as a result of small group interaction. This outcome would depend on the style of leadership and quality of conflict resolution in the group. Information flow may be improved as a result of interaction; but with a highly structured communication network and authoritarian leadership, communication flow might actually diminish. Similar points also can be made regarding organizational change. Each of the potential consequences depends to a considerable degree on the quality of the mix of other relevant variables in the model.

Hackman (1990) has identified three consequences for measuring the effectiveness of groups. He writes:

> First, is the degree to which the group's productive output . . . meets the standards of quantity, quality, and timeliness of the people who receive . . . that output.
> . . . The second dimension is the degree to which the [group] process . . . enhances the capability of members to work together interdependently in the future.
> . . . The third dimension is the degree to which the group experience contributes to the growth and personal well-being of team members. (pp. 6–7)

This seems like a good way to measure the ultimate success or effectiveness of the groups to which you belong.

What we have attempted to do in this chapter and throughout the book is to indicate ways to better understand and improve your functioning in small groups. There are no guarantees that these improved consequences will occur. In fact, as Katzenbach and Smith (1993) put it, "Teams are not the solution to everyone's . . . needs. They will not solve every problem [nor] enhance every group's results. . . . Moreover, when misapplied, they can be both wasteful and disruptive" (p. 24). However, considerable research cited earlier leads us to believe there is a distinct probability that you can and will become a more effective group participant if you are able to implement the ideas we have discussed.

The readings for this chapter help show how you can improve several small group consequences. Directly or indirectly, these articles touch on how to improve all six consequences discussed in this chapter. The article by Norman Maier even proposes a contingency model consistent with systems theory that suggests which types of problems are more likely to be solved using group decisions and which can be solved by the leader acting alone.

EXERCISES

1. Getting the Car Home

Divide the class in half. Let one half attempt to solve this problem individually, with no conversation allowed between and among participants. Record the number who solve the problem correctly as well as the average amount of time taken to solve it (sum the times of all persons and divide by the number of persons). Have the other half of the class form into groups of four or five people. Record how many groups correctly solve the problem and the average length of time taken per group.

Problem   You are stranded with a flat tire. In attempting to change the tire, you step on the hubcap containing the lug nuts (which hold the wheel on), and all five nuts are lost down a storm sewer. How do you get the car home?

2. Case Study Discussion

Read the following excerpts from an article on health care reform.

> *GOP SCOFFS AT CLINTON PLEDGE TO SIMPLIFY HEALTH CARE**
> By CHRISTOPHER CONNELL
>   President Clinton promises to simplify health care and free Americans from "the most bureaucratic system that exists anywhere in the world." But Republicans see less choice for patients—and even more red tape.

From *The Ann Arbor News,* December 30, 1993, p. A6.

"Simplicity is, 'I will do what I'm told by the government.' They'll tell me what I can buy, where I can buy it and how much I'll have to pay for it," complained Rep. Dick Armey, R-Texas.

"Thirteen hundred pages of red tape," sputtered House Republican Whip Newt Gingrich.

Clinton's critics are attacking two key features of his health reform plan. One is the creation of a powerful National Health Board that could set limits on private health insurance premiums; the other is a requirement that most Americans buy their coverage through new, government-run health alliances.

Another feature of the plan is that employers would be required to pay eighty percent of the health care costs of their employees. Business owners, especially in small businesses, say that these increased costs would either force them to lay off workers, or in some cases, go out of business.

Divide into groups of five and discuss the above case. When you are finished, each group should report its results to the class.

3. Personal Feedback Exercise

On the basis of the case study discussion in Exercise 2, answer the questions in Figure 7.2 for each person in the class (while every other person in the class does the same thing). Ultimately you will receive feedback from every other class member. These can be anonymous, or you may sign your name if you wish.

4. Case Study Discussion

Read the following excerpts from an article on the use of aborted fetus eggs.

UPROAR ERUPTS OVER FUTURE USE OF ABORTED FETUSES' EGGS
By WILLIAM TUOHY

Another controversy over fertilization techniques erupted Sunday in Britain amid reports that a method of producing test-tube babies from aborted fetuses is on the horizon.

Researchers said the technique, which has sparked intense ethical debate, might be able to produce a human baby within three years if the British Medical Association's ethics committee gives it the go-ahead as expected next month.

The latest developments in fertilization come after a 59-year-old woman gave birth to twins in a London clinic after undergoing artificial fertilization in Rome. Many doctors and officials argued that women past menopause are unsuitable mothers because of the vast differences between them and their offspring.

From *The Ann Arbor News*, January 3, 1994, p. A1.

FIGURE 7.2   PERSONAL FEEDBACK EXERCISE FORM

Comments for _____

Following are some general impressions I have formed of your performance over the course of the semester.

1. In the task or problem-solving areas, you seem to have the following
   strengths:

   weaknesses:

2. In terms of your ability to *communicate clearly and effectively* on an interpersonal level, you seem to have the following
   strengths:

   weaknesses:

3. In terms of your ability to *work with others on a social-emotional level,* you seem to have the following
   strengths:

   weaknesses:

4. In the following areas you seem to have improved during the semester:

5. Additional comments:

> Last week a British fertility clinic was embroiled in another controversy over implanting a white woman's egg into a black woman, following reports that the woman and her husband, a man of mixed race, wanted to ensure the color of the child.
>
> Member of Parliament David Alton . . . [said of] the new treatment, "This consumerist approach to the creation of life puts it on a par with an American fast-food outlet."

Get into groups of five and discuss the ethics of these practices. See if you can agree as a group on what should be done. Each group should report its results to the rest of the class.

READINGS: OVERVIEW

Most of us who work in small groups are interested to one extent or another in getting results. In the first article, Norman Maier offers a very practical discussion of the formula $ED = Q \times A$ briefly described in this chapter. This article also bridges the gap between communicating in small groups and applying those concepts and skills to meeting the needs of an organization.

In the final article, Schlesinger, Sathe, Schlesinger, and Kotter offer a comprehensive spectrum of seven methods for dealing with resistance to change.

Improving Decisions in an Organization

Norman R. F. Maier

The Pragmatic Test of Decisions

Most management situations are sufficiently complex so that solutions to problems or decisions that are to be made cannot be classified into correct and incorrect categories. Rather the alternative possibilities have relative merits, and the standards by which they are to be judged are not agreed upon. Frequently the criteria for judging them are unclear, or there is a lack of agreement on the correct standards to use. People may favor certain decisions because they fit the facts, because they like them, because they get support from those who must execute them, because they are the only ones that came to mind, because making a change in preference may cause them to lose face, because they like the person who suggested a particular decision, because the alternative favored is their brain child, because they participated in reaching it, and for a variety of other reasons. Some of these reasons may

From Norman R. G. Maier, Problem-Solving Discussions and Conferences *(New York: McGraw-Hill, 1963), pp. 1–9. Reprinted by permission of the estate of Norman R. F. Maier.*

be of assistance in the reaching of effective decisions while others may be a hindrance.

Regardless of why people favor certain solutions or decisions over others, the test of a decision's value is quite a different matter. If the pragmatic test is to be used, an effective decision would be the one that produced the desired objectives most completely, achieved the desired objective most efficiently (costwise, energywise, and with the least undesirable side effects), and carried with it the most valuable by-products. These three measures of success might sometimes be in conflict, but in any event they would all be dependent on the outcome of the decision.

In other words, decisions can best be evaluated in terms of subsequent events, and unfortunately it is then too late to change the decision. For example, General Eisenhower's decision to invade the French coast at a time when the weather report was doubtful is regarded as a good one because it turned out that the weather did not interfere with the plans. Had the weather turned out to be sufficiently unfavorable and created great losses, his decision would have been open to criticism. In this instance the weather information indicated that invasion was risky on the date set for the invasion. However, the alternative was to set another date and go through the costly preparation process again.

Decisions of this sort may be regarded as lucky, or we might suppose that the decision maker has some kind of intuition, some special wisdom, or some special information that guides him. Regardless of how we view such decisions, the factor of chance plays a part. Some people are wealthy because their ancestors happened to settle along a river bank that later became a thriving city. Even if we view the ancestors as having the intuition to settle at the right place, the payoff on these decisions did not occur in their lifetimes. It seems unlikely that potential real estate values were factors influencing these decisions, and hence it would be more appropriate to attribute the successes of the decisions to luck than to wisdom.

Granting that chance plays a part in successful decisions, we also must concede that some people seem to be lucky more often than others and that the difference exceeds what one would expect from the laws of probability. Some executives seem to have an uncanny way of making decisions that turn out to be highly successful; others may go through several bankruptcies. Although the borderline between luck and decision-making aptitude may sometimes be narrow, it is important to do what we can to reduce the chance factors to their bare minimum if we are to examine the factors that make for decision-making ability.

Since the final evaluation of the decision is only possible some time after the decision has been made, and since the evaluation of alternatives is often not available, we must confine our speculation to the ingredients of decision that have high probabilities for success. In examining alternate decisions we may appraise them from the point of view of their probable effectiveness.

For example, if a first-place baseball team is to play the seventh-place team, an even-money bet placed on the first-place team would be wiser, even if it turned out that the seventh-place team won. One cannot take unknowns into account in appraising decisions before the actual test. However, failure to consider all the factors and influences that are available before the decision is made will reduce its possibility for success. Thus the illness of two star players on the first-place team should not be overlooked.

The Dimensions of Effective Decisions

Two different dimensions seem to be relevant in appraising a decision's potential effectiveness. One of these is the objective or impersonal *quality* of the decision; the other has to do with its *acceptance* or the way the persons who must execute the decision *feel* about it. The usual conception of effective decisions has emphasized the quality dimension. This approach leads to a careful consideration of the facts of the case. The advice is to "get the facts; weigh and consider them; then decide." It is this emphasis that causes one to assume that there is a correct answer to a problem, a right decision to make. Although this position is sound in technological matters that do not involve people, one cannot assume that it is universally sound. It is this position that causes us to concentrate on getting more information and to assume that when decisions do not work out there must have been some oversight. Thus nations may debate peace plans for the world, attempting to improve the decision, when the fault may lie elsewhere. It is quite possible that any number of plans would be adequate if they received international acceptance. As soon as the behavior of people is involved, opinions and feelings introduce a second dimension.

It is important to clearly separate these two dimensions since, as we shall see, the ways for dealing with them are very different. Failure to differentiate the dimensions leads to complications in discussion because one person may be using terms such as "good" to describe the quality of the decision, another to describe its acceptability; and a third may be thinking in terms of the outcome, which depends on both.

Decisions may have varying degrees of acceptance by the group which must execute them; and it follows that, quality remaining constant, the effectiveness of decisions will be a function of the degree to which the executors of the decision like and believe in them.

For example, let us suppose that there are four ways to lay out a job and that the quality of these methods, from best to poorest, is in the following order: method A, method B, method C, and method D. Suppose further that the persons who must use these methods have a preference order as follows: method D, method B, method C, and method A. It is conceivable under these circumstances that method B would yield the best results even though it is not the decision of highest objective quality. Naturally one must consider the degrees of difference between each alternative; nevertheless, the fact remains that an inferior method may produce better results than a superior one, if the former has the greater support.

The formula for an effective decision *(ED)* therefore would require consideration of two independent aspects of a decision: (1) its purely objective or impersonal attributes, which we are defining as quality *(Q)*; and (2) its attractiveness or desirability to persons who must work with the decision, which we are defining as acceptance *(A)*. The first depends upon objective data (facts in the situation); the second on subjective data (feelings which are in people). Simply stated, the relationship may be expressed as follows:

$$ED = Q \times A$$

This separation of quality and acceptance somewhat alters the meaning of such expressions as "good" decisions and "correct" decisions. The term "goodness" might be used to describe degrees of quality, acceptance, or effectiveness and hence has little meaning when applied to decisions. The term "correct" similarly has different dimensions and in addition is limited because it is an absolute term and suggests that there are no moderately effective decisions, medium-quality decisions, and partially acceptable decisions.

It must also be recognized that the effect of acceptance on performance will vary from one problem to another. It is clear that when the execution of a decision is independent of people, the need for acceptance is less than when the execution is influenced by the motivations and attitudes of the people who must carry it out. Nevertheless, a respect for acceptance may be a worthwhile consideration in all group problem solving since a concern for a participant's satisfaction may influence his motivations and attitudes, which in turn would influence his contributions. For example, a marketing plan may have high quality and still have poor acceptance by a group of persons involved in designing the visual appearance of a package. Since the execution of the design and its reception by the public are independent of the initial planning group, it can be assumed that the success of the decision will be independent of the degree of acceptance of the decision-making group. However, what effect will such a decision have on a group if it has been railroaded through? If some members of the planning group are dissatisfied with the decision, may not this make them less valuable participants in the future? When we take the long-range point of view, dissatisfaction with a perfectly good decision can depress a group's future performance; whereas, high satisfaction with a decision may serve to upgrade future performance.

If we can assume the position that the acceptance of a decision by the group that must implement it is a desirable ingredient, what are the problem issues? First of all, we must examine how this ingredient is related to the other desired ingredient—quality.

It is one thing to say that in striving for effective decisions two criteria must be satisfied, but can one achieve both of these objectives simultaneously? High-quality decisions, on the one hand, require wisdom, and wisdom is the product of intelligence and knowledge. Decisions of high acceptance, on the other hand, require satisfaction, and satisfaction is the product of participation and involvement in decision making. Thus the method for achieving *quality* differs from the method for achieving *acceptance;* as a matter of fact they are in conflict.

Figure 1*A* describes this basic problem in aiming at two objectives. If we aim for both objectives, we may achieve neither. The traditional leadership approach is to aim for quality first, as in Fig. 1*B*. This means that the man responsible for decisions uses whatever resources he feels are needed in obtaining facts and opinions, and he may make free use of experts or consultants. However, the actual decision-making function resides in the leader who finally weighs the evidence and decides. Once a satisfactory quality has been achieved, the next step in this process is to obtain acceptance of the decision.

Traditional methods for achieving this secondary objective have ranged through (1) imposing the decision on subordinates who must execute it (dictatorial methods, using the motivation of fear); (2) playing the father figure and gaining acceptance through a sense of duty and trust (paternalistic methods, using the motivation of loyalty); (3) using persuasion types of approach which explain the virtues of the decision (selling methods, in which personal gains are stressed); and (4) using participative approaches which encourage discussion of decisions by subordinates but leave the final decisions to the superior (consultative management, in which the motivation is based on a limited degree of participation in which there is opportunity to discuss but no right to make a decision). Although this evolution of the decision-making process reveals improvement, the change has been confined to the aspect that is concerned with obtaining acceptance of decisions by subordinates. Throughout the history of the decision-making process, the quality ingredient has remained in the hands of the top man or group leader. Management philosophy is that the person held accountable for the decision should be the one who makes it. The fact that changes in methods for obtaining acceptance

FIGURE 1   QUALITY AND ACCEPTANCE AS TARGETS

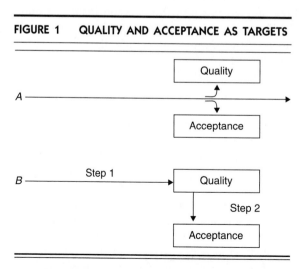

such matters as pay rates, he cannot expect the group to solve this type of problem through group decision.

In using group decision the superior serves as the discussion leader and presents the problem to his subordinates. His objective is to have the group resolve their differences through discussion while he remains neutral. He confines his activities to clarifying the problem, encouraging discussion, promoting communication, supplying information that may be at his disposal, and making appropriate summaries. His objective is to achieve unanimous agreement on a decision that is the product of the interaction in a group discussion.

Problems that fall into the high-acceptance category have to do with:

The fair way to distribute something desirable, be it a typewriter, a truck, office space, office furniture

The fair way to get something undesirable accomplished, be it unpleasant work, unattractive hours or shifts

The scheduling of overtime, vacations, coffee breaks, etc.

The fair way to settle disciplinary problems that involve violations of regulations, lack of cooperation, etc.

High-Acceptance, High-Quality Requirement

These are the problems that do not fall into the other two categories. At first this may seem to be the largest category of all, so that little seems to have been achieved by extracting the other two. However, in working with group problem solving, it soon becomes apparent that group decisions are often of surprisingly good quality. It is not uncommon for a supervisor to volunteer the information that the group's solution surpassed not only what he had expected, but what he could have achieved by himself. The fear that group decisions will be of poor quality appears to be greater than the hazard warrants. However, if the supervisor is anxious about the outcome, he is likely to interfere with the problem-solving process, rather than facilitate it. For this reason this category of problems should be handled by group decision only when the leader is experienced. Thus it is a category for which either group decision or leader decision is recommended, depending upon the supervisor's skills.

The fears of people frequently determine the motives they ascribe to others, particularly if they are members of an opposition group. For example, if a manager fears a drop in production, he unjustly assumes that his employees are motivated to produce less. Actually the motivational forces in employees form a complex pattern. They include not only what the employees want, but ways of protecting themselves from what they fear management wants to accomplish. With fear removed by the opportunity to participate, the outcome of a discussion often differs greatly from what is anticipated. Obstacles that seem insurmountable frequently disappear in thin air.

The Dynamics of Group Problem Solving

In order to illustrate the types of forces at work in a problem-solving interaction, it may be best to describe a case in the use of group decision. Specific incidents serve to bring theories and generalizations in closer contact with reality.

This case is selected because it is characteristic of the manner in which men solve problems involving attitudes toward prestige and seniority rights. At the same time it illustrates how the men on the job are aware of company objectives and do not take advantage of the company or of each other when the need for protective behavior is removed.

The problem arose because repair foremen in the telephone industry had a persistent problem in getting their men to clear "wet-weather drops."[1] A wet-weather drop is a defective line that runs from a pole to a building. These lines have to be replaced from time to time because water can seep through a break in the insulation and create a short. After a heavy rain there are reports of trouble, but since the difficulty is present only when the line is wet, the problem is a purely temporary one. During periods of expansion or when replacement material is at a minimum, many lines suffer from this wet-weather difficulty. If a station is out of order for this reason, the loss of service corrects itself and is not as serious as if the station were completely out of order. Hence the company, as well as the men, regards wet-weather drops to be minor and routine jobs in contrast to emergency jobs. Furthermore, repair men do not like to do this unimportant work, and they feel that anyone can do it without thinking. As a consequence, the men make little effort to get these jobs done. If the foreman decides to pressure men into bringing in a few wet-weather drops, he finds himself at a disadvantage. The men may promise to pick up one or two and then fail to do so. When asked why, they claim that they ran into extra difficulty on an emergency job and say, "You wanted me to do a good job on the other first, didn't you, boss?" Although the foreman may know the men are shirking, he never knows on what occasion the excuse is justified. It thus comes about that wet-weather drops are a headache to the foreman. When he gets far enough behind, he puts one man on the job full time and lets him clear wet-weather drops. The man in question feels degraded and wonders why he is picked on. To be as fair as possible, this job is usually given to the man with the least seniority. He may complain violently, but invariably the man with least seniority is in the minority. Among supervisory groups this practice is considered the fairest way to handle the situation, and they believe that the men want seniority to be recognized this way. They are completely unaware of the fact that this practice turns an undesirable job into one that has low status as well.

In a particular crew of twelve men the number of wet-weather drops was gradually increasing, and the time was approaching when something would have to be done about the matter. The foreman decided that this was a good problem on which to try group decision. He told his men that he realized no one liked to clear wet-weather drops and that he wanted to have their reactions on how the problem should be handled.

Of interest is the fact that no one in the group felt that the man with the least seniority should do the whole job. The man with most seniority talked against the idea of picking on the fellow with least seniority, saying that he had hated being stuck with the job when he had the least seniority and that he couldn't see why everybody shouldn't do a share of it. It was soon agreed that the job should be evenly divided among the crew. This crew divided up the job by assigning a work area for each man. In this way each man was to be responsible for the wet-weather drops in his area, and he was to be given a list of those. Each morning the local test desk was to designate for each man the wet-weather drop most in need of replacement. It was understood that he was to clear this one, if at all possible. This condition took care of clearing up the drops that were most essential from the point of view of the office. In addition, all agreed that each man should clear as many additional drops as his load permitted. However, when a man had cleared up all the wet-weather drops in his area, it was specifically understood that he should not be asked to help out another. This last condition clearly reveals an attitude built up over the years. It is evident that the reluctance to clear wet-weather drops hinged on the idea that when a man was conscientious, advantage was taken of him. Soon he got to be the "sucker" in the group or perhaps the foreman's pet. It was evident that all men were willing to do their parts but they did not wish to run the risk of being made a sucker. (Other foremen have testified that this defensive reaction made sense from the manner in which the job is frequently handled. The foreman wants to get the job done, and he begins to rely on those individuals who have cooperated in the past. Soon these men find they are doing all the undesirable jobs. It is just a matter of how long it takes a man to find out that he is losing out with the group.)

The results of this solution were immediately apparent. During the three-month period previous to the discussion, a total of eighty wet-weather drops had been cleared; during the week following the discussion, seventy-eight wet-weather drops were cleared and without any letup on the rest of the work. Within a few months the problem was practically nonexistent. The reaction of the men also bore out the effectiveness of the decision. Men discussed the number of drops they had cleared and showed a friendly competitive spirit. They discussed the time when they expected to be caught up and would only have to take care of wet-weather drops as they arose.

It should be noted that the men's notion of fairness was quite different from what the supervisor had anticipated. Although men strongly urge seniority privileges, they do not wish to give junior men a hard time. Rather, advantage is taken of junior men only when seniority rights are threatened. It is of special interest to note the protective reactions against the possibility that cooperation will lead to abuse. Once the protection was ensured, the men considered customer service. This recognition of the service is apparent from the fact that the crew wanted to clear the drops in the order of their importance. With defensive behavior removed, it is not uncommon for good quality solutions to emerge.

Dependence of the Solution's Quality on the Leader's Skills

The quality of group decisions can further be enhanced by improving the skills and the attitude of the discussion leader. Even with a minimum of skills the group decision approach can be effective with problems such as the following:

Setting standards on tardiness and absenteeism

Setting goals for production, quality, and service

Improving safety, housekeeping, etc.

Introducing new work procedures, changing standards, introducing labor-saving equipment, etc.

It is apparent that both quality and acceptance are needed in solving problems of this type, and for this reason they are the areas of greatest conflict in labor-management relations. However, the requirement of skill is more than methodology because it is something that cannot be decided, adopted, or purchased. It requires additional training in conference leadership, and this means an increase in a company's investment in management talents.

Conclusions

Problems may be divided into the following three types:

Type 1. Q/A problems: those for which the quality of the decision is clearly a more important objective than its acceptance. These may be successfully solved by the leader.

Type 2. A/Q problems: those for which acceptance of the decision is clearly a more important objective than its quality. These may be successfully handled by the group decision method in which the decision is made by the subordinates with the superior serving as a discussion leader.

Type 3. Q-A problems: those for which both quality and acceptance of the decision become major objectives. These problems may be handled in either of two ways, each requiring a different set of skills on the part of the leader. The alternatives are as follows:

Leader decision *plus* persuasive skills to gain acceptance or

Group decision *plus* conference leadership skills to gain quality.

The emphases in this book are on the second alternative because conference skills permit the effective use of a greater range of intellectual resources, thereby achieving high-quality decisions as a by-product.

Note

1. Taken from N. R. F. Maier, *Principles of Human Relations*, Wiley, New York, 1952.

Organizational Change Strategies and Tactics

Phylis F. Schlesinger, Vijay Sathe, Leonard Schlesinger, and John P. Kotter

Solving and avoiding organizational problems inevitably involves the introduction of organizational change. When the required changes are small and isolated, they usually can be accomplished without major problems. However, when they are large and involve many people and subunits, they often can cause significant problems.

Managing the change process is a critical skill for any manager. Very few organizations exist in a static state; the world is constantly changing. Outside the organization, in the space of a fiscal year, product development cycles go from two years to six months, because customers demand new products, better, and faster. Governments impose new regulations, and/or remove others. The financial environment becomes difficult to predict. Communications across organizations is intense and rapid, as the business environment becomes more global.

This kind of change in the competitive environment has an effect on organizations as well. They must seek and adopt more effective ways to set strategies, to market and manufacture products, to work effectively in an ever changing environment. Most organizations have to make major changes in

From Phylis F. Schlesinger, Vijay Sathe, Leonard Schlesinger, and John P. Kotter, Organization, 3d ed. *(Homewood, Ill.: Irwin, 1992).*

their management style, beliefs, systems, and perhaps even culture in order to meet this challenge. Whereas some companies make changes in their design factors and their management styles very easily, most do it with great difficulty. They become accustomed to their proven ways of managing, even if those ways are no longer as effective as they once were.

A Model for Assessing the Need for Change

Several factors need to be examined before one begins a change process. Managers can use the concepts of "fit" presented in the first parts of this text to analyze the organization's design problems. The ideas presented in this chapter will address ways to assess the need for organizational change, develop the "vision" for change, design implementation plans for change, and manage the change process. The ideas presented here can apply equally to managers at any organizational level.

Most organizations have a difficult time in preparing the organization for change. Once the organization is ready to change, it is often difficult to implement and sustain the process. Managers who are supporters of the change often meet resistance from many fronts. One president of a hotel company, for example, believes that the managers should be more attentive to the levels of service in their units. He exhorts them to change in a speech at the annual meeting; they all leave convinced that their unit will offer the best service imaginable. Once they return to their units, however, the speeches and new ideas fade in the day to day processes of the organization. Clearly, the change effort was not effective. If we look at the above example in terms of the model presented below, we can understand why.

There are many ways to conceptualize the change process.[1] We have found that change is more likely to be effective when the costs of making the change are outweighed by factors which create the motivation to change. The relationship can be explained as follows:[2]

$$Change = D \times M \times P > C$$

where D = the levels of dissatisfaction with the status quo, M = the new model for managing implicit in the change, P = the planned implementation process for making the change, and C = the cost of the change to the relevant stakeholders, the individuals, and groups in the organization.

Change can occur only when sufficient dissatisfaction (D) with the status quo is present in key individuals or groups, such as the Hotel President in

---

[1] See Michael Beer, *Organization Change and Development,* Scott, Foresman and Company, 1980; Richard Beckhard and Reuben T. Harris, *Organizational Transitions,* Addison-Wesley Publishing Company, 1987; and Rosabeth Kanter, *The Change Masters,* Simon and Schuster, 1983, for three examples.

[2] Michael Beer, *Organizational Change and Development,* Scott, Foresman and Co., 1980.

our example. These individuals have to articulate the new way of managing *(M)* which is necessary to make the changes. In our previous example, it was to pay more attention to customer service as a management tool. While most companies have articulated some kind of vision statement, the model for management is the way that managers have to put the vision into managerial practice. Finally, the organization has to have a process *(P)* for managing the change that is sufficiently well-planned, anticipates that resistance to the change will occur, understands where that resistance will come from, and outlines effective intervention methods for dealing with these changes. Unfortunately for our Hotel President, this is the piece he missed. Exhortation through speeches will not suffice. All of these variables combined must be greater than the cost *(C)* of the change economically and emotionally to the organization in question.

Creating Dissatisfaction

Most dissatisfaction comes when key organizational members recognize a crisis. A major customer suddenly shifts to another supplier. The bottom falls out of the market and managers are forced to make layoffs. Examples of organizational crises are as numerous as examples of the often traumatic change that results. However, a prescient manager is always looking for ways for the organization to improve continuously. S/he is constantly on the lookout for ways to make the organization more effective, and looks to communicate these ideas as a way to generate dissatisfaction with the status quo.

Often these ideas come from many sources. One source is from the competitive environment. Perhaps the hotel staff does not see the effects of poor service on customers—what difference can one angry customer make? Another source is the employees within the organization itself; the annual employee attitude surveys can be a powerful tool for diagnosing the culture and style of the organization. If the employees seem to be demoralized, dissatisfaction is present. In order to spread the word about the dissatisfaction present, to make it more known around the organization so as to arouse people to change, managers must communicate this concern through their letters, memos, actions, and expectations.

Developing a New Model for Managing

A vision of the future state, the structures and systems of the organization as well as the behaviors and attitudes of the employees, is essential for a change to occur. The vision a manager has of his/her unit or company's future can energize change, by uniting the people in a common goal. It also serves as a road map for change; establishing this model across the organization can be a planning exercise on just what the organizational problems are, and the solutions for them. Managers arrive at this vision through discussion, analysis, and observation. It should specify the "fit" of all the organization's elements, and be viable and adaptable over the long term.

At times the vision originates in a small part of the organization which itself serves as the role model for change. For example, one manufacturing company had a group of employees who focused on improving the cross-functional processes involved while they worked on developing a new product. Their results were so successful that they not only cut the introduction time from two years to one, but they also improved cross functional communication at the same time. Senior managers were so impressed by their efforts that they developed a "vision" of the organization as one which focused on process as well as on product, and developed a detailed model and plan for implementing process and product teams across the organization.

Managing the Process for Change

Having a vision of what ought to be does not translate directly into organizational life, however. Managers must work to develop a process for the implementation of the model they hold. This process is the sequence of events, meetings, speeches, communiques, celebrations, and design factor changes (personnel decisions, reward system changes, structural changes) directed at helping the model become a reality.

[There are a number of methods that] managers can use to implement the process of change. These include[3] building a coalition of backers and supporters, articulating and communicating the shared vision through symbols, signals, and rewards, assigning responsibility and accountability, ensuring communication, education, and training, and constantly monitoring the process as it goes forward. The particular strategies one uses to implement the desired change depends on many factors, most notably the amount and kind of resistance encountered, the position of the change initiator relative to the resistors, the sources of data and the energy of the change initiators for managing the implementation, and the stakes involved. These can be partially understood by looking at the costs of the change to those affected by it.

Costs of the Change

Change does not occur without costs to some parts of the organization. For example, the employee who has been used to performing one job the same

---

[3]Rosabeth Kanter, *The Change Masters,* Simon and Schuster, 1983.

way for years, who has developed a routine for work, may be terrified at the prospect of becoming a member of a self-managing work team where s/he is required to perform many tasks. The costs can be expressed in terms of the losses those with a stake in the change feel will occur. For some it is power, or a sense of competence, or a key relationship, or a sense of identity, or perhaps a key intrinsic or extrinsic reward. For whatever reason, understanding the costs to key individuals is crucial to planning the process of change.

It is useful for the change initiator to perform an assessment of each stakeholder affected by a change. What is that person's "stake" in the status quo? What do they believe they will lose? How can the cost of the change be decreased for that stakeholder? What techniques can one use to deflect the resistance that stakeholder will present? These data should be used in the planning of the change process itself.

Taken together, this model becomes a powerful tool for making sure a manager has considered all of the aspects of a change before embarking on one. Most managers can see the places where misfits or mismatches occur, and most have a particular view of where they would like to see the organization (or division or unit) be in the future. By understanding the nature and source of the resistance to the new model, the manager can plan the process to deal with that resistance.

Human Resistance to Change

Human resistance to change takes many forms—from open rebellion to subtle, passive resistance. It emerges for many reasons—rational and irrational. Some reasons are primarily self-centered; others are selfless.

Politics and Power Struggles

One major reason that people resist organizational change is that they see they will lose something of personal value due to the change. Resistance in these cases is often called "politics" or "political behavior" because people focus on their own interests and not the total organization.[4]

After years of rapid growth, for example, the president of one organization decided that its size demanded the creation of a new staff function—new-product planning and development—to be headed by a vice president. Operationally, this change eliminated most of the decision-making power that the

---

[4]For a discussion of power and politics in corporations, see Abraham Zaleznik and Manfred F. R. Kets De Vries, *Power and the Corporate Mind* (Boston: Houghton Mifflin, 1975), chap. 6; and Robert H. Miles, *Macro Organizational Behavior* (Santa Monica, Calif.: Goodyear Publishing, 1978), chap. 4.

vice presidents of marketing, engineering, and production had over new products. Inasmuch as new products were important in this organization, the change also reduced the status of marketing, engineering, and production VPs. Yet, status was important to those three vice presidents. During the two months after the president announced his idea for a new-product vice president, the existing vice presidents each came up with six or seven reasons why the new arrangement might not work. Their objections grew louder and louder until the president shelved the new job idea.

In another example, a manufacturing company traditionally employed a large group of personnel people as counselors to production employees. This group of counselors exhibited high morale because of the professional satisfaction they received from the helping relationships they had with employees. When a new performance-appraisal system was installed, the personnel people were required to provide each employee's supervisor with a written evaluation of the employee's emotional maturity, promotion potential, and so on, every six months. As some personnel people immediately recognized, the change would alter their relationship with most employees— from a peer helper to more of a boss/evaluator. Predictably, they resisted the new system. While publicly arguing that the new system was not as good for the company as the old one, they privately put as much pressure as possible on the personnel vice president until he significantly altered the new system.

Political behavior emerges in organizations because what is in the best interests of one individual or group is sometimes not in the best interests of the total organization or of other individuals and groups. The consequences of organizational change efforts often are good for some people and bad for others. As a result, politics and power struggles often emerge through change efforts.

While this political behavior sometimes takes the form of two or more armed camps publicly fighting it out, it usually is subtle. In many cases, it occurs completely under the surface of public dialogue. In a similar way, although power struggles are sometimes initiated by scheming and ruthless individuals, they are fostered more often by those who view their potential loss as an unfair violation of their implicit, or psychological, contract with the organization.[5]

Misunderstanding and a Lack of Trust

People also resist change when they incorrectly perceive that it might cost them considerably more than they will gain. Such situations often occur when people are unable to understand the full implications of a change or when trust is lacking in the change initiator-employee relationship.[6]

---

[5]Edgar Schein, *Organizational Psychology* (Englewood Cliffs, N.J.: Prentice-Hall, 1965), p. 44.
[6]See Chris Argyris, *Intervention Theory and Method* (Reading, Mass.: Addison-Wesley Publishing, 1970), p. 70.

For example, when the president of a small midwestern company announced to his managers that the company would implement a flexible work schedule for all employees, it never occurred to him that he might run into resistance. He had been introduced to the concept at a management seminar and decided to use it to make working conditions at his company more attractive, particularly to clerical and plant personnel. Shortly after the announcement to his managers, numerous rumors began to circulate among plant employees—none of whom really knew what flexible working hours meant and many of whom were distrustful of the manufacturing vice president. One rumor suggested that flexible hours meant that most people would have to work whenever their supervisors asked them to—including weekends and evenings. The employee association, a local union, held a quick meeting and then presented the management with a nonnegotiable demand that the flexible hours concept be dropped. The president, caught completely by surprise, decided to drop the issue.

Few organizations can be characterized as having a high level of trust between employees and managers; consequently, it is easy for misunderstandings to develop when change is introduced. Unless misunderstandings are surfaced and clarified quickly, they can lead to resistance.

Different Assessments of the Situation

Another common reason people resist organizational change is that their analysis of the situation differs from that of persons initiating the change. In such cases, their analysis typically sees more costs than benefits resulting from the change, for themselves and for their company.

For example, the president of one moderate-sized bank was shocked by his staff's analysis of their real estate investment trust (REIT) loans. Their complex analysis suggested that the bank could easily lose up to $10 million and that possible losses were increasing each month by 20 percent. Within a week, the president drew up a plan to reorganize the bank division that managed REITs. However, because of his concern for the bank's stock price, he chose not to release the staff report to anyone except the new REIT section manager. The reorganization immediately ran into massive resistance from the people involved. The group sentiment, as articulated by one person, was "Has he gone mad? Why is he tearing apart this section of the bank? His actions have already cost us three very good people [who quit] and have crippled a new program we were implementing [which the president was unaware of] to reduce our loan losses."

Persons who initiate change sometimes incorrectly assume that they have all relevant information required to conduct an adequate organizational analysis. They often assume that persons affected by the change have the same basic facts, when they do not. In either case, the difference in information that groups work with often leads to differences in analysis, which can lead to resistance. Moreover, insofar as the resistance is based on a more accurate analysis of the situation than that held by persons initiating the change, that resistance is good for the organization, a fact that is not obvious to some managers who assume resistance is always bad.[7]

Fear

People sometimes resist change because they know or fear they will not be able to develop the new skills and behaviors required. All human beings are limited in their ability to change their behavior, with some people more limited than others.[8] Organizational change can inadvertently require people to change too much, too quickly. When such a situation occurs, people typically resist the change—sometimes consciously but often unconsciously.

Peter Drucker has argued that the major obstacle to organization growth is managers' inability to change their attitudes and behaviors.[9] In many cases, he points out, corporations grow to a certain point and then slow down or stop growing because key managers are unable to change as rapidly as their organizations. Even if they intellectually understand the need for changes in how they operate, they sometimes cannot make the transition.

All people who are affected by change experience some emotional turmoil because change involves loss and uncertainty—even changes that appear positive or "rational."[10]

For example, a person who receives a more important job as a result of an organizational change will probably be happy. But, it is possible that such a person feels uneasy. A new and different job will require new and different behavior, new and different relationships, and the loss of some current activities and relationships that provide satisfaction. It is common under such circumstances for a person to emotionally resist giving up certain aspects of the current situation.

Still Other Reasons

People also sometimes resist organizational change to save face; to go along with the change would be an admission that some of their previous decisions or beliefs were wrong. They may resist because of peer pressure or because of a supervisor's resistant attitude. Indeed, there are many reasons why people resist change.[11]

---

[7]See Paul R. Lawrence, "How to Deal with Resistance to Change," *Harvard Business Review,* May–June 1954.

[8]For a discussion of resistance that is personality based, see Goodwin Watson, "Resistance to Change," in *The Planning of Change,* ed. Warren Bennis, Kenneth Benne, and Robert Chin (New York: Holt, Rinehart & Winston, 1969), pp. 489–93.

[9]The *Practice of Management* (New York: Harper & Row, 1954).

[10]See Robert Luke, "A Structural Approach to Organizational Change," *Journal of Applied Behavioral Science,* 1973.

[11]For a general discussion of resistance and reasons for it, see Gerald Zaltman and Robert Duncan, *Strategies for Planned Change* (New York: John Wiley & Sons, 1977), chap. 3.

Because of all the reasons for resistance to organizational change, it is hardly surprising that organizations do not automatically and easily adapt to environmental, technological, or strategic changes. Indeed, organizations usually adapt only because managers successfully employ strategies and tactics for dealing with potential resistance.

Tactics for Dealing with Resistance

Managers may use a number of tactics to deal with resistance to change. These include education/communication, participation, facilitation and support, negotiation, co-optation, coercion, and manipulation.[12]

Education/Communication

One of the most common ways to deal with resistance to change is education and communication. This tactic is aimed at helping people see the need for and logic of a change. It can involve one-on-one discussions, presentations to groups, or memos and reports. For example, as a part of an effort to make changes in a division's structure, measurement system, and reward system, the division manager put together a one-hour audiovisual presentation that explained changes and their reasons for changes. Over a four-month period, he made this presentation a dozen times to groups of 20 or 30 corporate and divisional managers.

Education/communication is ideal when resistance is based on inadequate or inaccurate information and analysis, especially if the initiators need the resister's help in implementing the change. But, this tactic requires at least a good relationship between the initiators and the others, or the resisters may not believe what they hear. It also requires time and effort, particularly if many people are involved.

Participation

Participation as a change tactic implies that the initiators involve the resisters or potential resisters in some aspect of the design and implementation of the change. For example, the head of a small financial services company once created a task force to help design and implement changes in the company's reward system. The task force was composed of eight second- and third-level managers from different parts of the company. The president's specific request was that they recommend changes in the company's benefits package. They were given six months and were asked to file a brief progress report with the president once a month. After making their recommendations,

---

[12]There are many ways to label change tactics. This list of seven tactics is one useful approach. Other writers use variations of this list.

which the president largely accepted, they were asked to help the firm's personnel director implement them.

Participation is a rational choice of tactics when change initiators believe they do not have all the information they need to design and implement a change or when they need the wholehearted commitment of others in implementing a change. Considerable research has demonstrated that participation generally leads to commitment, not just compliance.[13] But participation has drawbacks. It can lead to a poor solution if the process is not carefully managed, and it can be time consuming.

Facilitation and Support

Another way for managers to deal with potential resistance to change is through facilitation and support. As a tactic, it might include providing training in new skills, giving employees time off after a demanding period, or simply listening and providing emotional support.

For example, one rapidly growing electronics company did the following to help people adjust to frequent organizational changes. First, it staffed its human resource department with four counselors who spent most of their time talking to people who were feeling "burned out" or who were having difficulty adjusting to new jobs. Second, on a selective basis, it offered people "minisabbaticals," which were four weeks in duration and involved some reflective or educational activity away from work. Finally, it spent money on inhouse education and training programs.

Facilitation and support are best suited for resistance due to adjustment problems. The basic drawback of this approach is that it can be time consuming and expensive and still fail.[14]

Negotiation

Negotiation as a change tactic involves buying out active or potential resisters. This could mean, for example, giving a union a higher wage rate in return for a work rule change, or it could involve increasing an individual's pension benefits in return for early retirement.

Effective use of negotiation as a change tactic can be seen in the activities of a division manager in a large manufacturing company. The divisions in this company were highly interdependent. One division manager wanted to make some major changes in the division's organization. Yet, because of interdependencies, she recognized that she would be forcing some inconvenience and change on other divisions. To prevent top managers in other divisions from undermining her efforts, she negotiated with each division a

---

[13]See, for example, Alfred Marrow, David Bowers, and Stanley Seashore, *Management by Participation* (New York: Harper & Row, 1967).
[14]Zaltman and Duncan, *Strategies for Planned Change*, chap. 4.

written agreement that promised certain positive outcomes (for them) within certain time periods as a result of her changes and, in return, specified certain types of cooperation expected from the divisions during the change process. Later, whenever other divisions began to complain about changes or the process, she pulled out the negotiated agreements.

Negotiation is particularly appropriate when it is clear that someone will lose out as a result of a change and yet has significant power to resist. As a result, it can be an easy way to avoid major resistance in some instances. Like the other tactics, negotiation may become expensive—and a manager who once makes it clear that he or she will negotiate to avoid resistance opens up the possibility of being blackmailed by others.[15]

Co-optation

A fifth tactic managers use to deal with potential or actual resistance to change is co-optation. Co-opting an individual usually involves giving him or her a desirable role in the design or implementation of the change. Co-opting a group involves giving one of its leaders, or someone it respects, a key role in the design or implementation of a change. A change initiator could, for example, try to co-opt the sales force by allowing the sales manager to be privy to the design of the changes and by seeing that the most popular salesperson gets a raise as part of the change.

To reduce the possibility of corporate resistance to an organizational change, one division manager in a large multibusiness corporation successfully used co-optation in the following way. He invited the corporate human relations vice president, a close friend of the president's, to help him and key staff analyze some division problems. Because of his busy schedule, the corporate VP was not able to do much information gathering or analysis, thus limiting his influence on the diagnoses. But, his presence at key meetings helped commit him to the diagnosis and the solution designed by the group. The commitment was subsequently important because the president, at least initially, did not like some of the proposed changes. Nevertheless, after discussion with his human resource VP, he did not try to block them.

Co-optation can, under certain circumstances, be an inexpensive and easy way to gain an individual's or a group's support (less expensive, for example, than negotiation and quicker than participation). Nevertheless, it has drawbacks. If people feel they are being tricked into not resisting, they may respond negatively. And, if they use their ability to influence the design and implementation of changes in ways that are not in the best interests of the organization, they can create serious problems.

---

[15]For an excellent discussion of negotiation, see Gerald Nierenberg, *The Art of Negotiating* (New York: Cornerstone, 1974).

Manipulation

Manipulation, in this context, refers to covert influence attempts. Co-optation is a form of manipulation. Other forms do not have specific names but involve, for instance, the selective use of information and the conscious structuring of events so as to have some desired (but covert) impact on participants.

Manipulation suffers from the same drawbacks as co-optation, but to a greater degree. When people feel they are not being treated openly or that they are being lied to, they often react negatively. Nevertheless, manipulation can be used successfully—particularly when all other tactics are not feasible or have failed.[16] With one's back to the wall, with inadequate time to use education, participation, or facilitation, and without the power or other resources to use negotiation, coercion, or co-optation, a manager might resort to manipulating information channels to scare people into thinking there is a crisis coming that they can avoid only by change.

Coercion

The seventh tactic managers use to deal with resistance is coercion. They essentially force people to accept a change, explicitly or implicitly threatening them with the loss of jobs, promotion possibilities, raises, or whatever else they control. Like manipulation, coercion is a risky tactic because people resent forced change. Yet, coercion has the advantage of overcoming resistance quickly. And, in situations where speed is essential, this tactic may be the only alternative.

For example, when assigned to "turn around" a failing division in a large conglomerate, the chosen manager relied mostly on coercion to achieve the organizational changes she desired. She did so because she felt, "I did not have enough time to use other methods and I needed to make changes that were pretty unpopular among many of the people."

Using Change Tactics

Effective organizational change efforts are almost always characterized by the skillful use of a number of these change tactics. Conversely, less effective change efforts usually involve the misuse of one or more of these tactics.

Managers sometimes misuse change tactics simply because they are unaware of the strengths and limitations of each tactic (see Figure 1). Sometimes they run into difficulties because they rely only on the same limited number of tactics regardless of the situation (e.g., they always use participa-

---

[16]See John P. Kotter, "Power, Dependence, and Effective Management," *Harvard Business Review,* July–August 1977, pp. 133–35.

FIGURE 1 TACTICS FOR DEALING WITH RESISTANCE TO CHANGE

Tactic	Best for:	Advantages	Drawbacks
Education/ communication	Resistance based on lack of information or inaccurate information and analysis	Once persuaded, people will often help with implementing the change.	Can be very time consuming if large numbers of people are involved.
Participation	Situations in which initiators do not have all the information needed to design the change and where others have considerable power to resist.	People who participate will be committed to implementing change. Any relevant information they have will be integrated into the change plan.	Can be time consuming. Participators could design an inappropriate change.
Facilitation and support	Dealing with people who are resisting because of adjustment problems.	No other tactic works as well with adjustment problems.	Can be time consuming, expensive, and still fail.
Negotiation	Situations where someone or some group will lose in a change and where they have considerable power to resist.	Sometimes it is an easy way to avoid major resistance.	Can be too expensive in many cases. Can alert others to negotiate for compliance.
Co-optation	Specific situations where the other tactics are too expensive or are not feasible.	Can help generate support for implementing a change (but less than participation).	Can create problems if people recognize the co-optation.
Manipulation	Situations where other tactics will not work or are too expensive.	Can be a quick and inexpensive solution to resistance problems.	Costs initiators some credibility. Can lead to future problems.
Coercion	When speed is essential and the change initiators possess considerable power.	Speed. Can overcome any kind of resistance.	Risky. Can leave people angry with the initiators.

tion and persuasion or coercion and manipulation).[17] Sometimes they misuse the tactics simply because they are not chosen and implemented as a part of a clearly considered change strategy.

Change Strategies

In approaching an organizational change situation, managers explicitly or implicitly make strategic choices regarding the speed of the effort, the amount of preplanning, the involvement of others, and the relative emphasis of different change tactics. Successful change efforts are those in which choices are both internally consistent and fit some key situation variables.

The strategic options available to managers exist on a continuum.[18] See Figure 2. At one end of the continuum, the strategy calls for a rapid implementation of changes, with a clear plan of action and little involvement of others. This type of strategy mows over any resistance and, at the extreme, would involve a fait accompli. At the other end of the continuum, the strategy would call for a slower change process that is less clearly planned from the start and that involves many people in addition to the change initiators. This type of strategy is designed to reduce resistance to a minimum.[19]

With respect to tactics, the farther to the left one operates on the continuum in Figure 2, the more one uses coercion and the less one uses other tactics—especially participation. The opposite is true the more one operates to the right on the continuum—less coercion is used and other tactics are used more.

Exactly where a change effort should be strategically positioned on the continuum in Figure 2 is a function of four key variables:

1. *The amount and type of resistance anticipated.* The greater the anticipated resistance, other factors being equal, the more appropriate it is to move toward the right on the continuum.[20] The greater the anticipated resistance, the more difficult to simply overwhelm it and the more one needs to find ways to reduce it.

2. *The position of the initiator vis-à-vis the resisters, especially regarding power.* The greater the initiator's power, the better the initiator's relationships with the others; and the more the others expect that the initiator might

---

[17]Ibid., pp. 135–36.
[18]See Larry E. Greiner, "Patterns of Organizational Change," *Harvard Business Review,* May–June 1967; and Larry E. Greiner and Louis B. Barnes, "Organization Change and Development," in *Organization Change and Development,* ed. Gene Dalton and Paul Lawrence (Homewood, Ill.: Richard D. Irwin, 1970), pp. 3–5.
[19]For a good discussion of an approach that attempts to minimize resistance, see Renato Tagiuri, "Notes on the Management of Change," Working Paper, Harvard Business School.
[20]Jay Lorsch, "Managing Change," pp. 676–78.

FIGURE 2   STRATEGIC OPTIONS FOR THE MANAGEMENT OF CHANGE

Rapid changes	Slow changes
Clearly planned	Not clearly planned initially
Little involvement of others	Lots of involvement of others
Attempt to overcome any resistance	Attempt to minimize any resistance

Key Situational Variables
- The amount and type of resistance that is anticipated.
- The position of the initiators vis-à-vis the resisters (in terms of power, trust, etc.).
- The locus of relevant data for designing the change and of needed energy for implementing it.
- The stakes involved (e.g., the presence or absence of a crisis, the consequences of resistance and lack of change).

---

move unilaterally, the more one can move to the left on the continuum.[21] On the other hand, the weaker the initiator's position, the more he or she is forced to operate to the right.

3. *The locus of relevant data for designing the change and of needed energy for implementing it.* The more the initiators anticipate they will need information from others to help design the change and commitment from them to help implement it, the more they must move to the right.[22] Gaining useful information and commitment requires time and the involvement of others.

4. *The stakes involved.* The greater the short-run potential for risks to organizational performance and survival, the more one must move to the left.

Organizational change efforts that are based on an inconsistent strategy, or ones that do not fit the situation, run into predictable problems. For example, an effort that is not clearly planned but quickly implemented will almost always have unanticipated problems. Efforts that attempt to involve large numbers of people and at the same time try to move quickly will always sacrifice either speed or involvement. Efforts in which the change initiators do not have all the information that they need to correctly design a change but which nevertheless move quickly and involve few others sometimes encounter enormous problems.

---

[21]Ibid.
[22]Ibid.

Implications for Managing Organizational Change

Organizational change efforts are aided by an analysis and planning process composed of the following three phases:

1. Conducting a thorough organizational analysis—one that identifies the current situation, any problems, and the forces that are possible causes of problems. The analysis must clearly specify:

   a. The actual significance of the problems.

   b. The speed with which the problems must be addressed if additional problems will be avoided.

   c. The types of changes needed.

2. Conducting a thorough analysis of factors relevant to implementing the necessary changes. This analysis focuses on questions of:

   a. Who might resist the changes, why, and to what extent.

   b. Who has information that is needed to design the change and whose cooperation is essential in implementing it.

   c. The position of the change initiator vis-à-vis other relevant parties in terms of power, trust, normal modes of interaction, and so forth.

3. Selecting a change strategy based on the analysis in Phases 1 and 2, a set of change tactics, and then designing an action plan that specifies:

   a. What must be done.

   b. By whom.

   c. In what sequence.

   d. Within what time frame.

When initiating and managing an organizational change, it is conceivable that some or all of these steps will need to be repeated if unforeseen events occur or if new and relevant information surfaces. At the extreme, in a highly participative change, the process might be repeated a dozen times over a period of months or years. The key to successful organizational change is not whether these steps are repeated once or many times but whether they are done competently and thoroughly.

References

Acuff, Frank L., 1993. *How to negotiate anything with anyone anywhere around the world.* New York: American Management Association.

Adams, Debra, 1992. Empowerment splits union, board. *Detroit Free Press,* September 1: 1A, 6A.

Albanese, Robert, and David Van Fleet, 1985. Rational behavior in groups: the free-riding tendency. *Academy of Management Review* **11:** 244–255.

Amburgey, Terry L., Dawn Kelly, and William P. Barnett, 1993. Resetting the clock: the dynamics of organizational change and failure. *Administrative Science Quarterly* **38:** 51–73.

Ancona, Deborah Gladstein, 1990. Outward bound: strategies for team survival in an organization. *Academy of Management Journal* **33:** No. 2, 334–365.

Argyle, Michael, 1967. *The psychology of interpersonal behavior.* Baltimore: Penguin.

Aronson, Elliot, 1973. The rationalizing animal. *Psychology Today* **6:** 46–52.

———, and Judson Mills, 1959. Effect of severity of initiation on liking for a group. *Journal of Abnormal and Social Psychology* **59:** 177–181.

Asch, Solomon, 1952. *Social psychology.* Englewood Cliffs, N.J.: Prentice-Hall.

———, 1956. Studies of independence and conformity: a minority of one against a unanimous majority. *Psychological Monographs* **70:** No. 9 (Whole No. 416).

Associated Press, 1986a. Schools reject longstanding medical oath. *The Idaho Statesman,* May 18.

———, 1986b. Vegetarian graduates get paper diplomas. *The Idaho Statesman,* May 10: 2.

———, 1990a. Bay area delivers flood of "quake babies." *Ann Arbor News,* July 12: A1.

———, 1990b. City manages to get itself out of a (man) hole. *Ann Arbor News,* June 23: A2.

———, 1992. Nose rings? No. *Ann Arbor News,* July 6: A5.

Avianca pilots not trained to say "fuel emergency," 1990. *Detroit Free Press,* June 23: 4A.

Axtell, Roger E., 1991. *Gestures: the do's and taboos of body language around the world.* New York: Wiley.

Bales, Robert F., 1950. *Interaction process analysis.* Reading, Mass.: Addison-Wesley.

———, 1970. *Personality and interpersonal behavior.* New York: Holt, Rinehart and Winston.

———, and Fred Strodbeck, 1951. Phases in group solving. *Journal of Abnormal and Social Psychology* **46:** 485–495.

Barnard, William, 1991. Group influence and the likelihood of a unanimous majority. *Journal of Social Psychology* **131:** 607–613.

———, Carol Baird, Marilyn Greenwalt, and Ray Karl, 1992. Intragroup cohesiveness and reciprocal social influence in male and female discussion groups. *Journal of Social Psychology* **132:** 179–188.

Barnlund, Dean, 1968. *Interpersonal communication: survey and studies.* Boston: Houghton Mifflin.

Barol, Bill, 1990. Anatomy of a fad. *Newsweek,* September: 40–41.

Barrett, Marty W., and Thomas A. Carey, 1989. Communicating strategy: the best investment a CEO can make. *Mid-American Journal of Business* **4:** No. 1, 3–6.

Bass, B., C. Wurster, P. Doll, and D. Clair, 1953. Situational and personality factors in leadership among sorority women. *Psychological Monographs* **67:** No. 16 (Whole No. 366).

Batchelor, James, and George Goethals, 1972. Spatial arrangements in freely formed groups. *Sociometry* **35:** 270–279.

Bauduin, E. Scott, 1971. Obscene language and source credibility: an experimental study. Paper presented at the annual conference of the International Communication Association, Phoenix, Arizona.

Bazerman, Max H., and Margaret A. Neale, 1992. *Negotiating rationally.* New York: Free Press.

Beck, Joan, 1990. 2 Live Crew is more offensive than obscene. *Detroit Free Press,* June 25: 7A.

Beebe, Paul, 1986. Going in circles. *The Idaho Statesman,* May 11.

Benne, Kenneth D., and Paul Sheats, 1948. Functional roles of group members. *Journal of Social Issues* **4:** 41–49.

Bennis, Warren, and Burt Nanus, 1985. *Leaders: the strategies for taking charge.* New York: Harper & Row.

———, and Herbert Shepard, 1961. Group observation. In Warren Bennis, Kenneth Benne, and Robert Chin (eds.). *The planning of change.* New York: Holt, Rinehart and Winston, pp. 743–756.

Beyerlein, Michael, and Douglas Johnson, 1994. *Theories of self-managing work teams.* Greenwich, Conn.: JAI Press.

Bilodeau, J., and H. Schlosberg, 1959. Similarity in stimulating conditions as a variable in retroactive inhibition. *Journal of Experimental Psychology* **41:** 199–204.

Blackburn, Richard, and Benson Rosen, 1993. Total quality and human resource management: lessons learned from Baldridge award-winning companies. *Academy of Management Executive* **7:** 49–66.

Blair, Gwenda, 1988. *Almost golden: Jessica Savitch and the selling of television news.* New York: Simon and Schuster.

Blake, Robert, and Jane Mouton, 1970. The fifth achievement. *Journal of Applied Behavioral Sciences* **6:** 413–426.

Block, Peter, 1987. *The empowered manager.* San Francisco: Jossey-Bass.

Bloom, Benjamin S., and Lois J. Broder, 1961. Problem-solving processes of college students. In Theodore L. Harris and Wilson E. Schwahn (eds.). *Selected readings in the learning process.* New York: Oxford University Press, pp. 31–79.

Blotnick, Srully, 1986. Survey: women say affairs of the heart thrive at workplace. *The Idaho Statesman,* March 19: 2.

Boone, Louis E., and David L. Kurtz, 1994. *Contemporary business communication.* Englewood Cliffs, N.J.: Prentice-Hall.

Borisoff, Deborah, and David A. Victor, 1989. *Conflict management: a communication skills approach.* Englewood Cliffs, N.J.: Prentice-Hall.

Bostrom, Robert, 1970. Patterns of communicative interaction in small groups. *Speech Monographs* **37:** 257–263.

————, and Charles Rossiter, 1969. Profanity, justification, and source credibility. Paper presented at the annual conference of the International Communication Association, Cleveland, Ohio.

Bradford, David L., and Allan R. Cohen, 1984. *Managing for excellence: the guide to developing high performance in contemporary organizations.* New York: Wiley.

Bradley-Steck, Tara, 1987. High overhead: tall and thin executives receive fatter paychecks, university study reports. *Ann Arbor News,* March 3: A1.

Braybrooke, David, and Charles E. Lindblom, 1963. *A strategy of decision.* New York: Free Press.

Butler, Dore, and Florence L. Geis, 1990. Nonverbal affect responses to male and female leaders: implications for leadership evaluations. *Journal of Personality and Social Psychology* **58:** No. 1, 48–59.

Byrne, John A., 1993. Harvard B-School. *Business Week,* July 19: 58–65.

Cathart, Robert S., and Larry A. Samovar, 1988. *Small group communication* (5th ed.). Dubuque, Iowa: Wm. C. Brown.

Cissna, Kenneth, 1976. Interpersonal confirmation: a review of current theory and research. Paper presented at the annual convention of the Central States Speech Association, Chicago, April.

Clift, Eleanor, and Bob Cohn, 1993. President Cliffhanger. *Newsweek,* November 22: 26–29.

Cocks, Jay, 1990. Let's get crazy. *Time,* June 11: 40–41.

Conger, Jay A., 1989. Leadership: the art of empowering others. *Academy of Management Executive* **3:** No. 1, 17–24.

Conner, Daryl, 1993. *Managing at the speed of change.* New York: Villard Books.

Corcoran, Elizabeth, 1988. Groupware: beyond number crunching, computers aid management. *Scientific American,* July: 110–112.

Cosier, Richard A., and Charles R. Schwenk, 1990. Agreement and thinking alike: ingredients for poor decisions. *Academy of Management Executive* **4:** No. 1, 69–74.

Cotton, John L., 1993. *Employee involvement.* Newbury Park, Calif.: Sage.

Courtright, John A., Gail T. Fairhurst, and L. Edna Rogers, 1989. Interaction patterns in organic and mechanistic systems. *Academy of Management Journal* **32:** No. 4, 773–802.

Cousins, Norman, 1980. *Anatomy of an illness.* New York: Norton.

Covey, Stephen, 1990. *The seven habits of highly effective people.* New York: Simon and Schuster.

————, 1991. *Principle-centered leadership.* New York: Simon and Schuster.

Crane, Loren, Richard Dieker, and Charles Brown, 1970. The physiological response to the communication modes: reading, listening, writing, speaking, and evaluating. *Journal of Communication* **20:** 231–240.

Culbert, Samuel A., 1968. *The interpersonal process of self-disclosure: it takes two to see one.* New York: Renaissance Editions.

Dance, Frank E. X., and Carl E. Larson, 1972. *Speech communication: concepts and behavior.* New York: Holt, Rinehart and Winston.

———, and ———, 1976. *The functions of human communication.* New York: Holt, Rinehart and Winston.

Davis, Sammy, Jr., and Jane and Burt Boyar, 1989. *The Sammy Davis, Jr. story: why me?* New York: Warner Books.

Delbecq, André L., Andrew H. Van de Ven, and David H. Gustafson, 1975. *Group techniques for program planning: a guide to nominal group and Delphi processes.* Glenview, Ill.: Scott, Foresman.

DePree, Max, 1989. *Leadership is an art.* New York: Doubleday Publishing Group.

Dertouzos, Michael L., 1991. Communications, computers and networks. *Scientific American,* September: 62–69.

Dewey, John, 1910. *How we think.* New York: Heath.

Drucker, Peter, 1990. The emerging theory of manufacturing. *Harvard Business Review,* May–June: 94–102.

Dumaine, Brian, 1990. Who needs a boss? *Fortune,* May 7: 52–60.

———, 1993. The new non-manager managers. *Fortune,* February 22: 80–84.

Edwards, Allen, and L. E. Acker, 1962. A demonstration of the long-term retention of a conditioned galvanic skin response. *Psychosomatic Medicine* **24:** 459–463.

Eisenberg, Eric M., 1984. Ambiguity as strategy in organizational communication. *Communication Monographs* **51:** 227–239.

———, and Marsha G. Witten, 1987. Reconsidering openness in organizational communication. *Academy of Management Review* **12:** No. 3, 418–426.

Ellis, Donald G., and B. Aubrey Fisher, 1994. *Small group decision-making* (4th ed.). New York: McGraw-Hill.

Etzioni, Amatai, 1968. *The active society.* New York: Free Press.

Festinger, Leon, 1954. A theory of social comparison processes. *Human Relations* **7:** 117–140.

———, 1957. *A theory of cognitive dissonance.* Stanford, Calif.: Stanford University Press.

———, and Elliot Aronson, 1968. Arousal and reduction of dissonance in social contexts. In Dorwin Cartwright and Alvin Zander (eds.). *Group dynamics: research and theory* (3rd ed.). New York: Harper & Row, pp. 125–136.

Fiedler, Fred, 1967. *A theory of leadership effectiveness.* New York: McGraw-Hill.

———, and Martin Chemers, 1974. *Leadership and effective management.* Glenview, Ill.: Scott, Foresman.

Finkelstein, Sydney, 1992. Power in top management teams: dimensions, measurement, and validation. *Academy of Management Journal* **35:** 505–538.

Fisher, B. Aubrey, 1974. *Small group decision making: communication and the group process.* New York: McGraw-Hill.

———, 1980. *Small group decision making* (2nd ed.). New York: McGraw-Hill.

———, and Leonard C. Hawes, 1971. An interact system model: generating a grounded theory of small groups. *Quarterly Journal of Speech* **57:** 444–453.

Fisher, Kimball, 1993. *Leading self-directed work teams.* New York: McGraw-Hill.

Fisher, Roger, and Scott Brown, 1988. *Getting together.* Boston: Houghton Mifflin.

———, and William Ury, 1981. *Getting to yes.* Boston: Houghton Mifflin.

Fiske, Edward, 1990. Of learning and college: how small groups thrive. *The New York Times,* March 5: A1.

Footlick, Jerrold K., 1990. What happened to the family? *Newsweek,* Winter/Spring: 15–20.

Fox, Marilyn L., Deborah J. Dwyer, and Daniel C. Ganster, 1993. Effects of stressful job demands and control on physiological and attitudinal outcomes in a hospital setting. *Academy of Management Journal* **36:** 289–318.

Francis, Dave, and Don Young, 1992. *Improving work groups* (2nd ed.). San Diego, Calif.: Pfeiffer.

French, John, and Bertram Raven, 1959. The bases of social power. In Dorwin Cartwright (ed.). *Studies in social power.* Ann Arbor: Institute for Social Research, pp. 150–167.

Fruend, James C., 1992. *Smart negotiating.* New York: Simon and Schuster.

Fulk, Janet, 1993. Social construction of communication technology. *Academy of Management Journal* **36:** 921–950.

Gardner, John W., 1990. *On leadership.* New York: Free Press.

Geier, John, 1967. A trait approach to the study of leadership. *Journal of Communication* **17:** 316–323.

George, Maryanne, and David Morrow, 1992. Union was key in GM plant decision. *Detroit Free Press,* December 17: A1, A4.

Gersick, Connie J. G., 1988. Time and transition in work teams: toward a new model of group development. *Academy of Management Journal* **31:** No. 1, 9–41.

Gibb, Jack, 1961. Defensive communication. *Journal of Communication* **11:** 141–148.

Gibson, Jane Whitney, and Richard M. Hodgetts, 1986. *Organizational communication: a managerial perspective.* New York: Academic Press.

Gouran, Dennis, 1973. Group communication: perspectives and priorities for future research. *Quarterly Journal of Speech* **59:** 22–29.

Grantham, Russell, 1992. Office lovers may not wait to get home. *Ann Arbor News,* December 13: F1.

Gray, John, 1992. *Men are from mars, women are from venus.* New York: HarperCollins.

Greenhaus, Jeffery H., Saroj Parasuraman, and Wayne Wormley, 1990. Effects of race on organizational experiences, job performance evaluations, and career outcomes. *Academy of Management Journal* **33:** No. 1, 64–86.

Hackman, J. Richard (ed.), 1990. *Groups that work (and those that don't).* San Francisco: Jossey-Bass.

Haleblian, Jerayr, and Sydney Finkelstein, 1993. Top management team size, CEO dominance, and firm performance: the moderating roles of environmental turbulence and discretion. *Academy of Management Journal* **36:** 844–863.

Hall, Edward T., 1959. *The silent language.* Garden City, N.Y.: Doubleday.

Hammer, Michael, and James Champy, 1993. *Reengineering the corporation.* New York: HarperCollins.

Haney, William V., 1992. *Communication and organizational behavior* (6th ed.). Homewood, Ill.: Irwin.

Hare, A. Paul, 1962. *Handbook of small group research.* New York: Free Press.

———, and Robert Bales, 1963. Seating position and small group interaction. *Sociometry* **26:** 480–486.

Haroldson, Tom, 1989. Stress: for kids 10–14, it's fact of life, study finds. *Ann Arbor News,* September 6: B4.

Hatvany, Nina, and Vladimir Pucik, 1981. Japanese management practices and productivity. *Organizational Dynamics,* Spring: 5–21.

Hearn, G., 1957. Leadership and the spatial factor in small groups. *Journal of Abnormal and Social Psychology* **54:** 269–272.

Heider, Fritz, 1958. *The psychology of interpersonal relations.* New York: Wiley.

Hendrix, Kathleen, 1990. What do gangs, yuppies have in common? anthropologist sees same human drives. *Ann Arbor News,* June 27: B5.

Henrickson, Lorraine Uhlander, and John Psarouthakis, 1992. *Managing the growing firm.* Englewood Cliffs, N.J.: Prentice-Hall.

Hersey, Paul, and Kenneth H. Blanchard, 1993. *Management of organizational behavior* (6th ed.). Englewood Cliffs, N.J.: Prentice-Hall.

Hughes, Richard L., Robert C. Ginnett, and Gordon J. Curphy, 1993. *Leadership: enhancing the lessons of experience.* Homewood, Ill.: Irwin.

Huszczo, Gregory E., 1990. Training for team building: how do you avoid the 10 common pitfalls of team-training approaches? *Training and Development Journal,* February: 37–43.

Insko, Chester, John Schopler, Stephen M. Drigotas, Kenneth A. Graetz, James Kennedy, Chante Cox, and Garry Bornstein, 1993. The role of communication in interindividual-intergroup discontinuity. *Journal of Conflict Resolution* 37: 108–138.

Janis, Irving, 1982. *Victims of groupthink* (2nd ed.). Boston: Houghton Mifflin.

Jarobe, Susan P., 1988. A comparison of input-output, process-output, and input-process-output models of small group problem-solving effectiveness. *Communication Monographs* **55:** 121–142.

Jemmott, John B. III, and Elida Gonzales, 1989. Social status, the status distribution, and performance in small groups. *Journal of Applied Social Psychology* **19:** No. 7, 584–598.

Jick, Todd D., 1993. *Managing change.* Homewood, Ill.: Irwin.

Jones, Richard P., 1981. Nude sunbathing. *Flint Journal,* September 6: c6.

Jourard, Sidney M., 1964. *The transparent self: self-disclosure and well-being.* Princeton, N.J.: Van Nostrand.

Kameda, Tatsuya, Mark F. Stasson, James H. David, Craig Parks, and Suzi Zimmerman, 1992. Social dilemmas, subgroups, and motivational loss in task-oriented groups: in search of an "optimal" team size. *Social Psychology Quarterly* **55:** 47–56.

Karlins, Marvin, and Edyth Hargis, 1988. Inaccurate self-perception as a limiting factor in managerial effectiveness. *Perceptual and Motor Skills* **66:** 665–666.

Karrass, Chester L., 1993. *The negotiating game.* New York: T. Crowell.

Katz, Daniel, and Robert Kahn, 1978. *The social psychology of organizations* (2nd ed.). New York: Wiley.

Katzenbach, Jon R., and Douglas K. Smith, 1993. *The wisdom of teams.* Cambridge, Mass.: Harvard Business School Press.

Keller, Robert T., 1986. Predictors of the performance of project groups in R & D organizations. *Academy of Management Journal* **29:** No. 4, 715–726.

Kelly, Francis J., and Heather Mayfield Kelly, 1986. *What they really teach you at the Harvard Business School.* New York: Warner Communications.

Keltner, John, 1970. *Interpersonal speech communication.* Belmont, Calif.: Wadsworth.